"While Luther's approach to exe
grammatic than Ignatius's, his re
and meditation—in the midst of the eschatological battle with Satan, the
world, and his own desires that similarly plague believers each day—led
him just as sure-footedly into the depths of Scripture and back into daily
life. In this book, Isaac explores the many dimensions of Luther's meditative, devotional discipline with keen insight into the Reformer's prayer life
and the challenges of twenty-first century Christian existence. This volume
captures not only Luther's instructions and model for bringing Scripture
into daily life, but also the spirit of dependence on God that shaped his
encounters with Scripture. With his astute sensitivity to both historic text
and our contemporary environment, Isaac demonstrates how lively and apt
Luther's example is for us today."

—**Robert Kolb**
Professor of systematic theology, emeritus
Concordia Seminary, Saint Louis

"Martin Luther was not only the central figure in the Protestant Reformation
of the sixteenth century, but also a spiritual master whose words give guidance to all Christians today. This volume explores his spirituality through his
threefold rule of prayer, meditation and testing. A good introduction to the
heart of Luther's faith."

—**Timothy George**
Founding dean of Beeson Divinity School
General editor, *Reformation Commentary on Scripture*

"Some theologians transcend their day and generation in significance, both
theologically and practically. Luther is just such a one, yet many people are
probably more familiar with the spectacular moments of his public life than
with the devotional convictions and practices that formed the foundation
of his spiritual strength. In this book, Gordon Isaac takes Luther's famous
triplet—prayer, meditation, and spiritual trials—and uses it as a means of
making the Reformer's insights relevant to the Christian today, both for
personal devotion and (of particular note) practical life in the community.
Highly recommended."

Carl R. Trueman
William E. Simon Fellow in Religion and Public Life
Princeton University

PRAYER, MEDITATION

— & —

SPIRITUAL TRIAL

PRAYER, MEDITATION

— & —

SPIRITUAL TRIAL

Luther's Account of Life in the Spirit

GORDON L. ISAAC

Prayer, Meditation, and Spiritual Trial: Luther's Account of Life in the Spirit

© 2017 Hendrickson Publishers Marketing, LLC
P. O. Box 3473
Peabody, Massachusetts 01961-3473
www.hendrickson.com

ISBN 978-1-68307-018-4

Printed in the United States of America

First Printing—October 2017

Library of Congress Cataloging-in-Publication Data

A catalog record for this title is available from the Library of Congress
Hendrickson Publishers Marketing, LLC ISBN 978-1-68307-018-4

To all those who recognize the cross as a signpost for free travelers.

CONTENTS

INTRODUCTION

Luther is endlessly fascinating. From his earliest days in the monastery at Erfurt he seemed destined for some great work. The anxieties and melancholies that drove him to an intense study of the Bible did not overwhelm the young Augustinian. Instead, he found his own pathway, quite apart from the Scholasticism of his day. His meditation on Scripture was not done for the sake of intellectual purposes but for the feeding of his soul. This was necessary as the trials in his life became more prominent. He had to give answer to high church officials, and he debated the theologians of his time. He stood before the emperor of the Holy Roman Empire and was excommunicated by the pope. He was the most published author of the sixteenth century, yet he also had time to plead the case of refugees in his beloved Wittenberg and preach over two thousand sermons in the town church. He rubbed shoulders with the important figures of his time, and yet he lived with the common people. In addition to all this, Martin and his wife Katie took in many houseguests. It is no irony to say that his was a life of contemplation and action.

There is always something new to learn about Luther. Perhaps one reason for that is the impressive written legacy Luther managed to leave behind. His writings are collected in a critical edition in over one hundred thick volumes known as the Weimar Edition (*Weimarer Ausgabe*). It is said that he wrote the equivalent of eighteen hundred pages per year—all before the convenience of computers and word processing! But it is not only the sheer volume of his creative output that is so impressive. The quality of his prose, the power of his expression, and the precision of his translating all helped to codify the modern German language with the publication of the Luther Bible. This, along with his ability to craft aphorisms and memorable, moving passages of preaching caused a prominent scholar in the field to call Luther a *Sprachereignis*, a "word event."

Prayer, Meditation, and Spiritual Trial: Luther's Account of Life in the Spirit is an attempt to let Luther speak and instruct again in his fresh way. This is not an attempt to tell the story of Luther as in a full-length biography, although there are moments when Luther's point is best illustrated with an example from his life. Neither is this an exposition of the entirety of Luther's complex, subtle, and powerful theology—there are several standard works referenced in the endnotes for interested readers. The aim of this work is to set out Luther from a particular angle, a specific perspective.

Simply put, the shape and the pattern of Christian life takes the form of prayer, meditation, and spiritual struggle. Luther is convinced that these three rules are deeply embedded in Scripture and can be seen in the lives of patriarchs and matriarchs of the faith. In fact, Luther says that these are the three rules for practicing proper theology. This is a singular statement that cannot be rushed past too quickly. When a theologian of Luther's stature makes such a statement, it is worth pondering and putting into the context of our theological existence.

The exercise of viewing Luther's thought with these three rules in mind brings with it the possibility of seeing things in a new light. No one who has any exposure to Luther and his keen interest in teaching the laity would be surprised to think that he urged the praying of the Psalms and the Lord's Prayer. But it might come as a bit more surprising that he also advocated for a prayerful meditation on the catechism, and even a methodical praying of the Ten Commandments! It is my hope that those who only know the Reformer of serious polemics and doctrinal controversy will also catch a vision of the spiritual resource, both doctrinal and practical—for the two cannot be separated—that Luther offers. In this book, we will explore what Luther has to say about prayer, meditation, and spiritual trial—all through the lens of the "theology of the cross" (*theologia crucis*)—culminating in Luther's account of life in the Spirit.

Chapter 1 begins with a description of the three rules for doing proper theology. Luther outlines the wrong way to do theology as well as the right way to do theology. As we will see throughout this book, he points to a disciplined practice of the three rules, which he recommends for all those who would become theologians. Confronted as we are with the full array of delights and reversals in this world, the question of existence knocks at our door whether we know how to answer or not. Luther directs us toward finding the "right path," helping us understand our spiritual struggles—our *theological* existence—in this world and how best to respond to them.

Chapter 2 concentrates on the first rule: prayer. Luther's teaching on the subject of prayer is direct and lively. We find that there is a dynamic interplay between the one who prays, Scripture, and the Spirit. To put it in the language of the catechism: we are brought up short by the law (Ten Commandments), we are forgiven by the word of promise (the Apostles' Creed), and the ongoing life of the believer—the breathing in and out of living faith—is manifest in prayer (the Lord's Prayer). The Spirit ignites our prayer and teaches us to pray.

Chapter 3 treats the second rule: meditation. Luther's teaching on meditation is no less direct and lively. We find that Luther urges contemplation on the external word that bars the way to any inward spiritual journey of our own making. Reading, learning, and savoring the text lead us away from our own story of sin and alienation into the world of the Bible and the story of God and his promise. The grace of God thus shapes the believer in intellect and affections so that we love what God loves and we turn away from what God hates. The external truth of Scripture is applied to heart by means of the Spirit, who brings us into all truth.

Chapter 4 takes up the third rule: spiritual trial. The fact that Luther identifies spiritual struggle as an essential element for pursuing proper theology sets him apart from most theologians. His realism on this point is refreshing. But it is more than just an assertion that every life will have some pain. His convictions regarding spiritual trial go back to the fact that God is revealed in hiddenness. On the cross God's victory over sin, death, and the devil has all the appearance of a defeat. That the unending life of God is revealed in the death of Jesus Christ means that there is no direct approach to God. His revelation must of necessity come under the forms of suffering and the cross. The Spirit intercedes and fights for the Christian in the depths of spiritual trial.

Chapter 5 summarizes Luther's account of life in the Spirit by way of a thought experiment, using Abraham as a paradigm. Luther describes the patriarch as "Abraham the believer": he believed God, and it was reckoned to him as righteousness. As such, Abraham is a pilgrim or a holy wanderer who follows the voice of God, and his holy wanderings take him to many places where he can serve his neighbor in love. This pilgrimage, or holy wandering, is not like its medieval counterpart—which is an attempt to accrue merit—but is an act of worship undertaken in freedom on the basis of God's gift. It is also not geographical in nature, but one that realigns all of life's relations. We see that Abraham is a practitioner of the three rules and thus an exemplar of one who lives life in the Spirit.

At the time of publication of this book, people all over the world are commemorating the five-hundredth anniversary of the posting of the Ninety-Five Theses (October 31, 1517), usually accounted the beginning of the Protestant Reformation. Martin Luther proceeded with that action out of doctrinal concern and pastoral necessity. Many in his parish were negatively affected by the practice of indulgences. His desire was to lighten the load of the laity so that the promise of God in Christ would not be obscured. It is my goal in this written undertaking to show that prayer and meditation as we undergo various spiritual trials are vital to how we live our lives in the Spirit. For those of us today in a world perhaps in more turmoil than ever before, Luther still has something important and even helpful to teach us after all these years.

CHAPTER 1

THEOLOGICAL EXISTENCE

The Three Rules

In the *Preface to the Wittenberg Edition of Luther's German Writings*, written in 1539, Luther points out a correct way of studying theology:

> It is the way taught by King David (and doubtlessly used also by all the patriarchs and prophets) in the one hundred nineteenth Psalm. There you will find three rules, amply presented throughout the whole Psalm. They are *Oratio, Meditatio, Tentatio.*[1]

Prayer, meditation, and spiritual trial become the shorthand used by the mature Luther for theological existence or lived theology. This singular approach to the Christian life consists of only three interrelated patterns, yet it opens out onto an experience that embraces God in the most comprehensive fashion. This succinct statement of Luther is so deceptively simple that it might be easy to miss the gravitas of what is being said. Prayer, meditation, and spiritual trial are the form and the pathway of Christian existence.

Technically speaking, one could make the argument that the three rules are not for the average person but for those with a special vocation to serve as pastors and teachers.[2] The advice is given to those who want to study profitably in the Holy Scriptures and to those who must write books. Luther claims that if one keeps up the correct way of studying theology,

> You will become so learned that you yourself could (if it were necessary) write books just as good as those of the fathers and councils, even as I (in God) dare to presume and boast, without arrogance and lying, that in the matter of writing books I do not stand much behind some of the fathers.[3]

It may well be that Luther had a select group in mind as he wrote his preface. However, Luther's use of the term "theologian" in an everyday sense needs to be recalled. In his early writings, Luther speaks of two ways of being a theologian: there is the way of the cross and the way of glory.[4] It is not at all clear that Luther was attempting to talk of a conflict only on the academic level. Theology is a much more daily and useful subject.

In point of fact, Luther's three rules tell us how to study theology, but they also wonderfully capture the way we should live as Christians. It would seem that Luther is quite unaware of the separation that is sometimes made in current thinking when we differentiate between the mere study of theology and the practice of theology. For Luther, the study of theology is really nothing less than the making of a theologian (*faciunt theologum*). Luther is not so interested in saying, "Such and such theology says this . . ." as he is, "a theologian does this . . ." The difference between saying and doing is very great. Theology is thus not a matter of academic study only, but rather a matter of divine wisdom applied to a life lived in time and space through the Spirit.

I rather like the way that Gerhard Forde puts the matter when he says, "All of us are theologians in one way or another."[5] We are not speaking about being professional theologians, whose work is teaching, lecturing, and writing books. Being a theologian is rather more natural to our being. It simply means that because life comes to us as it does, we end up asking the big questions. Why does my friend have such a horrible life? Why doesn't God let some of the "good guys" win? The overwhelming experience of beauty may bring us to an experience of God and creation. Or in the daily business of living, in conversation, or attending a funeral, we begin thinking about God and the meaning behind all of this in our lives. When we wonder about injustice and ponder what is to be done—this is how natural it is to become a theologian.

Becoming a theologian is something that happens to us all. If we get it right, then we are blessed by it; if not, then we are cursed by it. The question is not whether we will become theologians; it is only a matter of whether we will be good theologians or bad theologians. It is worth our while, therefore, to spend some time thinking about God and life in the Spirit—and what kind of theologians we ought to be. This book is an invitation to consider how it is that prayer, meditation, and spiritual struggle carry us along in becoming theologians who will bring honor to God's name and who will be of service to our neighbor.

The Wrong Path

Luther's preface comes in two parts: the first is a sharply formed critique of the contemporary and fashionable theology that pushed the Bible to one side, and the second is a description of the correct way of studying theology. It has been pointed out that it would be easy to isolate these two sections of the preface in order to go directly to the correct way of studying theology.[6] But it will help us in our understanding of the correct way of studying theology if we take a moment to look at the false way of studying theology, according to Luther. What we will find is that the concerns set forward in the early part of the preface are identical to the kinds of critique directed against Scholastic theology throughout Luther's career.

Luther emphasizes the loss of the divine word, the Holy Scriptures. The loss has not come about because of malice but due to inattention. It is not the first time but is apparently something to which sinful human nature is subject. Even as the book of the law was lost in the time of the kings of Judah (2 Kings 22:8), so the Bible was lost to the people of Luther's day. The writings of the many fathers and councils had squeezed out the Bible and had replaced it with books, books, and more books. There were now so many books that Luther complained, "It has begun to rain and snow books and teachers, many of which already lie there forgotten and moldering."[7]

Luther takes a jab at those who have written some of these books. He describes the arrogance in which they wrote their books, hoping that they would "eternally be on sale in the market and rule churches." Power, influence, and a desire for fame were apparently as much a problem in the sixteenth century as in our own. These unworthy motives for writing simply cannot stand up to the true fathers who wanted "to accomplish something good."[8] Here Luther uses the negative effects the overabundance of books had in Christendom to express the hope that after "the over-zealousness of this time has abated, that my books also will not last long."[9] Luther's desire is not to distract from the Bible but to bring it attention and praise.

Another way in which Luther can describe the same problem is to say that we have been cut off from the source of pure water. The fresh spring has been lost and overgrown. Those of us who are thirsty are relegated to drinking water downstream. The great struggle is to recover the true source and find clean water so necessary for life. In an image that echoes the ecological disasters of our own time and the terrible toll they take on humanity and the harm that is done to God's good creation, Luther is looking for the pure water that alone can satisfy. The point that Luther wants to make in all this is that we cannot do better than God's word. As he puts it rather succinctly, "Neither councils, fathers, nor we, in spite of the greatest and best success possible, will do as well as the Holy Scriptures, that is, as well as God himself."[10]

Luther cites Augustine as an example of one who has swum against the stream to find the pure source:

> Herein I follow the example of St. Augustine, who was, among other things, the first and almost the only one who determined to be subject to the Holy Scriptures alone, and independent of the books of all the fathers and saints. On account of that he got into a fierce fight with St. Jerome, who reproached him by pointing to the books of his forefathers; but he did not turn to them. And if the example of St. Augustine had been followed, the pope would not have become Antichrist, and that countless mass of books, which is like a crawling swarm of vermin, would not have found its way into the church, and the Bible would have remained on the pulpit.[11]

The meaning of the Bible as the true source is underlined by the sharp contrast between the words of men and the words of God. Luther likens the countless mass of books to a "crawling swarm of vermin." He blames, among other things, the decrees and decretals of the popes, as well as the books of the sophists, for casting a shadow on Scripture and allowing it to be put "under the bench."

The Right Path

After a rather polemical beginning, Luther attaches an important addition: "Moreover, I want to point out to you a correct way of studying theology, for I have had practice in that."[12] The "way" or path Luther speaks of is grounded in the Bible and is found throughout Psalm 119. In fact, it is none other than King David himself, as Luther informs us, who teaches the three rules. "If you study hard in accord with his example, then you will also sing and boast with him in the Psalm, 'The law of thy mouth is better to me than thousands of gold and silver pieces.'"[13]

Prayer is the starting point that actually precedes reading the Bible. Turning aside from human reason and the presumption that God can be perceived through speculation, Luther urges the theologian to bend the knee in prayer. This kind of prayer does not consist in the pious words of someone on a path of self-improvement. This prayer is to be prayed out of the desperation of heart as displayed by David, who cries out, "Teach me, show me, instruct me." This prayer seeks the tangible action of God on earth as opposed to seeking God as he might be in heaven.[14] As a result, Luther urges an attitude of receptivity: "But kneel down in your little room [Matt. 6:6] and pray to God with real humility and earnestness, that he through his dear Son may give you his Holy Spirit, who will enlighten you, lead you, and give you understanding."[15] Prayer is entrance into a dialogue where the one kneeling does not dictate the terms but is summoned to humility instead of presumption.

Luther states that a Christian might be unable to read the Bible. Even so, that person can still learn and know the Ten Commandments, the Apostles' Creed, and the Lord's Prayer. The total content of Scripture, preaching, and everything a Christian needs to know is contained in these three items. From Luther's point of view, learning to pray the catechism is the place to start for those who seek to grow spiritually. The practice of praying the commandments and the creed may indeed sound strange to the ears of many modern Christians, but that is precisely what Luther did! The proper prayer of the believer begins with the text of Scripture; prayer emanates from and returns to the sacred page. Luther urged the laity to follow him in this practice.

Meditation comes next. Perhaps we cannot say that it sequentially follows, considering that praying the catechism is itself a form of meditation. But meditation on the Bible forms a major role in Luther's theology. Bible reading, which constitutes one important aspect of meditation, is informed by the monastic ideals in which Luther was trained. Contemplation on the text, chewing it over and over again, marks out Luther's commitment to hearing God's word. For example, I believe that monastic practice stands behind Luther's statement in his preface to the book of Romans that the more we deal with the text, the more precious and the sweeter it becomes.[16]

Meditation comes in various shapes and sizes. Some people use meditation in their religious expressions or spiritual quests to detach themselves from the visible world to ascend to the invisible world. It is thought that by doing so one comes into contact with what is spiritual as opposed to that which is merely temporal. Luther uses the term in a different sense altogether. For Luther, the proper object of meditation is Christ himself, the Word of God. In him, both external matters and internal matters are bound together by God's design. The Spirit uses the external things of God to get to our hearts and heads. Meditation on God's word, then, brings us face to face with how God shows himself: the Word become flesh. This blocks the human attempt to know God as he is in himself. Instead, Scripture urges us to know God in afflictions and in the holy cross, the actual history of the crucified Christ. When meditated upon, Scripture brings us back to earth from our religious wanderings and speculation. In this way, the story of redemption as revealed in Christ circumscribes the life of the hearer. Scripture itself is the mirror in which the true reflection of existence is seen.

After meditation, Luther turns his attention to *Anfechtung*. Struggle, or spiritual trial, comes to every person in one form or another in this life. This truth plays an important role in Luther's understanding and in the living out of the faith. The believer is never at rest but is in incessant combat against the "flesh," the "world," and the "devil." Just about the time when one is settled and feeling secure, something dire takes place. It may be as simple a matter as growing weary and stumbling. Or, it could be that the devil takes one's good works and turns them into sin in a great conflict of spirit. Or, it might be that the simple matter of living as a Christian in the world is squeezed and forced by the overwhelming demands that come from life in a complex and complicated world. There are forces that wear us out and make us renounce our faith or that cause us to become indifferent or impatient.

David complains in his psalms about various enemies, backbiters, and those looking to spill his blood. His experience, Luther would assert, is not so far from our own. How does the believer square the experience of conflict, doubt, and turmoil with heartfelt and certain faith? Aren't doubt and faith opposites that cannot be reconciled? The astounding and startling fact is that Luther recognizes the close proximity of doubt and grace. In his discussions of faith, Luther does not banish the difficulties, fears, and uncertainties; instead, he attempts to address them in a number of ways.

First and foremost, Luther pronounces that it is precisely in the midst of inner conflict that God the Holy Spirit comes to work in our lives. The Spirit alone can help us by interceding for us with sighs too deep for words (Rom. 8:26). But also we find Luther giving advice and creating scripts and a vocabulary of faith to aid believers who are in the midst of struggle. For example, in the event one becomes engaged in an argument about how good one is, Luther gives the following advice:

> But you must learn to say: Devil, you're coming at the wrong time. No devil is going to argue with me now, but rather I shall talk with my Lord Jesus Christ, that I may learn that he suffered for me and died and rose again for my sins, and that God will bring me with him on the last day.[17]

These kinds of "scripts" or "dialogues" form what we might call today Christian self-talk, which creates a pattern of thinking, acting, and believing that plays an important role in spiritual growth and formation.

My contention is a simple one. Luther taught the three rules not only to those who had a special call to ministry but also to the laity in simple evangelical treatises of various kinds. He taught the laity how to pray, meditate, and suffer spiritual trial or struggle. This triad forms, in the broadest possible terms, Luther's account of life in the Spirit. These rules are by no means static but contain within them the dynamic of a life that is traversing difficult terrain. The struggle and uncertainty drive the believer to pray on bended knee. Prayer, in its turn, is based on the words of God in the Psalter, the Ten Commandments, the Apostles' Creed, and the Lord's Prayer. The meditation of prayer and study brings to light the story of God's people, who in daily repentance are turned and called by the Spirit toward the eternal life of God. If we enter at any point of the triad, we are confronted with the Spirit who calls, gathers, and enlightens the whole Christian church on earth. When viewed in their interrelatedness, the three rules function as one movement directed by God's Spirit. There are not three rules but one that characterizes life in the Spirit.

The Theology of the Cross

It is commonplace in Luther studies to speak of Luther's approach to theology as a "theology of the cross" (or *theologia crucis* in Latin). This distinctive terminology and powerful description came early in Luther's career as he wrested himself away from the prevailing Scholastic approaches to the questions of his day. At this juncture, it may serve our purposes to take the time to elucidate more particularly what a theology of the cross means in Luther's terms. This will then put us in a position to describe how this terminology relates to Luther's three rules of prayer, meditation, and spiritual trial.

When Luther was first asked to give an account of his new evangelical theology before his Augustinian Order, the resulting presentation was published as the Heidelberg Disputation of 1518. The twenty-eight theological and twelve philosophical theses and proofs contain a response, in dialectical form, to the spent force of Scholasticism in its various expressions. By discussing the problem of human and divine works, of works and the law, of free will, and of the distinction between a theologian of glory and a theologian of the cross, Luther means to set out a proposal for a fresh approach, or perhaps better, to establish the possibility of a fresh hearing of God's word unencumbered by human wisdom and unnecessary attachments to philosophical presuppositions. Luther was convinced that theology has a decided character all its own, quite apart from the philosophizing of an Aristotle or a Plato.

At the heart of Luther's presentation is a distinctive way of perceiving the things of God that one can come to only by despairing of one's own ability. Taking his lead from the apostle Paul, Luther insists that "the word of the cross is folly to those who are perishing, but to us who are being saved it is the power of God" (1 Cor. 1:18). In the critical portion of the Heidelberg Disputation, Luther puts it in the following manner:

> 19. That person does not deserve to be called a theologian who looks upon the invisible things of God as though they were clearly perceptible in those things which have actually happened [Rom. 1:20].

> 20. He deserves to be called a theologian, however, who comprehends the visible and manifest things of God seen through suffering and the cross.

> 21. A theologian of glory calls evil good and good evil. A theologian of the cross calls the thing what it actually is.[18]

A theologian of glory attempts to use enduring principles such as virtue, justice, and goodness to penetrate the actual events of history to see what God is doing and willing in heaven. A theologian of glory begins with the conviction that everyone has a basic conception of God. Though human reason is marred by sin, one can still know the good, even though one cannot always do the good. In this way of thinking, there is an essential continuity between humankind and God. To make the case for God, one can proceed by referring to things invisible or by making a case through apologetics.

On the basis of this continuity, it is only reasonable to bypass the suffering of the cross to concentrate on virtue, the good, and good works. This particular kind of "God logic" applies to the theologian of glory. "Therefore he prefers works to suffering, glory to the cross, strength to weakness, wisdom to folly, and, in general, good to evil."[19] When one looks away from the one place where God has revealed himself, it is inevitable that a false set of priorities arises. That is what Luther means when he says, "A theologian of glory calls evil good and good evil" (thesis 21). It is evil to call the imperfections of human works good as though that is a natural conduit to God, and it is equally wrong to call the good of the cross evil.

In the following passage, Luther continues contrasting a theologian of glory and a theologian of the cross:

> A theologian of glory does not recognize, along with the Apostle, the cruci-
> fied and hidden God alone [1 Cor. 2:2]. He sees and speaks of God's glorious
> manifestation among the heathen, how his invisible nature can be known from
> the things which are visible [cf. Rom. 1:20] and how he is present and power-
> ful in all things everywhere. This theologian of glory, however, learns from
> Aristotle that the object of the will is the good and the good is worthy to be
> loved, while the evil, on the other hand, is worthy of hate. He learns that God
> is the highest good and exceedingly lovable. Disagreeing with the theologian
> of the cross, he defines the treasury of Christ as the removing and remitting
> of punishments, things which are most evil and worthy of hate. In opposition
> to this the theologian of the cross defines the treasury of Christ as impositions
> and obligations of punishments, things which are best and most worthy of
> love. Yet the theologian of glory still receives money for his treasury, while the
> theologian of the cross, on the other hand, offers the merits of Christ freely.
> Yet people do not consider the theologian of the cross worthy of consideration,
> but finally even persecute him.[20]

Luther points out that a theologian of glory has presuppositions about God and
God's work that block any meaningful way to a definition of God that springs
from the crucifixion of Jesus. A theologian of glory learns from Aristotle about
the will and what is good. This capitulation to a philosophical route to knowledge of God reverses the way of the cross in favor of the way of human wisdom.
Instead of looking to God's self-revelation in his hiddenness on the cross, the
theologian of glory seeks God in a different manner. The end result could not
be more pronounced.

Luther's provocative point is to say that there is no essential continuity between humanity and God except that which is established by the work of God
in Christ. A theologian of the cross does not proceed with the conviction that
everyone has a basic conception of God. It is just the opposite:

> So, also, in John 14[:8], where Philip spoke according to the theology of glory:
> "Show us the Father." Christ forthwith set aside his flighty thought about seek-
> ing God elsewhere and led him to himself, saying, "Philip, he who has seen
> me has seen the Father" [John 14:9]. For this reason true theology and recog-
> nition of God are in the crucified Christ, as it is also stated in John 10 [John
> 14:6]: "No one comes to the Father, but by me." "I am the door" [John 10:9],
> and so forth.[21]

Luther's urgency in the disputation is to say that it does no one any good to recognize God in his glory and majesty, unless one recognizes him in the humility
and shame of the cross. True theology recognizes God in the crucified Christ.
This is counterintuitive. Humanly speaking, the last place we would expect to
find God is in the lowliness of a baby in a manger, or in the humility of one
dying on a cross; nevertheless, that is the truth of the revealed Word and it is
the manner in which a theologian of the cross proceeds.

By setting out these thoughts in this particular manner, it becomes clear that Luther proves himself to be a faithful interpreter of Scripture and especially of Paul. Luther rejects the knowledge of God depicted (and rejected) by the apostle in Romans 1 and instead sides with the "foolishness of preaching" in 1 Corinthians. Since it is impossible to know God through human wisdom, the only alternative is preaching the crucified Christ. "For the foolishness of God is wiser than men, and the weakness of God is stronger than men" (1 Cor. 1:25). Luther knows that moving in this direction puts him in direct opposition to the deeply entrenched structures of the day. This is shown in the following passage from the *Explanations of the Ninety-Five Theses*:

> From this you can now see how, ever since the scholastic theology—the de- ceiving theology (for that is the meaning of the word in Greek)—began, the theology of the cross has been abrogated, and everything has been completely turned up-side-down. A theologian of the cross (that is, one who speaks of the crucified and hidden God), teaches that punishments, crosses, and death are the most precious treasury of all and the most sacred relics which the Lord of this theology himself has consecrated and blessed, not alone by the touch of his most holy flesh but also by the embrace of his exceedingly holy and divine will, and he has left these relics here to be kissed, sought after, and embraced. Indeed fortunate and blessed is he who is considered by God to be so worthy that these treasures of the relics of Christ should be given to him; rather, who understands that they are given to him. For to whom are they not offered? As St. James says, "Count it all joy, my brethren, when you meet various trials" [James 1:2]. For not all have this grace and glory to receive these treasures, but only the most elect of the children of God.[22]

In the first few lines of this passage, Luther sets the theology of the cross over against the Scholastic theology of his day. He then returns quickly to his pre- ferred terminology of "the theologian of the cross." As he does so, Luther makes evident that this way of theologizing is not abstract, as though one could have knowledge of God in a purely speculative manner. The theologian of the cross is one who has been grasped by the preaching of Christ crucified. The experience of being confronted with Christ, who has given himself for the sins of the world in his sacrifice on the cross, effects a change. Luther sets out a theology of the cross as a particular kind of wisdom that opposes the speculation so rampant in medieval theology. The knowledge of God thus takes the form of an intense experiential wisdom, or as Luther would say, a *sapientia experimentalis*.

This very brief presentation of Luther's theology of the cross reveals that it is a thoroughgoing approach to the task of theology. It is not a chapter in theology; it is a particular approach to the theological task. Or, to use mod- ern terminology, the theology of the cross is a theological methodology or a critical criterion for proper theology that has distinctive boundaries and that is exclusive in character. It is not merely theoretical knowledge of God, but it is knowledge of God grounded in day-to-day living. From Luther's point of view, there are only two ways to theologize: there is the way of glory, and there is the way of the cross.

What Luther presented before his chapter of the Augustinian Eremites was not an isolated interpretation of a biblical passage or two. As Robert Kolb asserts, "He presented a new conceptual framework for thinking about God and the human creature."[23] Luther's particular theological approach emphasizes the following matters: (1) distinguishing God as he has revealed himself in his reconciling work on the cross, from God in himself who cannot be comprehended by sinful humanity; (2) relying on the word of God rather than on human ability; (3) recognizing that God works in mysterious and unexpected ways, often in a form opposite of what one might expect; and (4) accepting that spiritual trial has a role to play in the revelation of God on the cross, and in the daily dying and rising of the Christian.

Luther's logic runs in the following manner: God in his majesty is too great for fallen human nature to grasp. By means of a mask, he covers himself and presents himself to us clothed in humanity. But having fallen under the slavery of the disobedience of sin and the influence of the Deceiver, when humanity did not recognize or receive Christ when he came to his own. To break the power of sin, death, and the devil, Christ yielded his life upon the cross and achieved reconciliation for humanity with God. Those who recognize the objective reality of the cross at once know themselves to be crucified with Christ. Faith in the word of God that conveys Christ allows us to die to our old ways of living and to endure evil and suffering in the course of caring for our neighbor.

God Hidden and Revealed

Throughout Luther's theology, a distinction is made between the human attempt to find and know God, and the knowledge and encounter that God grants through his word. Luther uses a wide array of expressions to show the antithesis. He can speak of "God in himself" versus "God as he reveals himself." Or he can speak of "the naked God" and "the God clothed in his promises." Or again, as he famously put it,

> We have to argue in one way about God or the will of God as preached, revealed, offered, and worshipped, and in another way about God as he is not preached, revealed, offered, and worshipped. To the extent that God hides Himself, and wills to be unknown to us, it is no business of ours.[24]

The God who stands outside the reach of human reason is the same God who has shown himself faithful in the person of Jesus Christ; they are one and the same. Luther's point is to say that God in his majesty is to be left alone. He does not desire that we seek after him as he is in himself; he desires that we seek him as he is clothed and displayed in his Word. To find God in his naked power would bring only death, but to find him in the suffering of Jesus on the cross conveys life.

Luther feels compelled to reject the attempt of the theologian of glory to see God as he is in his works. He asserts this opposition not only to the way of speculation regarding God in general, but more particularly, Luther rejects any human attempt to take the initiative in finding God. Autonomous attempts simply feed human self-reliance and arbitrariness that are foundations for *superbia*, the human pride that insists on dealing with God on the basis of human ideas rather than obediently meeting him where he has designated. More often than not, this also means the attempt to see God face to face, forgetting that "man shall not see me and and live" (Exod. 33:20).

> The people of Israel did not have a God who was viewed "absolutely," to use the expression, the way the inexperienced monks rise into heaven with their speculations and think about God as He is in Himself. From this absolute God everyone should flee who does not want to perish, because human nature and the absolute God—for the sake of teaching we use this familiar term—are the bitterest of enemies. Human weakness cannot help being crushed by such majesty, as Scripture reminds us over and over.[25]

Luther holds out a stern reprimand for those who would seek to know God as he is in heaven, and it is precisely against some in the religious orders that he used sharp words of warning. The attempt to "storm heaven" in this manner can only lead to being overpowered by that majesty.

God desires to be known where he has revealed and offered himself. With the nation Israel, it was the tabernacle, the mercy seat of the Ark of the Covenant, and the temple in Jerusalem. God directs his people to seek him in a given place within particular limitations. God sojourns with Israel throughout its varied history: through their wilderness wanderings, the conquest and establishment of Jerusalem, and into exile. It is a specific history of real acts and signs, and God's revelation comes in and with those signs.

> Since our corrupted nature is completely unable to grasp the Divinity, we are not able to bear the sight of God as he is. God has therefore chosen to take hold of our nature which is corrupted and infected with satanic poison and to involve it in these external manifestations and sacraments so that we may be able to grasp him.[26]

Now in the age following Christ's resurrection, there is no longer a geographical limitation. Christ himself is the new temple and the mercy seat of God. Only in him is God now present to his people. All of the promises of God find their "yes" in him (1 Cor. 1:30), and it is in him that the father's heart of love is displayed. If we seek God outside of Christ, then we are sure to go wrong.

> Just as after God revealed himself in Christ, the human being, we properly say and believe that all those who do not grasp this human being born of Mary simply cannot grasp God. Even if they say that they believe in God, the creator

of heaven and earth, they nevertheless in fact believe in an idol fashioned by their own hearts, because apart from Christ there is no true God. . . . Christ is the throne of grace [Hebrews 4:16], in whom all things are found, and apart from him nothing can be found.[27]

The theologian of the cross knows that the one way to distinguish properly between the hidden God and the revealed God is to look to Christ. This sets down a clear and focused pattern that calls into question the way of glory, while at the same time establishing a true and proper theology. Luther rejects the theology of glory on the epistemological level (how we gain knowledge of God), as well as on the ethical level (how we relate to God). The theology of glory seeks to *know* God directly in his divine power, wisdom, and glory. At the same time, the theology of glory seeks to *relate* to God through works. Both are expressions of human self-exaltation. Both are ways in which the human pride becomes inflated, or to use the words of Luther, "puffed up, blinded, and hardened."[28]

Luther asserts that God wishes to be known and honored, or related to, according to a different standard. The cross is opposed to both the rationalistic and the moralistic elements of the theology of glory. The theology of the cross recognizes God in his indirect revelation in suffering. This is the manner chosen by God to make "foolish the wisdom of the world" (1 Cor. 1:20). The theology of the cross calls women and men to relate to God, not through ethical achievement but through the gift of transforming faith. The person for whom this is true has been brought from a self-interested moralism to a self-giving life of faith toward God and works toward their neighbor.

Relying on the Word of God

As the scriptural record tells us, "The wisdom of their wise men shall perish" (Isa. 29:14). He does so by hiding himself under suffering and the cross. There is no direct approach to God that is confirmed through human understanding. Thus relying on the word of God is the only approved method, or the only approved reception of the presence of God in the world. The foolishness of God in preaching is held out to us. It is not God in himself that we receive but the crucified Christ in suffering that meets us in this world marked by sin, confusion, and injustice. So it is that the way in which we know God and relate to God takes the form of a different kind of wisdom.

Here we begin to see Luther's transition from the cross of Jesus Christ to the cross of the Christian. Accepting the cross of Christ is a judgment on human wisdom and the natural tendency to think according to a theology of glory. Toward the end of Luther's exposition of thesis 21 he says, "The friends of the cross say that the cross is good and works are evil, for through the cross works are destroyed and the old Adam, who is especially edified by works, is crucified."[29] The cross is a judgment against the attempt to achieve standing with

God through works. What is more, the cross stands as an attack upon the old Adam and begins its work of bringing low and reducing to nothing that person who "misuses and defiles the gifts of God."[30]

Becoming a theologian of the cross is not a simple matter of choosing one theory over another. Recognition of the cross of Jesus Christ as the objective and exclusive place of God's revelation comes only in and with knowing that we are crucified with Christ. This is not theoretical knowledge but experiential in the sense that it is only those who have been brought low who can make that acknowledgment.

It is fascinating to observe the moves Luther makes in his exposition. In the explanation of thesis 21, he speaks of how the cross destroys works and crucifies the old Adam. In thesis 23 he states categorically, "The law brings the wrath of God, kills, reviles, accuses, judges, and condemns everything that is not in Christ."[31] The cross thwarts humanly devised approaches. Again, in his explanation of thesis 24, Luther speaks in a manner that is unmistakably existential: "He, however, who has been emptied [cf. Phil. 2:7] through suffering no longer does works but knows that God works and does all things in him."[32] The cross puts the individual in a place where no works can be offered as a possible way to achieve fellowship with God. This is the death of the old Adam who is "edified by works." Someone who has been gripped by the cross is thus brought low and comes to the place of utter despair of one's own ability. The suffering of the cross belongs to both Christ and the believer. At the nadir of his exposition, Luther says, "It is this that Christ says in John 3[:7], 'You must be born anew.' To be born anew, one must consequently first die and then be raised up with the Son of Man."[33] The cross of Christ therefore also becomes the cross of the believer.

The dynamic of Luther's thought continues in thesis 25, as he states, "He is not righteous who does much, but he who, without work, believes much in Christ."[34] It is the one who lives in faith who is righteous. One can almost feel the transition that takes place in this portion of the Heidelberg Disputation. He has been speaking about being brought low, but at this juncture he speaks of new life. It is not through works that one is righteous; rather it is the righteousness of faith that produces works. The believer is transformed to become "Christ's action and instrument."[35] We become theologians of the cross through the death and resurrection that produce faith.

It is in this sense that relying on the word of God is so important. From Luther's exposition, the one with whom God deals is a sinner who feels nothing but the wrath of the law and is thus brought low, despairing of all innate ability. But it is precisely this person who dares everything in relying on Christ, who dies as a ransom for many. The truth that we are righteous apart from the works of the law is to be believed in spite of all appearances. Firmly trusting in the incarnate, preached, and inscripturated Word of God becomes foundational for us in adjusting to the reality of God revealed in hiddenness. "Anyone who has a god, but does not have his word, has no god at all."[36]

God Works under the Form of the Opposite

All genuine knowledge of God and all true human self-understanding come through the cross. This is a strange and paradoxical truth that points to the fact that God reveals himself in hiddenness. In the cross, the power of God is displayed through helplessness and suffering. The righteousness of God is on display in the person of an indicted criminal under the death penalty. The life of God is shown and offered in Christ's death. The paradoxes mount as we continue by saying that God's grace is hidden under his wrath and his benefits are brought about through intense loss. The reality of God stands in contradiction to the standards of the world. It is hidden under the cross in trouble and in disaster.[37]

When the world looks on the cross of Christ, it can only seem to be something other than the wisdom of God. As the apostle Paul pointed out, it is a scandal to the Jews and folly to the Greeks. In Luther's time, the assessment was no different. Even the theology of the glory expected the attributes of God to somehow parallel the power paradigm of a medieval king. How can someone be recognized as king who experiences such a shameful death? Human reason shakes its head in denial of the truth of God in the cross. The world can judge only on the basis of what transpires; and it would seem that God, if there is a God, turns away from evil and does nothing about it. Either he is feeble and powerless or he is unjust. In the matter of experience, distinguishing between God and the devil is a difficult matter. Even Luther acknowledges this logic: "He [God] makes himself look like a devil."[38]

We might be able to understand the devil parading as God, but God making himself look like the devil? What could Luther possibly mean by such a statement? At the very least, this is Luther's way of pointing to the fact that God is hidden. There is no easy way from our ideas of God to God as he is in himself. If God is omnipotent, then it stands to reason that he is responsible for all things. Luther is being honest in saying that it is impossible to separate God from the evil things in the world, at least in terms of appearance. Luther is able and willing to put this in the starkest terms. Perhaps this is also the reason why Luther, on the other side of things, can speak about salvation in Christ Jesus in such bold, lyrical, and inspired ways.

The salvation that God brings breaks the expectations of the world and even those of the faithful. The faithfulness, the truthfulness, and the justice of God cannot be arbitrated on the basis of human reason and what we see in the world. Christians cannot make easy determinations about the meaning of historical events, but they must rely on the word of God and the promises God makes about the future. Luther recognizes that believers are thrown in prison, John the Baptist was beheaded, and Christ himself was crucified, but the fact that the wicked are allowed to flourish for a period of time does not negate the truthfulness and justice of God. "The *theologia crucis* is Luther's version of a theodicy. He did not try to justify God through explanations but recognized that all explanations wither and collapse in the face of the reality of evil and the reality of the good and almighty God who revealed his essence on the cross."[39]

In the end, Luther recognizes that there is no explanation adequate to reconcile the goodness of God with the injustice of the world. There is a split in our image of God; on the basis of human reason, we can only imagine that God, if there is a God, is not for us but against us; it is only on the basis of what God has done for us in Christ that we know his essence is love and that he extends life to us through the forgiveness of sins. By allowing that God works under the form of the opposite, however, space is preserved for God to be God. It is an admission that human reason does not have all the answers to the complicated reality of this world. It is only through the revelation of God in the cross that we are presented with the fatherly heart of love through the self-giving action of the Son. Faith in the living Christ heals the breach that occurs in our image of God precisely because it is there that the eternal love of God is manifest and the promises of God find their fulfillment under the form of the opposite.

Spiritual Trial as a Part of God's Revelation and Christian Experience

Spiritual trial is an essential element of Luther's theology of the cross. It is the nature of faith to endure being contradicted by reason and assaulted by the actions of God, who works under the form of the opposite. Faith is aligned against the conclusions of human reason that put God to the test. Reason and the experience of the world are only able to see God as feeble and impotent, or to see God as a monster willing to endure or even promote evil. In this circumstance, Christian existence comes into question and the danger of deep contradiction, unbelief, and despair are close at hand. To believe means to live in antithesis to the doubts posed by empirical reality and to trust in the One who is revealed in hiddenness.

The opposition between faith and experience are felt keenly when the woes and troubles of life press in hard against us. The human heart finds it hard to withstand the pressures and the grinding uncertainty that wears away our strength and joy of living. The word of the promise speaks of the resolution of all things at the end of time, on the Day of the Lord, but that future is still hidden. The hidden future makes the present difficulties loom larger, and our perspective becomes captive to the moment. In these straits, the hidden salvation of God cannot be seen. To believe means to abandon the viewpoint of reason and to venture everything on Christ. God is able to see to the end of our troubles. "For this reason we must give heed to what he says in his word rather than to our own nearsighted heart."[40]

Doubt and temptation come to every life. One almost expects that the "no" of Satan and of the world are inevitable. But what makes the situation all the more unbearable is when we must conclude that this "no" coincides with the "no" of God's own will. This struggle with the idea that God has rejected us is treated in a memorable fashion in Luther's Postil sermon on the Syrophoenician woman.[41] The story tells of a poor woman worried about her daughter who was afflicted by a devil. Everything about the case is unpromising. Even as she begins to approach Jesus, she must face the fact that she is not a child of Abraham and has no natural audience with the Christ. She then experiences a series of rebuffs that would have turned most people away: first, through silence on the part of Jesus; next, through the rejection of the disciples; and finally, through the stern words of Jesus, "It is not right to take the children's bread and throw it to the dogs" (Matt. 15:26). What is so difficult and perplexing is that Jesus himself takes up a position identical to the heart in its self-accusation and distress. In all of this, however, the woman persists in faith and never gives up the good news she had embraced in him. Luther therefore writes: "We must also do the same and learn to cling firmly to His Word alone, even if God with all His creatures would act differently than this Word says about Him."[42] Jesus' encounter with the Syrophoenician woman teaches us something important: "This was written for all our comfort and instruction so that we may know how deeply God hides his grace from us, so that we would not consider Him according to our perception and thinking but strictly according to His Word."[43]

Robert Kolb points out that Luther's theology of the cross served to outline his way of thinking and his practice of theology. It contains essential elements of his theology and shapes the way Luther approaches the biblical text, and it frames the way he applies the text to the lives of believers in conflict. The gospel-centered approach of Luther is highlighted in Kolb's useful summary of five fundamental axioms:

1. Believers are to distinguish the hidden God, who lies beyond the grasp of human comprehension, from the revealed God.

2. This God has disclosed his essence by giving himself for the sins of the world in Christ's sacrifice on the cross.

3. Believers are to rely on faith in God's Word over human reason.

4. Believers are to perceive how God acts in human lives by hiding himself under what seems to be contrary to his will and his love.

5. Believers are to be encouraged in the midst of their battle against Satan and every form of evil he uses as they live the life of daily dying and rising in repentance.[44]

Having spent some time now describing Luther's theology of the cross, we see that it is not a concept always easy to get a handle on. Gerhard Forde suggests that it is indeed not always easy to get at the distinction between a theology of glory and a theology of the cross. The language used for each is so similar that the point can sometimes be lost. A theologian of glory, just as a theologian of the cross, will inevitably speak about the concepts of "God," "creation," "sin," "grace," and "redemption." How can we make the distinction? In a deceptively simple move, Forde suggests that it might be easier to understand the matter if we say that Luther made a distinction between a theology *of* the cross and a theology *about* the cross. A theology of glory seeks to attract the slumbering soul and address the human will, and by virtue of this approach it becomes a theology *about* the cross, and explanation is its stock-in-trade. A theology of the cross, however, assumes that the will is bound and by virtue of this approach it becomes a theology *of* the cross that is enacted upon the hearer through the living word of God with death and new life as its *modus vivendi*, and preaching and offering the promise through the sacraments is its stock-in-trade.[45]

The theology of glory, as Forde points out, may well grant the need for grace. The only dispute will be about the degree of grace needed. Those who are "liberal" will most likely describe it as a form of moral persuasion or spiritual encouragement. Those who are "conservative" will speak of the difficulty of extracting ourselves from sin and thus exalt the power of grace.

> But the hallmark of a theology of glory is that it will always consider grace as something of a supplement to whatever is left of human will and power. It will always, in the end, hold out for some free will. Theology then becomes the business of making theological explanations attractive to the will.[46]

It is interesting to note in this regard that a theology of the cross transcends the liberal/conservative divide that so dominates much theological debate. As such, we can see how it serves as a critical criterion for determining what true theology and recognition of God is all about.

But if Luther himself describes his manner of going about the theological task as a theology of the cross, then why is it that in the introduction to his German works he speaks of prayer, meditation, and spiritual trial? Or to put the question in a slightly different way: What is the relationship between Luther's theology of the cross and the three rules? How do these two concepts and sets of terminology fit together? Answering this question would take us into details well beyond the scope of this study, but it can be said that Luther's two formulations need not be seen in oppositional terms.

When Luther was asked to present his new evangelical theology to his Augustinian Order, he formulated his theology of the cross in a set of compact theological/philosophical theses. These concepts and language were formulated in polemic opposition to Scholasticism and the Erasmian humanism of his day. The content of Luther's theological outlook and insight is contained in his Heidelberg Disputation of 1518 with particular force. Further, it must also be said that the theology of the cross constitutes a criterion for theological thinking and serves as a critique for all human religion. This remains constant throughout Luther's career, even though the context (and thus the terminology) changes. On the other hand, in 1539 Luther speaks of the three rules as the proper method for pursuing theology. The method or form of theological existence is shaped by prayer, meditation, and agonizing struggle. This method, with its distinctive roots in the monastic tradition as enhanced by the biblical humanism of the day, remained in place throughout Luther's career as a teacher of the Bible. Prayer, meditation, and agonizing spiritual struggle are the pathway in which the experience of God takes place. To state it simply, the *theologia crucis* is the *content* while the three rules are the *method* for Luther's life as a theologian.[47]

In the end, it would seem that we have come back around again to the critical formula we began with: prayer, meditation, and spiritual trial. This triadic formula presents itself as something more than a phrase constituting a criterion for all theology; rather, it is an approach to the subject matter of theology not as an academic science but as a lived reality. As such, Luther's approach brings together such things as prayer and work, illumination and thinking, and grace of the Spirit and the study of the arts. These are things that broke apart under the pressure of the Enlightenment into historical considerations on the one hand and personal piety on the other.

Oswald Bayer points out that in spite of overlapping interests, the formula presents a clear alternative to the program of Anselm's motto *fides quaerens intellectum* ("faith seeking understanding"), which has been and continues to be a guiding principle for theology. Augustine was convinced that a knowledge of God presupposed faith, and that faith seeks to understand in order to praise God more fully. Anselm, in the preface to his *Prologion*, uses the phrase in opposition to the idea that we understand in order to believe. Rather, he was convinced that apart from faith there would be no understanding. Faith seeking understanding as a program proceeds without much disturbance from Augustine to Anselm until Hegel and then through to Karl Barth. It is notable that this approach does not include *tentatio* as a fundamental and constitutive element.[48] This is because the historical nature of theological existence is not highlighted. Theology conducted in this manner is a science that centers on contemplation.

The triadic formula of Luther stands as an understanding of theology that is more a matter of wisdom than science, although science is not excluded. In fact, science is included in wisdom. As such, wisdom seeks to hold together the scientific inquiry of the subject without neglecting the fact that all knowledge is achieved from a particular starting point that cannot be erased by the inquiry itself. Wisdom brings with it a recognition of the world in which we live and the vital connection each one has with it. Thus with wisdom we have a pathway of learning and growing. It is never complete, but it is always on the way. Wisdom seeks to bind together the theoretical and the practical and grounds them in a third reality, the life of gratitude. Science has only one principle, and this becomes its boundary. Wisdom on the other hand has to do with experience, and since it encompasses science it relativizes the priority that is given to pure intellect in science and establishes it in a balance within a wider discussion.

It is important to point out, according to Bayer, that Luther's formula opens up what he calls *Spielraum*—room to operate or explore (literally, "to play")—in the many open areas of inquiry, such as Scripture and Spirit, word and church, time and history, and experience and suffering.[49] This openness of the three rules excludes any understanding of theology that is a mere rehearsal of an exclusive or dominant theory or explanation of the sphere of activity of theology. In place of the binary schema of theory and praxis, Luther places his understanding in a threefold approach that includes knowledge, action, and faith. Luther does not allow himself to be placed under a particular traditional definition of theology, although he can freely interact with them all. What is of importance is the critical understanding that grows in the tension of prayer, meditation, and spiritual trial.

Theological Existence as Vocation

Luther's teaching of these three rules to the laity is the constant factor that attests to the central focus on theological existence we find in his theology. Citing just a few examples should be enough to show how Luther imparts "wisdom for the road," so to speak. Here we find Luther training the laity in the three rules and thus encouraging theological existence in light of prayer, meditation, and agonizing spiritual struggle.

The first example is found in Luther's 1519 work, "A Simple Way to Pray."[50] In this treatise, which is much more than a simple exposition of the universal prayer of Christians, Luther sets out prayer for the laity in the context of the three rules. The seven petitions of the Lord's Prayer lead the participant through an acknowledgment and naming of God as Father through prayer for the kingdom, daily bread, forgiveness, and deliverance from temptation and evil. This deceptively simple prayer encompasses the entirety of the Christian life. Luther, in plainly written exposition, leads believers to a deeper understanding of the "how" and the "what" of prayer, and also to recognition of sin, repentance, and trusting in the Triune God.

Luther based this exposition on his series of sermons on the Ten Commandments, which he gave from December 1516 to February 1517. After this, he gave a series of sermons on the Lord's Prayer during the 1517 Lenten season. Luther's friend and fellow theologian, Johann Agricola (1494–1566), produced a publication from these sermons on the Lord's Prayer. Luther, however, was dissatisfied with this publication and produced his own version. Between 1519 and 1522, it went through thirteen editions with four different publishing houses, which is a testimony to its popularity.[51]

Let us briefly observe how Luther teaches the three rules in this exposition. Since it is titled "A Simple Way to Pray," prayer is obviously the focus of the work. In this treatise, Luther carefully provides—along with copious illustrations—an introduction to prayer, its nature and use, petitions from the Lord's Prayer, and a brief summary and arrangement for these petitions. Luther teaches, exhorts, gives examples, and rehearses various kinds of prayer a layperson might utter. One such example comes at the end of the third petition:

> O Father, do not let me get to the point where my will is done. Break my will; resist it. No matter what happens let my life be governed not by my will, but by yours. As no one's own will prevails in heaven so may it also be here on earth.[52]

The address and response, which is the beginning of all theological existence, naturally moves into the act of repentance. God's address "I AM the LORD your God" is the beginning of theological existence, and our response to this address is that dialogue we call faith.

Recognizing God as the boundary of human existence and seeking to honor his name at the outset dictates the course of the Christian life. Sin is recognized and a continued meditation upon Scripture is undertaken. Regarding the fourth petition of the Lord's Prayer, Luther says that "sermons and doctrines which do not bring and show Jesus Christ to us are not the daily bread and nourishment of our souls, nor will they help us in any need or trial."[53] The recognition of sin, the receiving of forgiveness in Christ, and moving to faith is the pathway contained in the Lord's Prayer. This is done not to *avoid* trial but rather in the *midst* of trial. For prayer, as it acts upon us, humbles us because it compels us to confess our sin, but it also raises us up and overcomes our weakness through the mercy of Christ. "Every word of God terrifies and comforts us, hurts and heals; it breaks down and builds up; it plucks up and plants again; it humbles and exalts [Jer. 1:10]."[54]

Falling into the hands of the living God is a death *and* a resurrection, and Luther's exposition of the Lord's Prayer makes that perfectly clear. Quoting the book of Job, Luther insists that life is nothing but struggle against sin; and citing the apostle Peter, he warns about the prowling devil who seeks someone to devour.[55] We should not be like an idle or a runaway knight "who wants neither to be attacked nor to enter combat."[56] Rather, we are to be like the true knight who overcomes trial. "We cannot prevent trials and temptations from overtaking us, but with our prayer and our invocation of God's assistance we can stave off their victory over us."[57] Although more could be said about this exposition, it is resoundingly clear that these three rules provide the context and approach of this early work by Luther.

We find a second example in Luther's 1521 treatise titled "A Sermon on the Three Kinds of Good Life for the Instruction of Consciences."[58] This colorful sermon speaks in graphic terms using the threefold construction of Solomon's Temple as a foundational metaphor.[59] The outer court consists of external ceremonies, fasting, the wearing of special clothing, and the practice of specifically religious activities. We must advance from the outer court to the nave and thereby learn what is of greater importance. In this area of the temple, we learn the meaning of conscience, virtue, and authentic good works. Here we learn that the joyful and willing performance of these important things is hindered and rendered impossible due to the nature of the human heart. Finally, we come to the inner sanctuary, the Holy of Holies. In his final stage of evangelical doctrine, Luther holds up before us Christ and his promises. Here, Luther presents Christ, faith, and the coming of the Holy Spirit as the manner in which a new life is constituted.

Through this sermon, Luther intended to help the laity break free from their entanglement with old ways and ideas. Luther's claim that a believer is justified by faith alone stood in opposition to what they had been taught. Like the Jewish people during the days of the temple, the people of Luther's day were accustomed to ceremonies, holy days, rules regarding fasting, and the kinds of good works prescribed by the Roman Catholic Church. Through his sermon, Luther sought to release their bound consciences into the freedom of the gospel. From Luther's point of view, focusing on the word of God in Christ is the only way to accomplish this. At the dramatic high point of the sermon, Luther says that the one who seeks God himself will find him; on the other hand, he who seeks reward will never find him and makes his reward his god.

> For these reasons a man has to go down on his knees for grace and deny himself. To this end, then, God has built the sanctuary and *Sanctum sanctorum* for us. Here he has set Christ before us and promised that he who believes in him and calls on his name shall at once receive the Holy Spirit. As he says in John 16, "The Father will send the Holy Spirit in my name."[60] A man who denies himself and calls upon Christ in genuine trust is certain to receive the Holy Spirit. Where Christ's name is, there the Holy Spirit follows. He who calls on Christ in faith, however, possesses his name, and the Holy Spirit most certainly comes to him. When the Spirit comes, however, look, he makes a pure, free, cheerful, glad, and loving heart, a heart which is simply gratuitously righteous, seeking no reward, fearing no punishment. Such a heart is holy for the sake of holiness and righteousness alone and does everything with joy. Look! Here is really sound doctrine! This shows what a conscience is and what good works are! It is to go into the *Sanctum sanctorum*, to pass into the sanctuary. That is the last thing on earth that any man can do. This is the road to heaven. No man remains wicked; on the contrary, all become righteous. This road is quite the opposite of the atrium, for it has no regard for the external things of the churchyard. Indeed, one sees only what enemies of this road they are and how dangerous they are.[61]

It is important to note here how Luther—following in the trailblazing pathway of Paul, John, and the other apostles—reconstructs the whole world with Christ as its Alpha and Omega, its source, its center, and its goal. This liberty of mind and the freedom of thought with which Luther proceeds are produced by the powerful witness of Jesus, the One who atones for sin and brings the gift of a divine righteousness. This gospel of freedom is not bound by old orthodoxies; neither is it satisfied to rehearse the need to follow human regulations, as though ceremonial accuracy and routine were the source of divine pleasure. Hearers of this sermon are presented with the Christ who makes all things new, and they are called to meditate on the Christ who is placed before us in his promise. This meditation brings with it the Holy Spirit and the new life of faith, the creation of a loving heart, and freely given righteousness.

With this focus on the gospel of freedom, we would not expect a languid and drawn-out exposition of the three rules. But note what is close at hand: the quoted passage begins with a man falling on his knees in prayer (*oratio*) in order to deny himself and to receive grace, and then he focuses on meditation (*meditatio*) on Christ and his promise. All this is done under the shadow of the affliction and adversity of the land. With characteristic flair, Luther says, "Tragically it has come to pass that there has never been a people on the face of the earth that has had a bigger atrium, more holy foods, more holy garments, more holy days, more holy places, than Christians now have!"[62] The danger comes from the pope and canon law. This spiritual trial (*tentatio*) is one from which Luther prays for God's deliverance. Being set free comes by that change of mind that happens in Christ through the Spirit. It comes by receiving the Spirit, and the Spirit is received at the cross. It enters into us as we are enveloped in the love of God and as we are perpetually renewed—not in the old manner of the dead letter, or in fidelity to established rules or usages. Even in this example, it seems that Luther believes that renewal happens as we follow along a path marked out by prayer, meditation, and spiritual trial, as we are led by the Spirit.

The third example comes from Luther's 1522 treatise titled *The Estate of Marriage*.[63] This was produced during a time of extraordinary stress in Luther's life. After receiving warnings from Rome, the public decree announcing Luther's excommunication was published on January 3, 1521. Hard on the heels of that, Luther was summoned to recant at the assembly known as the Diet of Worms, something he refused to do. Given his outlaw status, very few believed that the safe passage granted to Luther would be honored. For that reason and fearing for the life of his star professor, Frederick the Wise had arranged for Luther to be whisked away to safety. The plan was so carefully crafted that even the elector himself could honestly say he did not know Luther's whereabouts. From May 1521 to March 1522, under the assumed name of Junker Jörg ("Knight George"), Luther resided at Wartburg Castle in Eisenach, Germany. Here Luther threw himself into his work during this time of seclusion, managing a masterful translation of the New Testament from Greek into German in just ten weeks. Although it was not the first German translation of the Bible, it became the most popular and the most influential. It was sometime between March and December of 1522 that Luther's *The Estate of Marriage* was published.

It is not an exposition of the Lord's Prayer, nor is it a focused meditation on Scripture. Rather, it is a treatise touching on a life issue of great importance— marriage. To answer the restraints of papal law, Luther set out his concerns in three parts: part one deals with the laws of consanguinity and the question of who may be legally married; part two deals with who may be legally divorced; and part three deals with how the estate of marriage is conducive to the salvation of one's soul and how one may live a Christian and godly life in that estate.

Luther speaks of the fact that the estate of marriage had fallen into disrepute. He points out how pagan books had been written disparaging marriage, and how complaints against marriage were commonplace among those who did not recognize it as God's work. To summarize, Luther quotes the worldly adage regarding marriage, "Brief is the joy, lasting the bitterness."[64] "When that clever harlot, our natural reason (which the pagans followed in trying to be most clever), takes a look at married life, she turns up her nose."[65] Too many thought that the effort involved in marriage was simply not worth it; it was just too difficult to make it work. A married person must care for his or her spouse. Even in the best of relationships there are times when this is no small task. There is a constant need to provide food and shelter for each other. The married person must put aside individual wishes in deference to the other. Even in the best of relationships, patience can be stretched to the breaking point. For all these reasons, human reason often looks on marriage with a jaundiced eye. Human reason does not see marriage as a work ordained by God for the good of creation. Instead, it focuses on the drudgery that a married person must endure and the inconvenience of children. Over against human reason, Luther sets this response:

> What does Christian faith say to this? It opens its eyes, looks upon all these insignificant, distasteful, and despised duties in the Spirit, and is aware that they are all adorned with divine approval as with the costliest gold and jewels. It says, "O God, because I am certain that thou hast created me as a man and hast from my body begotten this child, I also know for a certainty that it meets with thy perfect pleasure. I confess to thee that I am not worthy to rock the little babe or wash its diapers, or to be entrusted with the care of the child and its mother. How is it that I, without any merit, have come to this distinction of being certain that I am serving thy creature and thy most precious will? O how gladly will I do so, though the duties should be even more insignificant and despised. Neither frost nor heat, neither drudgery nor labor, will distress or dissuade me, for I am certain that it is thus pleasing in thy sight.[66]

The response of faith, even in the face of real hardship and trial, is to acknowledge that marriage is the good work of God. As Luther presents it here, marriage comes in the form of a confession of faith—indeed, as a prayer from the heart that resolves to act in the world in a particular way.

Marriage carries with it duties and responsibilities that are ordered by God. Entering joyfully into fulfilling those tasks is a prayerful act of worship. In some cases, this means caring for children. These young lives are brought into the bosom of a family so that Christian works might be lavished upon them. This brings into view the importance of the family and the role of parents. As Luther puts it,

Most certainly father and mother are apostles, bishops, and priests to their children, for it is they who make them acquainted with the gospel. In short, there is no greater or nobler authority on earth than that of parents over their children, for this authority is both spiritual and temporal. Whoever teaches the gospel to another is truly his apostle and bishop. Miter and staff and great estates indeed produce idols, but teaching the gospel produces apostles and bishops. See therefore how good and great is God's work and ordinance![67]

One theme in this treatise has to do with the trial and suffering that go along with marriage. The natural desire to escape this kind of trial and suffering blocks human reason from recognizing marriage as the gift of God, but the light of faith sees things differently. Faith views the insignificant and distasteful duties of marriage through the Spirit. These tasks are done to freely serve others, which also pleases God.

In this treatise, Luther begins with the trial and the temptation of human reason rather than meditation on the word of God or prayer. What we find, however, is that the agonizing struggle in life leads to a consideration of the word of God in its manifold witness regarding marriage. Further, it is interesting to note that the response of faith to the doubts of human reason on this topic come from Luther in the form of a confession, a prayer of belief. In this example of Luther's preaching, as in the two examples before, we see how the three rules stand in close proximity, forming the dynamic interchange of theological existence. The threefold approach to the matter of theology is one that Luther teaches to the laity in his early period, long before he sets out the formula in 1539.

The idea that Luther's three rules are central to the Wittenberg Reformation is confirmed in the writings of his followers. One such example comes from Johann Mathesius (1504–65), a student of Luther's and compiler of some of his Table Talks. In a sermon given in 1560, he states:

Three things make a theologian: *Meditatio, oratio, und tentatio* (meditation, prayer, and trial). One should consider and pay close attention to the words of Scripture and must earnestly entreat the Lord of the Bible and his Spirit, who is the gatekeeper of God's library. In addition, one should have been tested and have gained some experience in the school of the cross, even as Christ himself was led into the wilderness by the Spirit and tested by the devil before he began his public ministry in his thirtieth year.[68]

Again, in the same sermon he says, "A preacher should do three things: read the Bible avidly, pray earnestly, and remain a disciple and a student. In this way he will be a great doctor."[69] Apparently the lessons that Johann Mathesius learned from the Wittenberg Reformer stuck with him. From these comments, we can deduce that the three rules were a common way of thinking and living out life in the Spirit. We turn now to a more thorough exposition of the three rules.

CHAPTER 2

PRAYER

Prayer is the first of the three rules. Or, perhaps better, I should say that it is the beginning of the making of a theologian. This is how Luther sets out the matter in brief form:

> In the first place, you should know that the Holy Scripture is such a book as to make the wisdom of all other books foolishness, because it is the only book that teaches about eternal life. Therefore you should immediately despair of your reason and understanding. They will not gain you eternal life, but, on the contrary, your presumptuousness will cast you and others like you out of heaven (as happened to Lucifer) into the abyss of hell. But kneel down in your little room [Matt. 6:6] and pray to God with real humility and earnestness, that he through his dear Son may give you his Holy Spirit, who will enlighten you, lead you, and give you understanding.
>
> As you can see, David keeps praying in the above-mentioned Psalm [Ps. 119], "Teach me, Lord, instruct me, lead me, show me," and many more words like these. Although he well knew and daily heard and read the text of Moses and other books besides, he still wants to lay hold of the real teacher of Scripture himself, so that he may not grasp it in a disordered way with his reason and become his own teacher. For such practice gives rise to factious spirits who allow themselves to nurture the delusion that Scripture is subject to them and can be easily grasped with their reason, as if they were Markolf or Aesop's Fables, for which no Holy Spirit and no prayers are needed.[1]

One of the most notable characteristics of this presentation of the first rule is the intense interplay among Holy Scripture, prayer, and the Holy Spirit. In Luther's thinking, prayer is intimately connected with the word and the Spirit. Holy Scripture makes the wisdom of all other books foolishness because it teaches about eternal life. But since Scripture is not subject to human reason, the illumination and the leading of the Holy Spirit is necessary in order for the believer to come to understanding. That calls for prayer in the style of David, who cries out, "Teach me, Lord, instruct me, lead me, show me." The point is to "lay hold of the real teacher of Scripture himself" so that a disordered approach to the text can be avoided. Instead of relying on human reason (*ratio*), Luther urges the adoption of prayer (*oratio*). Only through this "orational" appropriation of Scripture can human presumption be replaced with a hearing of faith.

The goal of prayer is thus to find oneself in the hands of the Holy Spirit, who will enlighten the mind through the text of Scripture.

The importance Luther attached to the matter of prayer can be seen in the number of booklets, sermons, and other instructions he wrote for a lay audience. Even if we restrict ourselves to a rather short and random list, we still find a wealth of resources that tell us a great deal of what Luther would have us know about prayer. In 1517, Luther prepared his first book for the printers.[2] His work, *The Seven Penitential Psalms*, provides commentary on the texts that were especially prayed during the Lenten season. Although Luther ultimately broke with the penitential system of the medieval church, he retained the use of these psalms as an expression of Christian repentance. This is in keeping with the saying that stands at the head of the Ninety-Five Theses, "When our Lord and master Jesus Christ said, 'Repent' [Matt. 4:17], he willed the entire life of believers to be one of repentance."[3]

An Exposition of the Lord's Prayer is a series of sermons collected together to instruct the laity in what and how to pray.[4] The booklet appeared under several different titles and at least three different forms between 1518 and 1522. It was extremely popular, judging by the fact that between 1519 and 1522 the Reformer's own version went through thirteen editions printed in Wittenberg, Leipzig, Basel, and St. Ursula's Monastery. A Venetian printer, we are told, who had read the work but did not know the identity of the author, was reported by Johann Mathesius to have exclaimed, "Blessed are the hands that wrote this. Blessed are the eyes that see it. Blessed shall be the hearts that believe this book and cry to God."[5]

In 1522, *Personal Prayer Book* (*Betbüchlein*) was published.[6] The occasion for this more comprehensive prayer book had to do with the rapid growth of the Reformation while Luther was absent from Wittenberg (April 1521–January 1522). As mentioned in the previous chapter, immediately after his appearance at the Diet of Worms, where Luther's confession of faith was made before the emperor, Luther was kidnapped for his own safety and taken to Wartburg Castle. The hiatus was necessary because of the personal danger presented to Luther, but the time away from Wittenberg also left the progress of the gospel in less stable and reliable hands. Upon his return it was evident that something needed to be done to communicate the new evangelical piety in terms that could be understood and appropriated by the laity. His *Personal Prayer Book* of some forty pages incorporated the outward form of some of the highly regarded prayer books of the Roman Church but modified the content in crucial ways.

Luther's prayer book contains expositions of the Ten Commandments, the Apostles' Creed, the Hail Mary, and several psalms. While the inclusion of these items was not unusual in itself, the evangelical interpretation of Luther is unmistakable. Later editions of the prayer book included a "Sermon on the Holy," "Revered Sacrament of Baptism," a "Sermon on Confession and Sacrament," and a "Sermon on Preparation for Death." The 1529 edition of *Personal Prayer Book*, among other inclusions, contained a Latin calendar with a verse for each month, as well as a Passion History consisting of fifty full-page wood-cuts of Bible events and stories showing the drama of salvation. The original prayer book of approximately forty pages swelled to two hundred eight pages with these added features. In its first year of publication, it went through nine editions, with fourteen more between 1523 and 1530.[7]

Almost five centuries later, it is hard for us to realize the centrality and importance of the prayer-book tradition. We can, however, get an idea by look-ing at the shifting tides of the Reformation in England precisely on the basis of changes made to the prayer book as it transformed during the reigns of Henry VIII, Edward VI, Mary, and Elizabeth I. The final production of *The Book of Common Prayer* by Thomas Cranmer and others contains all the historical twists of those difficult years.[8]

In the case of Luther and his prayer book, the stakes were also very high. So it is that he complains about the prayer books of his age as being harmful and objectionable: "They drub into the minds of simple people such a wretched counting up of sins and going to confession, such un-Christian tomfoolery about prayers to God and his saints!"[9] Luther wanted to undertake a reforma-tion of the literary genre, but he simply did not have the time. Instead, he wrote *Personal Prayer Book* and attached the following words to the preface:

> I urge everyone to break away from using the Bridget prayers and any others which are ornamented with indulgences or rewards and urge all to get accus-tomed to praying this plain, ordinary Christian prayer. The longer one devotes himself to this kind of praying, the more pleasant and dear it becomes. To that end may this prayer's Master, our dear Lord Jesus Christ, help us, to whom be blessings in all eternity. Amen.[10]

Luther was convinced that the total content of Scripture was contained in the Ten Commandments, the Apostles' Creed, and the Lord's Prayer. From his point of view, there is no need to add anything additional—indeed, to do so could be dangerous. That is why he wanted to set out an unencumbered form for learning prayer directed to the needs of the laity.

In 1529, Luther's Small and Large Catechisms eclipsed *Personal Prayer Book*,[11] becoming central to Luther's educational reform in the church and es-tablishing the prayer life of the Christian as a foundational feature.[12] Once again, we see that Luther's pattern for prayer is based on the Lord's Prayer. Luther was convinced that praying this prayer given to us by the Master, while paying at-tention to its content and form, was the best possible way to learn how to pray. But it is interesting to note that in spite of the fact that the catechisms filled the educational needs of the evangelical churches in Germany, Luther still found reason to write more on the topic of prayer.

In 1535, *A Simple Way to Pray* was published and dedicated to Peter Besk-endorf, a master barber and surgeon.[13] A longtime friend of Luther, Beskendorf had asked him for a simple way to pray that a common layperson could use. The thirty-four-page booklet Luther produced came directly out of Luther's experience. Its compelling and direct style evidences a lifelong practice of prayer. The following memorable opening paragraphs contain a vivid portrait of Luther in his quest for prayer in the Spirit:

> First, when I feel that I have become cool and joyless in prayer because of other tasks or thoughts (for the flesh and the devil always impede and obstruct prayer), I take my little psalter, hurry to my room, or, if it be the day and hour for it, to the church where a congregation is assembled and, as time permits, I say quietly to myself and word-for-word the Ten Commandments, the Creed, and if I have time, some words of Christ or Paul, or some psalms, just as a child might do.

> It is a good thing to let prayer be the first business of the morning and the last at night. Guard yourself carefully against those false, deluding ideas which tell you, "Wait a little while. I will pray in an hour; first I must attend to this or that." Such thoughts get you away from prayer into other affairs which so hold your attention and involve you that nothing comes of prayer for that day.[14]

Luther knows that the habit of true prayer is something that takes time to develop and nurture. He also knows that prayer will not necessarily flow effortlessly the first time believers try to pray and that there are many pressures that push us away from it. In *A Simple Way to Pray*, Luther teaches his friend Beskendorf—and all his readers—what to do in order to avoid becoming "lax and lazy, cool and listless toward prayer."[15]

What are some of the foundational thoughts of Luther on prayer? How would he go about teaching someone to pray? If we want to know what Luther thinks about a particular topic, then taking a look at his catechisms is a good place to start. The introduction to his exposition of the Lord's Prayer in the Large Catechism sets out in brief compass Luther's frame of reference with respect to the important matter of prayer. Here we find Luther's comments in a catechetical context, treating prayer by way of command, promise, and the need that impels prayer.

The catechetical context has already been mentioned. Luther sees prayer at the heart of the Christian life, and his work as a theologian of the cross and pastor motivates him to constantly be on the watch for ways to instruct and inspire the laity in their efforts to pray. Luther's exposition of the Lord's Prayer in the Large Catechism—which has been called "a continuing lesson in the theology of the cross,"[16] as well as "The battle-cry of faith"[17]—is yet another example. In fact, the instructional or the catechetical approach of Luther is so central that Oswald Bayer has spoken of Luther's theology as "catechetical systematics."[18]

The exciting story of how Luther transformed the medieval catechetical structure has been told elsewhere.[19] The medieval ordering of the essential elements of the catechism is as follows: the Lord's Prayer, the Apostles' Creed, the Ten Commandments, and the Ave Maria. This ordering is oriented to the penitential system of merit. Unfortunately, the old penitential system offered only one piece of advice, although in different forms, compelling believers to do more, making them feel they are never doing enough. This form of "tread-mill" Christianity only trapped a person on a never-ending quest of uncertainty. Psychologically, there could be only two possible responses: a smug self-righteousness for the self-assured, or despair for the anxious and sensitive.

Luther's approach has a different starting point. Instead of beginning with advice for a good life that would ultimately lead to contrition, a full repentance of sin, and resulting salvation, Luther begins with the proclamation of God's word to the human heart. Luther's ordering of the catechism is as follows: the Ten Commandments, the Apostles' Creed, and the Lord's Prayer. This reordering reflects Luther's conviction that the gospel is the central need of the human heart. No longer oriented to the medieval penitential system, Luther seeks to allow the elements of the catechism to do their divine work in transforming the hearer through law and gospel. As Timothy Wengert says of Luther, "He jettisoned the medieval penitential order, which moved from faith to contrition to satisfaction, and replaced it with an evangelical one based upon his understanding of justification by faith alone and its hermeneutic: the distinction between law and gospel."[20] The radical word of sin and forgiveness then led quite naturally to prayer, which was now understood not as merit but as the cry of the believer calling upon God for help in every area of life:

> Three things a person must know in order to be saved. First, he must know what to do and what to leave undone. Second, when he realizes that he cannot measure up to what he should do or leave undone, he needs to know where to go to find the strength he requires. Third, he must know how to seek and obtain that strength. It is just like a sick person who first has to determine the nature of his sickness, then find out what to do or to leave undone. After that he has to know where to get the medicine which will help him do or leave undone what is right for a healthy person. Then he has to desire to search for this medicine and to obtain it or have it brought to him.

> Thus the commandments teach man to recognize his sickness, enabling him to perceive what he must do or refrain from doing, consent to or refuse, and so he will recognize himself to be a sinful and wicked person. The Creed will teach and show him where to find the medicine—grace—which will help him to become devout and keep the commandments. The Creed points him to God and his mercy, given and made plain to him in Christ. Finally, the Lord's Prayer teaches all this, namely, through the fulfillment of God's commandments everything will be given him. In these three are the essentials of the entire Bible.[21]

Clearly, for Luther, the catechism is a matter of diagnosis (law), treatment (gospel), and medicine (prayer). The Lord's Prayer is the culmination or inevitable outcome that expresses a life grasped by the gospel and renewed in relationship with the God of creation, redemption, and sanctification. The catechetical context for Luther's teaching on prayer shows the force of this line of thinking; it also shows how very central prayer is to the gospel of Jesus Christ.

In the introduction to the Lord's Prayer in the Large Catechism, Luther impresses upon his readers the importance of prayer by way of the commandments:

> The first thing to know is this: It is our duty to pray because of God's command. For we heard in the Second Commandment, "You are not to take God's name in vain." Thereby we are required to praise the holy name and to pray or call upon it in every need.[22]

The command to pray is just as binding as God's command not to have any other God but him, not to kill, not to steal, and not to bear false witness. If we want to be Christians, then we must pray.

It may come as a surprise that Luther, the theologian of freedom, begins his treatment with a presentation of the law, or obligation (we might think he would begin with a reiteration of the gospel). His starting point might be surprising from that point of view, but it serves to stir and to comfort the human heart. In the first instance, Luther points out that it is not left up to our choice whether to pray or not. The command stands as an accusation against any effort to wiggle out of the responsibility. I might ask myself, "What difference do my prayers make in the big scheme of things?" I might be tempted to give up any attempt to pray and think, "What is the use in prayer anyway?" But against these thoughts the command is unwavering: "You shall and must obey!"[23]

In addition, Luther points out that the natural impulse of the human heart is to flee from God and not turn to him in "prayer, praise, and thanksgiving."[24] But for those who think that God neither wants nor cares about their prayers, the command has a different effect. In this circumstance, the command to pray is a source of comfort, for in it God "makes it clear that he will not cast us out or drive us away, even though we are sinners; he wishes rather to draw us to himself so that we may humble ourselves before him, lament our misery and plight, and pray for grace and help."[25] Thus when we pray to God, we know that we are doing what God commands and that it is pleasing to him. This is indeed a comforting thought for the conscience that is bruised.[26]

The second reason to pray, beyond the command itself, is the promise attached to prayer:

> God has made and affirmed a promise: that what we pray is a certain and sure thing. As he says, in Ps. 50[:15], "Call on me in the day of trouble; I will deliver you," and Christ says in the Gospel of Matthew 7[:7–8], "Ask, and it will be given you," etc. . . . "For everyone who asks receives." Such promises certainly ought to awaken and kindle in our hearts a longing and love for prayer.[27]

God wants us to call him Father and to rely on him for all our earthly and eternal good. To place ourselves in the hands of God is to trust and believe in God's goodness. This is made possible by the generosity and extravagance

God shows us in Christ Jesus, in whom all the promises of God find their "yes" (1 Cor. 1:30).

Luther acknowledges that since it is easy to pray in a less than wholehearted manner, the question may arise, "Why should God hear my prayers? I am insignificant and deeply flawed by sin." To this attitude Luther has a sharp answer: those who pray like this do not have their eye on God's promise but on their own works, and they "are angering God, grossly dishonoring him, and accusing him of lying."[28] The fact is that God himself "desires nothing more from us than that we ask many and great things of him. And, on the contrary, he is angered if we do not ask and demand with confidence."[29] Prayer in confident faith flows out of the promise of God's word. As Luther says,

> In this life our old skin always smacks of the nature of its origin. The wine takes on the taste of the barrel. Therefore it must always be cleaned out. Our life, however, is set firmly on the foundation of the apostles and prophets so that in these remains we can always say, "I am a child and an heir of God." We can say this not because of ourselves but because of the most far-reaching promises, for the sake of which we are certain that we shall be heard.[30]

In this way, the barrel is cleaned out and we continue in the way of life. Prayer catches us up into that divine dialogue where we learn again and again what it means to trust in the "far-reaching" promises of God.

In addition to the command, the promise, and the fact that "God takes the initiative and puts into our mouths the very words and approach we are to use,"[31] we should be encouraged and drawn to pray because of the distress that surrounds us and causes us to cry out. Luther points out that we all have sufficient needs to fill our prayers. The odd thing, however, is that through the forgetfulness of sin we are not always aware of them, "we do not feel or see them."[32] Were we to feel our need acutely, were we to see the serious trouble that crouches at the door, there would be no need to generate devotion; prayer would come spontaneously. "God therefore wants you to lament and express your needs and concerns, not because he is unaware of them, but in order that you may kindle your heart to stronger and greater desires and open and spread your apron wide to receive many things."[33]

Prayer, as Luther describes it, embraces life. It moves the heart from those pathways that so crudely and coldly trade in indifference. Instead, by creating the habit of praying daily for our physical needs, the coming of God's kingdom, forgiveness, and deliverance from evil, we find ourselves at the feet of the God who always delights in showing mercy. Prayer undertaken in this way causes us to be aware of the world and the God who works in it, often in hidden ways. The task of those who pray is to approach God boldly and confidently. From this posture the task, in Luther's view, is to "remind God of his commandment and promise, knowing that he does not want them despised."[34] Importuning God on the basis of the commandment and the promise is a sure place to stand.

Luther asserts that prayer is a work of the "First Table," referring to the first three commandments as used in the Lutheran order of the Ten Commandments: "You shall have no other Gods," "You shall not take the name of the Lord your God in vain," and "Remember the Sabbath Day to keep it Holy."[35] These three commandments pertain to our relationship with God. The "Second Table" involves our neighbor. This selection from Luther's lectures on Genesis is typical:

> Here then, we have the highest form of worship, which is pleasing to God and later on was commanded in the First Table, and which includes the fear of God, trust in God, confession, prayer, and preaching.
>
> The First Commandment demands faith, that you believe that God is a Helper in due time, as Ps. 9:9 declares. The Second demands confession and prayer, that we call upon the name of God in danger and give thanks to God. The Third, that we teach the truth and only forms of worship of God which God demands; He does not demand sacrifices, money, and other things. He demands the First Table, that you hear, meditate on, and teach the Word; that you pray, and that you fear God. Whenever this is done, there will follow spontaneously, as it were the forms of the worship or the works of the Second Table. It is impossible for him who worships in accordance with the First Table not to keep the Second Table also.
>
> Similarly, the first psalm declares (Ps. 1:2–3): "He who meditates on the Word of God day and night is like a tree planted by rivers of water, which yields its fruit in its season and whose leaves do not fall to the ground." This is the clear and unfailing result. He who believes God and fears God, who calls upon God in troubles, who praises and thanks Him for His blessings, who gladly hears His Word, who constantly meditates on the words of God, and who teaches others to do the same, cannot harm his neighbor, can he? Or disobey his parents? Or kill? Or commit adultery?
>
> The First Table therefore must be presented first; people must first be instructed about the true worship of God. This produces a good tree, from which later on good fruits result. Our adversaries follow the opposite procedure; they want fruits to exist before there is a tree.[36]

Here, Luther depicts the relation of the God of creation to the created world entirely through the concept of law. The first commandment requires faith, which allows God to be God for the believer. The second commandment requires confession of sin and a crying out in prayer, which constitutes a proper use of God's name. The third commandment binds us to truth and true forms of worship, which keep us from building up false human ceremonies and direct us to a proper use of his word. Where the First Table is followed, a proper relationship to God is established. This makes it possible for the Second Table to be fulfilled as well.

Luther ties his explanation of the work of the First Table with one of his most beloved gospel images: "The First Table therefore must be presented first; people must first be instructed about the true worship of God. This produces a good tree, from which later on good fruits result."[37] The relationship between faith and works is likened to the tree (faith) that ultimately produces fruit (works). In this way, the work of the First Table is prior to the work of the Second Table.

God's command and promise are the starting point for all prayer. The command to have faith in the one true God (the first commandment) is directly related to the command not to take the name of the Lord in vain (the second commandment). The one rests in the other. Faith and prayer are related as heart and mouth. As the apostle Paul writes, "If you confess with your mouth that Jesus is Lord and believe in your heart that God raised him from the dead, you will be saved" (Rom. 10:9). The connection between belief and confession is axiomatic. The dynamic between faith and prayer participates in the truth of our confession of faith and the struggle to bring that to voice in the face of everyday trial. Thus it is possible to say that prayer is simultaneously the cry *of* faith as well as the cry *for* faith.[38]

Luther at Prayer

As we have seen, the making of a theologian begins in the practice of prayer. This was certainly the case with Luther. At this point in our study, it may be useful to take a close look at a few instances from his life as illustration. While there is a wide array of possible places to touch down, there are two very instructive moments worth highlighting: one of disappointment and one of great encouragement. The first is when Luther failed in his responsibility to say the canonical hours as prescribed by his Augustinian Order. This put him in the unenviable situation of having to say prayers as an obligation and therefore experiencing prayer as an intensifying burden. In a very real way, this represents the low point in Luther's experience of prayer. The second moment reveals an instance in which Luther derived great joy from answered prayer. He cried out to God and received a specific and tangible answer from his heavenly Father. In his later life, he refers back to this event as an exceptional example of the power of prayer.

To give a bit more background, prayer was a way of life in the Augustinian Order that Luther joined in 1505. Monastic life revolved around the canonical hours, which consist of offices (or services) of devotion observed at various points throughout the day and which were required for all monks. These offices would begin in the middle of the night with Matins. When the bell rang, the monk would get dressed, leave his cell, cross himself with holy water, kneel in respect toward the altar, and go to his assigned place. Matins began with the reading of Scripture and was followed by prayer. Prime, or the first hour of the day, followed at six o'clock in the morning, which was followed by Terse at nine, and then Sext at twelve. Mass for the monastery community was celebrated midmorning, and after the midday meal the monks observed an hour of rest. The office of Nones was sung in the afternoon and then Vespers toward evening. After the evening meal, the day concluded with the singing of Compline—after which silence was observed in the monastery.

The services of the day were extremely important, as observing them was the means by which the monastic community accrued merit (spiritual credit) and thus benefited the world around them. It was through the saying of the Mass, observing the canonical hours, and praying the rosary, as well as holding to the monastic life in general, that a monk could obtain merit for himself and merit for others. Later in his career, Luther put the matter in his usual direct fashion:

> What was I looking for so long in the cloister? Why did I read or pray so many Masses, canonical hours, and rosaries? Why did I expect comfort from the dead saints? Why did I go here and there on pilgrimages and for indulgences? All this was done—and no one can deny it—to expiate our sins, to reconcile God, and to be saved.[39]

Observing the canonical hours was certainly at the heart of monastic piety, and in its original form was meant to express the life of faith. But, as the tradition of Divine Office became increasingly hostage to the economics of the penitential system of the High Middle Ages, the saying of these prayers began to carry a different burden. Instead of prayer being a gift from God, it often became a works-righteous endeavor that, if taken to the extreme, meant the expulsion of the work of Christ—that is, replacing what he did on the cross with the merits earned by the monks.

Luther experienced the saying of canonical hours as a bit of legalism in a very personal way. When assigned as professor of Bible at the University of Wittenberg, Luther's schedule revolved around teaching classes and the administrative duties that fell to him. This meant he would often miss the saying of one of the hours or another. As a theologian, he was allowed the flexibility to make up for the missed service by saying it on his own. But because of the busy schedule of the university, this meant he would have to do them on the weekend, which was his prime study time in preparation for upcoming classes. Church historian Martin Brecht tells the story of how one of the Erfurt theologians paid someone else to say his hours. Luther, however, chose to fast and say his hours himself during his precious time over the weekend.[40] When the conflict with the indulgence controversy continued to increase and he became further occupied with his writings, Luther fell several months in arrears in saying his prayers. To try to catch up with this obligation and maintain his work in other areas became increasingly hopeless.

After experiencing prayer as a mere obligation and a deadening law, we could imagine that Luther would want to give up on prayer altogether. Indeed, we find his assessments of prayer in the monastery of a sharp kind. Luther criticizes the mumbled and inattentive praying of the hours. He points out the person who stands in church turning the pages of the prayer book, rattling his beads, while his mind wanders far from the confession of his lips:

> That is not praying. God says to such a one through his prophet Isaiah, "This people prays to me with their lips, but their heart is far from me" [Isa. 29:13]. Thus we also find some priests and clerics who slaver out their canonical hours without heartfelt desire and still dare to say unabashed, "Well, now I am happy. I have now settled my account with our Lord," and think that they have thereby satisfied God.[41]

He makes the caustic declaration that the real reason for all the prayers is the prebend, or monies received from the endowment of masses and other activities. The works-righteous atmosphere in which the prayers were offered swept aside the true nature of prayer as gift. Luther indicates something of the uncertainty of the prayers that were offered when he places these words in the mouth of one of the monks: "It is my duty to chant my canonical hours and to count my beads in this way, but I do not know whether God is pleased with this, takes delight in it, and will hear my prayers."[42]

In this story of Luther and the praying of the canonical hours, we have a glimpse of the rigors of monastic life with its strict accounting of sins, the vigils, and the mortification of the body through watching and fasting. The story could be told in order to emphasize the inevitability of the reform of the canonical hours that would soon take place during the Reformation period. If told in this way, then we simply corroborate the idea that Luther was destined to sweep away this practice of praying the Divine Office. Of course, Luther's own statements make that view plausible. The reality of Luther's relation to the Divine Office is, I think, a bit more nuanced than that. Rather than demolishing the set times for prayer and substituting for it a preference for individual prayer, we find Luther in his liturgical reforms retaining the daily offices of morning and evening prayer in the church. We find him giving attention to how these services will benefit the laity and help them to mature in the faith. Further, Luther's reforms seem to be consistent with earlier monastic ideals regarding prayer, which had been lost over the years. The admonition to "pray without ceasing" (1 Thess. 5:17) characterizes the monastic approach to prayer. All of life is a prayer during which, from time to time, we pause to practice set times for prayer, or the Divine Office. In essence, Luther's changes in the canonical hours are a move to retrieve this ideal. Of course, by doing so, Luther also turns his back on insisting that saying the canonical hours is required or that it is a law.[43]

If Luther's experience of dealing with the obligation of saying the canonical hours was one of the low points of his experience with prayer, then certainly one of the high points came as he prayed for his friend and colleague, Philipp

Melanchthon. The winter of 1539–40 had dealt harshly with Melanchthon, and declining health and a presentiment of his impending death caused him to make out his will in November. His mood was somber and circumspect as he made his way to the Colloquy in Hagenau. It is reported that on his way he murmured, "I have lived my life in ecclesiastical meetings, but presently I shall die in one!"[44] Too ill to make it all the way to Hagenau, however, Melanchthon was forced to stop in Weimar. The concern over his life was so serious that the elector, John Frederick, sent his court physician, Georg Sturz, to attend to him, and Luther and Caspar Cruciger, Lutheran theologian and close friend of Melanchthon, were summoned from Wittenberg.

When Luther entered the sickroom, he was shocked to see the dying Melanchthon. Philipp's countenance was fallen, his eyes were sunken, his senses diminished, he had stopped communicating, and his hearing was gone. He did not acknowledge anyone and refused food and drink. Upon seeing this, Luther was deeply affected and said, "God protect us! How the devil has disfigured this instrument [of God]!" Immediately Luther turned to the window and began to pray earnestly.

> At that time, said Luther, our Lord God had to receive it. For I threw the entire sack before the door, and rubbed his ears with all the promises to hear prayers that I could recall from Holy Scripture, so that he had to hear me, were I to believe all those other promises.[45]

It is altogether appropriate to say that "Luther's chutzpah toward God in that moment was not so much a sign of hubris as it was of faith."[46] "Throwing sacks" and "rubbing ears" are indeed playful and wonderfully colloquial phrases that well express the urgency and intimacy of Luther's petition. The picture here is that of Luther importuning the Lord on behalf of his ailing friend. Luther reminds the Lord that this is his business, and he does so through Holy Scripture. Luther repeats God's promises as petition, as inducement, indeed, as an act of faith. Importuning God is a practice that requires diligence. In this sense, prayer is not clinical or "scientific" but is driven by need and carried along by the strength of the relationship.

The account goes on to say that after Luther prayed, "he took Philipp by the hand and said, be of good spirit, Philipp; you will not die." Luther reminded him that God does not will the death of the sinner, but he desires that the sinner might turn and live. God prefers life over death. That being the case, he urged Philipp by saying, "Believe in the Lord who kills and makes alive again, who injures and binds up, who strikes down and can make whole again."

In the intensity of the moment Melanchthon began to breathe a bit deeper, and he looked directly at Luther. He couldn't speak for some time, but when he did he told Luther that God had started him on a good journey and that he ought to let him depart. There couldn't be a better ending for him. At this Luther shook his head and said, "By no means, Philipp, you have to serve our

Lord God some more. . . . Do you hear? Shortly you must eat some food for me or I'll excommunicate you!"[47] After eating a little, Melanchthon began to regain his strength.

While Luther is well aware that all prayer is heard, he also realized that not all prayer is answered in the affirmative, which is why Luther experienced such overwhelming joy from God's answer and Melanchthon's recovery. His relief and exuberance are palpable in a letter he sent to his wife, Katie (Käthe), a few days later.

> Grace and peace! Dear maiden Käthe, gracious Lady von Zolsdorf,[48] and whatever other titles pertain to Your Grace! I must submissively bring to the attention of Your Grace that I am doing well here. I am gorging like a Bohemian and swilling like a German,[49] thanks be to God, amen. The reason is that Master Philipp was truly dead, and has arisen from death just like Lazarus! God, the dear Father, hears our prayer—that we see and experience—even though we still do not believe it. Let no one say "Amen" to our terrible unbelief.[50]

Later on in his life, Luther still referred to Melanchthon's recovery, attesting to how the prayer of the church accomplishes great miracles: "In our time, three have been raised from the dead; me—and I have often been near death—my wife Käthe, who was also at death's door, and Master Philipp Melanchthon who in 1540 lay deathly ill in Weimar."[51] Prayer is a bold act resting on the promise of God. As Luther puts it,

> Ah, how great a thing is the prayer of the godly? How powerful it is before God that a poor human should speak with high majesty in heaven and not be afraid before him, but know that God smiles on him with a friendly countenance on account of the will of Jesus Christ, his loving son, our Lord and Savior! Here the heart and the conscience must not run away, neither remain in doubt because of its unworthiness, nor allow itself to be terrified.[52]

We are not to give in to the thought that we might not be heard. Instead, we are "to remain confident of heart, certain and believing, that what we have prayed for in faith in Christ has already been heard."[53] First, believers must call on the name of the Lord, and then they need to be bold in bringing requests. That was certainly the approach that Luther exemplified in his lifetime.

Praying the Lord's Prayer

Luther had the highest possible praise for praying the Lord's Prayer:

> Since our Lord is the author of this prayer, it is without a doubt the most sublime, the loftiest, and the most excellent. If he, the good and faithful Teacher, had known a better one, he would surely have taught us that too.[54]

This endorsement is noteworthy in that Luther often commends the psalms as especially good and edifying prayers. But while the psalms embrace the main points of the Lord's Prayer, Luther contends that they do not express them as clearly.

Apparently, Luther had reason to direct attention to the Lord's Prayer and to sing its praise. In the ferment of popular piety of his day, the Lord's Prayer had some stiff competition. Also very popular were various other prayers, including those attributed to Saint Brigitta. These special prayers purported to grant spiritual advantages to the devoted who recited them with the right attitude. This problem was serious enough to prompt Luther to complain that the Psalter, rosaries, and Franciscan Crown prayers had superseded the Lord's Prayer.[55] Luther's opinion on that matter was straightforward, "It would be better for you to pray one Lord's Prayer with a devout heart and with thought given to the words, resulting in a better life, than for you to acquire absolution through reciting all other prayers."[56] The very idea that prayer was said to accrue merit was offensive.

In *An Exposition of the Lord's Prayer for Simple Laymen* (1519), we find Luther speaking to two issues: the manner in which we are to pray, and the words we are to use. This reflects the Gospel accounts where Jesus instructs his disciples in these very things. As the Master begins to teach the disciples to pray, he rails against the hypocrites who pray to show off their piety and who heap up many words, thinking this is the best way to pray. Jesus urges the disciples not to be like them and proceeds with setting out the "Our Father." In time-honored fashion, Luther follows suit, saying, "From these words of Christ we learn about both the words and the manner, that is, they tell us how and for what we are to pray. It is vital that we know both."[57] In characteristically direct manner, Luther tells us that,

> Our prayer must have few words, but be great and profound in content and meaning. The fewer the words, the better the prayer; the more words, the poorer the prayer. Few words and richness of meaning is Christian; many words and lack of meaning is pagan. Therefore Christ says that the disciples should "not heap up empty phrases as the Gentiles do." And in John 4 he tells the Samaritan woman, "Those who worship God must pray to him in spirit and in truth." The Father desires such worshipers.[58]

Praying in the Spirit is the opposite of outward sham or oral prayer. Thoughtless mumbling or chattering out of obligation may be prompted out of obedience—a good motive—but it does not embody the full intention of the Lord's command to pray. Thus the manner of true prayer is a matter of the heart.

Luther gleaned many insights on this topic from the early church fathers. Particularly influential is Saint Cyprian, whose treatise on the Lord's Prayer was highly regarded. The African bishop urges us not to pray with "uncouth voices," or with "turbulent loquaciousness," but with modesty, "because the hearer is not of the voice but of the heart."[59] The God to whom we pray certainly hears our prayers, but he does so by looking upon the heart. In the last book of the Bible we read, "I am he who searches mind and heart" (Rev. 2:23). Cyprian, along with the rest of the early church fathers, recognized that disjunction between the lips and the heart was not only possible, but it was indeed the plight of the sinful and the inattentive. Modeling ourselves after those who proceed with "a hidden prayer but with manifest faith" is what is required.[60]

Luther, along with Cyprian and the early church fathers, places great emphasis on the heart in prayer. This comes through as the Reformer tells the story of Agathon:

> This man, living in the desert, carried a stone in his mouth for thirty years to teach him silence. But how did he pray? Without a doubt inwardly with his heart, which, after all, appeals to God more than anything else. In fact, it is the one mode of praying that God regards and seeks. It is, admittedly, helpful to hear the words, for they stimulate thought and true prayer. As was said before, the spoken words have no other purpose than that of a trumpet, a drum, or an organ, or any other sound which will move the heart and lift it upward to God.[61]

Prayer is indeed a matter of the heart for Luther. If prayer has hold of the heart, then the believer's entire being is taken up in its appeal to God. In this way, the heart is moved and instructed by the Spirit.

The section on community prayer in the Rule of Saint Augustine is short but explicit: "When you pray to God in psalms and songs, the words spoken by your lips should also be alive in your hearts."[62] As an Augustinian friar, Luther was bound to live by this rule. He was intimately familiar with it as well as with some of Augustine's comments on this matter. The intent of prayer should have at its center the heart's yearning and love for God. When we are found in the one true God, we believe, hope, and love. Prayer is thus the incitement to grow more intent in this truth and to exercise ourselves in this relationship so that the daily cares and activities of life do not mask or dampen the uninterrupted longing that faith engenders.

Luther takes delight in teaching through the Lord's Prayer in a number of his works. As we will see below, he structures the prayer into an introduction, seven petitions, and a final conclusion.

Introduction: "Our Father, Who Art in Heaven"

At the beginning of the Lord's Prayer, we see words that reveal God's warm and friendly dealings with those who pray. The best way to begin the prayer is to know how we are to address, honor, and treat the person to whom we submit our petition.

> Now, of all names there is none that gains us more favor with God than that of "Father." This is indeed a friendly, sweet, intimate, and warmhearted word. To speak the words "Lord" or "God" or "Judge" would not be nearly as gracious and comforting to us. The name "Father" is part of our nature and is sweet

by nature. That is why it is the most pleasing to God, and why no other name moves him so strongly to hear us. With this name we likewise confess that we are the children of God, which again stirs his heart mightily; for there is no lovelier sound than that of a child speaking to his father.[63]

Luther's language here demonstrates the great mercy that attends prayer. At the outset there is mercy, tenderness, and above all relationship.

In our day there are many for whom the term "father" is not associated with good memories. Many of us have known or have heard of fathers so preoccupied with their work that there was nothing left for the family. These fathers were so aloof and unresponsive that they were no fathers at all. Some have known verbally or sexually abusive fathers, leaving ghastly wounds on those in the family unit. I know a woman who as a little girl remembers her father slapping her in the face mercilessly for some insignificant issue. The incidence of these negative images of human fathers seems to be magnified in the complex and alienating society in which we live. This has given rise to an understandable reaction. In some theological circles, attempts have been made to substitute female images and other alternatives for the male images that denote domination and oppression as opposed to nurture and sustenance.

For those who may be offended by Luther, the scriptural tradition, and the liberal use of the term "Father," we need to understand that Luther here is not calling on the image of human fathers to describe God; it is just the opposite. Luther is making a case from the Scripture that describes God as good.[64] He is the one whose covenant faithfulness is from everlasting to everlasting. He has gathered a people to himself, and his steadfast love endures forever. Thus human relationships are to be judged by his holy standard. From Luther's point of view, when we say "Our Father," we are uttering words that refer solely to God, in whom we can place ultimate confidence. He pledges himself to give us aid and mercy. He is ready to assist anyone who calls on his name. "Thus all who are heavy-laden, and even those who do not know the meaning of these words, may well pray this prayer. In fact, I regard it to be the best prayer, for then the heart says more than the lips."[65]

Prayer, as Luther describes it, is entered into with a sense of reverence, joy, and discovery, for it is a gift from God. We are told how to pray, what to pray, and the manner in which God does the hearing. It is also a great benefit that Christ himself gives us the exact words to learn. God has crafted this prayer precisely so that by it we might learn to pray and learn to know the One to whom we pray. In the process, we have the additional advantage of self-knowledge—that is, learning to know who we are in relationship to the One who has made us.

"Hallowed Be Thy Name"

The first petition of the Lord's Prayer deals with the use and misuse of God's name. As Luther says in the Small Catechism, "It is true that God's name is holy in itself, but we ask in this prayer that it may also be holy in and among us."[66] He goes on to argue that we received God's name when we became Christians at baptism. Since the gift of his name is the greatest treasure we have, "we should be most concerned that God's name receive due honor and be kept holy and sacred."[67] By praying as his children, we are reminded of our duty and are aligned to the work being done in us as well as the work to make God's name holy in the world. How is God's name made holy among us? "Whenever the Word of God is taught clearly and purely and we, as God's children, also live holy lives according to it."[68] The clarity and precision of the Small Catechism is hard to exceed. It emphasizes the centrality of God's word and the need to allow that word to shape the thoughts and actions of his people. This is a corporate prayer at the same time that it is an individual prayer. As such, it prays for the realization of the word of God in the community of faith as well as its realization in the individual who prays this prayer.

Luther also outlines some of the ways in which the name of God is profaned among us. First, it is profaned when there is false teaching that would lead others astray, using "his name to dress up their lies and make them acceptable; this is the worst desecration and dishonor of the divine name."[69] Second, it is also profaned when there is an open violation of the Ten Commandments and a disregard for proper living. This is especially despicable when it happens that Christians are "adulterers, drunkards, gluttons, jealous persons, and slanderers."[70] For the name of God to be dishonored and blasphemed because of God's own people is particularly onerous. Luther sums up the force of the first petition when he says,

> So you see that in this petition we pray for exactly the same thing that God demands in the Second Commandment: that his name should not be taken in vain by swearing, cursing, deceiving, etc., but used rightly to the praise and glory of God. Whoever uses God's name for any sort of wrong profanes and desecrates this holy name.[71]

The petition is for the sake of the world, to exalt the name of God in it, and to pray that anything that diminishes God's name would itself be diminished, whether in the world or in those who pray it.

"Thy Kingdom Come"

Even as God's name is holy in itself without our prayer, so also, "God's kingdom comes on its own without our prayer, but we ask in this prayer that it may also come to us."[72] Where God's name is honored, there will be a resulting kingdom. His rule shall be established and the justice of his reign will be in evidence. This petition opens our eyes to the work God is doing in the world, and this prayer openly states our desire to be a part of that kingdom. We ask in this petition that his kingdom would be in evidence among us and that it would prevail among us. How would Luther describe the kingdom of God?

Answer: Simply what we heard above in the Creed, namely, that God sent his Son, Christ our Lord, into the world to redeem and deliver us from the power of the devil, to bring us to himself, and to rule us as a king of righteousness, life, and salvation against sin, death, and an evil conscience. To this end he also gave his Holy Spirit to deliver this to us through his holy Word and to enlighten and strengthen us in faith by his power.[73]

We pray the second petition that all this would be realized among us who have already been claimed by baptism. But the prayer further asks for the growth of God's kingdom in the world even among those who have not yet bowed the knee. We ask that the kingdom would advance so that there would be more partakers of the grace and salvation won in Christ. In this way, praying the second petition is praying in harmony with the *missio Dei,* the mission of God.

Luther points out that it is bold to pray along these lines. "From this you see that we are not asking here for crumbs or for a temporal, perishable blessing, but for an eternal, priceless treasure and for everything that God himself possesses."[74] Praying for the coming of the kingdom is venturing out on God's promises. It is something larger than any human heart would dare to do unless God himself sanctioned it.

But because he is God, he claims the honor of giving far more abundantly and liberally than anyone can comprehend—like an eternal, inexhaustible fountain which, the more it gushes forth and overflows, the more it continues to give. He desires nothing more from us than that we ask many and great things of him. And, on the contrary, he is angered if we do not ask and demand with confidence.[75]

We can be bold in praying for the coming of the kingdom because of the inexhaustible generosity of God the Father, Son, and Holy Spirit.

Perhaps a good way to summarize this petition is to say that it is a prayer for the coming of the Holy Spirit. It is the Spirit who produces faith. It is the Spirit who reaches and enlightens through God's holy word. It is the Spirit who applies the benefits of the redemption won in Jesus Christ to the lives of believers and to the life of the world. Perhaps it is the Small Catechism that answers most directly when we ask how it is that the kingdom comes. "Answer: Whenever the heavenly Father gives us his Holy Spirit, so that through his grace we believe his Holy Word and live godly lives here in time and hereafter in eternity."[76]

"Thy Will Be Done on Earth, as It Is in Heaven"

When we pray in the third petition of the Lord's Prayer, "thy will be done," we are certainly praying for God's commandments to be fulfilled. This has both a negative and a positive side. Luther explains,

Briefly stated, it refers to distinguishing the old self, the old Adam in us, as the holy Apostle teaches us in many passages (for example, Romans 6). The old Adam is simply the evil leaning in us toward wrath, hatred, unchastity, greed, vainglory, pride, and the like. These evil impulses were inherited from Adam and born in us through our mothers. From these stem all kinds of evil deeds such as murder, adultery, robbery, and similar transgressions of God's commandments, which cannot happen without disobedience to God's will.[77]

Recognizing and distinguishing the old Adam places us in a position in which we recognize the differentiated self. We are not now what we will be in the future. Prayer has this power of bringing the eschaton to bear on our life in the present. We pray against our old self, and by so doing we exercise the new life of faith in its daily returning to God and the practice of hallowing his name.

Trying to describe the radical nature of the gospel, this is how Luther puts it in his commentary on Hebrews:

> For absolutely no doctrine, be it civil, ecclesiastical, or philosophical and in any way human, can direct man and make him upright, since it leads only so far that it establishes good behavior, while man remains as he has been of old. And so of necessity it makes nothing but pretenders and hypocrites; for those dregs of the heart and that bilge water of the old man, namely, love of himself, remain. Therefore it deserves to be called an evil doctrine, since it is not able to offer rectitude. But the Gospel says: "Unless one is born again of water and the Spirit, he cannot enter the kingdom of heaven" (John 3:5). And thus the Gospel preserves nothing of the old man but destroys him completely and makes him new, until hatred of himself utterly roots out love of himself through faith in Christ. Therefore all boasting of erudition, wisdom, and knowledge is useless; for no one is made better by these, no matter what good and laudable gifts of God they are. Indeed, besides the fact that they do not make a man good, they become a covering for wickedness and a veil over the disease of nature, so that those who are pleased with themselves because of them and seem to themselves to be good and sound are incurable.[78]

Praying the Lord's Prayer is in this sense a conversion and a turning from self-love to the love of God. Prayer is a constant shaping of the believer's life that is not learned in a day but becomes the work of a lifetime.

This focus on the humiliation of the individual is more typical of Luther's early writings like the lectures on Hebrews. His exposition of this petition in the Larger Catechism seems to focus much more on the forces aligned against the believer: the devil and all his angels; the world as our enemy, including religious and civil structures; and the flesh, otherwise known as the old Adam. The prayer of the third petition is thus a prayer that the devil, our enemies, and anyone who suppresses the word of God would not prevail. Rather, the believer prays for the holy and pure will of God to be done for the preservation of peace, the health of the world, and the flourishing of individuals. Luther points out that in these petitions, we offer up interests that concern God himself, but in so doing we also pray on our own behalf.

Luther sets out the following as a kind of summary of the meaning behind this petition:

> Dear Father, your will be done and not the will of the devil or of our enemies, nor of those who would persecute and suppress your holy Word or prevent your kingdom from coming; and grant we may bear patiently and overcome whatever we must suffer on its account, so that our poor flesh may not yield or fall away through weakness or sloth.[79]

As he puts it, this prayer is a protection against the spiritual forces that rage and storm against the good will of God. The prayers of God's people taking up the third petition make room for the kingdom of God in time and space.

"Give Us This Day Our Daily Bread"

The spiritual praying that Jesus Christ teaches his disciples does not disregard physical need. "In fact, God gives daily bread without our prayer, even to all evil people, but we ask in this prayer that God cause us to recognize what our daily bread is and to receive it with thanksgiving."[80] From God's hand comes every good gift, and in this petition we pray with thanksgiving and praise recognizing this fact. Contrariwise, we pray against anything that might disrupt or disturb people's access to the abundance of God's provision. Luther's insight into the petitions includes praying for and praying against:

> When you say and ask for "daily bread," you ask for everything that is necessary in order to have and enjoy daily bread and, on the contrary, against everything that interferes with enjoying it. You must therefore expand and extend your thoughts to include not just the oven or the flour bin, but also the broad fields and the whole land that produce and provide our daily bread and all kinds of sustenance for us. For if God did not cause grain to grow and did not bless and preserve it in the field, we could never take a loaf of bread from the oven or to set upon the table.[81]

There is a strong link between daily bread and the creation from which it comes. We might say that Luther evidences a creation spirituality that sees the relationship between God and the believer as mediated in very physical ways. This allows Luther to pray heartfelt prayers for favorable weather and a good harvest. The desire to live as a Christian is not in conflict with a life lived in devoted harmony with the cycle of the created order.

Luther is also quite willing to pray against anything that would disrupt or prevent the peace of important daily business and associations. Without a proper government, we cannot receive and enjoy the good things of the earth in security and happiness. It becomes necessary to pray against the dissension, strife, and war that would take away our daily bread. Therefore, praying for good government and peace is part of this petition as well.

Luther considers the fourth petition regarding daily bread as a comprehensive one that deals with all kinds of relations on earth. It would be possible to make a long prayer of it, enumerating in detail the food, drink, and clothing we seek from God's hand. From there we could range more widely to include our dwelling place and our extended family structure. Beyond that we could pray for our work, "faithful neighbors and good friends."[82] Luther goes on to speak of our need to pray for wisdom for "emperor, kings, and all estates."[83]

Luther emphasizes the comprehensive nature of this petition and how it covers such a broad range of connections and relations on earth. This is highlighted by the fact that Luther sees the matter from the vantage point of the eschaton:

> But especially is this petition directed against our chief enemy, the devil, whose whole purpose and desire it is to take away or interfere with all we have received from God. He is not satisfied to obstruct and overthrow the spiritual order, by deceiving with his lies and bringing them under his power, but he also prevents and impedes the establishment of any kind of government or honorable and peaceful relations on earth. This is why he causes so much contention, murder, sedition, and war, why he sends storms and hail to destroy crops and cattle, why he poisons the air, etc. In short, it pains him that anyone should receive even a mouthful of bread from God and eat it in peace. If it were in his power and our prayer to God did not restrain him, surely we would not have a straw in the field, a penny in the house, or even an hour more of life—especially those of us who have the Word of God and would like to be Christians.[84]

The struggle of receiving our daily bread in faith is due to the opposition active in the world. Praying the fourth petition in this manner is directed *for* our daily needs and *against* anything that would interfere. Such a prayer allows the believer to awaken to the goodness of God's provision, and it stands as a restraint upon the spiritual forces that would hinder the growth of God's kingdom.

"And Forgive Us Our Debts, as We Forgive Our Debtors"

In this petition we bring to voice our constant need for the saving cover and comfort that comes in the forgiveness of sins. "Not that he does not forgive sins even apart from and before our praying; for before we prayed for it or even thought about it, he gave us the gospel, in which there is nothing but forgiveness. But the point here is for us to recognize and accept this forgiveness."[85] Living in the forgiveness of sins as the gospel instructs us is not easy. Abiding sin clings, and it is easy to justify ourselves in actions that partake of anger, resentment, and impatience. This is true because fallen human nature "does not trust and believe God and is constantly aroused by evil desires and devices, so that we sin daily in word and deed, in acts of commission and omission."[86] With such a restless conscience, it is necessary to come again and again to this petition to be reminded of the gift that comes in God's gracious pronouncement. Luther states it succinctly when he says, "Unless God constantly forgives, we are lost."[87]

Luther takes time to identify two results that proceed from the forgiveness of sins. First, forgiveness leads to a glad confidence with God. In this petition, we pray that God would not regard our sin or punish us as we deserve. We call on the mercy of God and lean on his gracious will. As God forgives according to his promise, he creates a bold and confident spirit. The knowledge that our sin is forgiven and that our lives are secure in the finished work of Christ creates a joyful and confident heart. This certainty makes it possible for us to dare to pray.

Second, the forgiveness of sins necessitates a reciprocal response. Even as we have been forgiven by God—despite constant transgressions—we too are to forgive "our neighbor who does us harm, violence, and injustice, bears malice toward us, etc."[88] It follows that to receive the forgiveness of God and to live in it means we extend to others what has been extended to us. Luther points out the consequences of not doing this:

> If you do not forgive, do not think that God forgives you. But if you forgive, you have the comfort and assurance that you are forgiven to heaven—not on account of your forgiving (for he does it altogether freely, out of pure grace, because he has promised it, as the Gospel teaches) but instead because he has set this up for our strengthening and assurance as a sign along with the promise that matches this petition, Luke 6[:37], "Forgive, and you will be forgiven." Therefore Christ repeats it immediately after the Lord's Prayer in Matt. 6[:14], "If you forgive others their trespasses, your heavenly Father will also forgive you."[89]

Luther makes much of the fact that this sign and promise are attached to the petition. When we pray, we recall the promise of the forgiveness of sin; we know that God has placed his seal on it, which makes it as certain as an absolution pronounced by God himself. The condition is established "in order to strengthen and gladden our conscience."[90] The forgiving of others is not considered by Luther as a simple "ought," but as a sign that you will be forgiven.

"And Lead Us Not into Temptation"

Luther points out that retaining and persevering in all the gifts for which we pray is no small matter. This cannot be accomplished "without failures and stumbling."[91] The Lord's Prayer calls us to a fresh moment in which we cry out to begin again. One may be doing well and have the assurance of the forgiveness of sins, a good conscience, and patience to spare, "yet such is life that one stands today and falls tomorrow."[92] So it is that we must pray again in each new situation so we will not fall and yield to temptations and trials.

Temptations, as Luther informs us, come in three kinds: the flesh, the world, and the devil. The flesh is anything that stands opposed to the Spirit, or the will of God. As Luther puts it, "We live in the flesh and carry the old creature around our necks; it goes to work and lures us daily into unchastity, laziness, gluttony and drunkenness, greed and deceit, into acts of fraud and deception against our neighbor."[93] The evil tendencies that run like a vein of coal in the hidden recesses of the human nature are what Luther means by the "old Adam." Next comes the world that does not so much entice as it assails with its overwhelming cultural force. The Christian pilgrim is confronted with war, injustice, violence, slander, pride, vengeance, "along with fondness for luxury, honor, fame, and power."[94] All of these forces swirl together to make an unholy setting full of temptation and trial. "Then comes the devil, who baits and badgers us on all sides, but especially exerts himself where the conscience and spiritual matters are concerned."[95] His desire is to tear us away from faith, hope, and love and to cause us to "scorn and despise both the Word and works of God."[96] The devil seeks to draw the faithful into unbelief, despair, and many other dehumanizing sins.

> This, then, is what "leading us not into temptation" means: when God gives us power and strength to resist, even though the attack is not removed or ended. For no one can escape temptations and allurements as long as we live in the flesh and have the devil prowling about us. We cannot help but suffer attacks, and even be mired in them, but we pray here that we may not fall into them and be drowned by them.[97]

Luther urges the Christian pilgrim to "run here and seize hold of the Lord's Prayer and to speak to God from the heart, 'Dear Father, you have commanded me to pray; let me not fall because of temptation.'"[98] This kind of prayer is the best resistance to the trials and temptations that inevitably come to us all.

Conclusion: "But Deliver Us from Evil" and "Amen"

"Keep us from the Evil One" is the force of this phrase in the original Greek. The petition "seems to be speaking of the devil as the sum of all evil in order that the entire substance of our prayer may be directed against our archenemy. For it is he who obstructs everything for which we ask: God's name or honor, God's kingdom and will, our daily bread, a good and cheerful conscience, etc."[99] Since the devil is a liar and a murderer, he incessantly seeks the downfall of anything directed toward the good as God intended it. Therefore, this petition is a way to sum up and pray against the misfortune that would keep the kingdom of God from coming in its fullness.

Luther adds one last reflection to his exposition of the Lord's Prayer. He says that we do not pray by chance but because God has promised to grant our requests. This admonition to wholehearted prayer is gathered up nicely in the following paragraph from an early treatise:

> Therefore the little word "Amen" means the same as truly, verily, certainly. It is a word uttered by the firm faith of the heart. It is as though you were to say, "O my God and Father, I have no doubt that you will grant the things for which I

petitioned, not because of my prayer, but because of your command to me to request them and because of your promise to hear me. I am convinced, O God, that you are truthful, that you cannot lie. It is not the worthiness of my prayer, but the certainty of your truthfulness, that leads me to believe this firmly. I have no doubt that my petition will become and be an Amen."[100]

Luther's contribution to the teaching on the Lord's Prayer is characterized by his hermeneutical approach of law and gospel, or use of command and promise. His exposition is meant to make clear our need for prayer and its experiential nature. It drives us toward the proper use of the name of the Lord, the coming kingdom, daily bread, the forgiveness of sins, and the handling of temptation as it comes our way. Luther deals with the Lord's Prayer as one who is familiar with its contours and implications. He seeks to have others love it and use it as a resource for life lived in conflict.

Praying the Psalter

Luther's love affair with the Psalms is impossible to hide. At every turn we find the Reformer writing about the Psalms, lecturing on the Psalms, or more importantly, singing the Psalms. They were his constant companion throughout his life and were dearer to him than almost any of his possessions. He prayed them as a monk and learned all one hundred fifty by heart. In good monastic fashion, he not only learned the Psalms and their lessons but also meditated upon them as something to be tasted and savored. For the truths uttered by the Holy Spirit in the Psalms cannot be fully known unless they are taken in by the eyes, sung by the heart, experienced in the inner being, and appropriated by the intellect.

Luther contended that in the Psalter we have the Bible in miniature: the events of God's salvific history stand behind the prayers of his people. The Psalter is the prayer book of the church.

It is really a fine enchiridion or handbook. In fact, I have a notion that the Holy Spirit wanted to take the trouble himself to compile a short Bible and book of examples of all Christendom or all saints, so that anyone who could not read the whole Bible would here have anyway almost an entire summary of it, comprised in one little book.[101]

The Bible is a huge volume, and in the Middle Ages, few had read the entire text from Genesis to Revelation. So, summarizing the faith quickly and simply was long seen as desirable. The idea of an enchiridion or handbook is one that has a correspondingly long history in the church, Augustine having written one as well as many other teachers in the church.[102] Luther uses singular language in stating that the Psalms are just such a summary.

Luther believed, however, that the Psalms were not simply a summary of doctrine but also a record of the interaction of God's people as they found themselves in the push and pull of life. The record is not of "silent saints," as he calls them—saints who do various actions or works, but from whom one learns nothing of their struggle. Instead, we find Luther admiring the Psalms for their breathtakingly honest emotion and the trustworthy character of the reflected witness:

> Finally there is in the Psalter security and a well-tried guide, so that in it one can follow all the saints without peril. The other examples and legends of the silent saints present works that one is unable to imitate; they present even more works which it is dangerous to imitate, works which usually start sects and divisions, and lead and tear men away from the communion of saints. But the Psalter holds you to the communion of saints and away from the sects. For it teaches you in joy, fear, hope, and sorrow to think and speak as all the saints have thought and spoken.[103]

The great virtue of the Psalms is that when faithfully sung they lead our thinking and shape our response. The Psalms trace out, as it were, the pathways of David, Solomon, and others as they engage in worship before the Lord. Their words—whether sorrowful or joyful, in despair, crying out for comfort, or pleading and yearning for a true thirst for God—form a pattern of godly interaction that reveals more than mere action. Through them, we catch a glimpse of the thoughts and the most deeply held longings of human existence. It's as though we can look into the psalmists' hearts and know their deepest thoughts about the most important issues of life. In the Psalms, the whole range of human emotion is depicted and spoken with such clarity and feeling that anyone who faithfully prays these prayers will learn something about conversation with God.

Luther points out that even though many legends of saints and their miracles and good works have been published and become well known, the book of Psalms still has the best examples for the Christian.

> For here we find not only what one or two saints have done, but what he has done who is the very head of all saints. We also find what all the saints still do, such as the attitude they take toward God, toward friends and enemies, and the way they conduct themselves amid all dangers and sufferings. Beyond that there are contained here all sorts of divine and wholesome teachings and commandments.[104]

When Luther mentions the one "who is the very head of all saints," he is referring of course to Christ. Notice that as far as Luther is concerned, Christ himself is not only indicated in some of the messianic psalms, but that Christ himself prays the Psalms! So that when we as believers pray the Psalms, we pray them as the Savior did.[105]

As already mentioned, in the Psalms Luther sees a summary of the Bible. In addition, we also find examples of saints who have wrestled with God in the hard places of their lives, and who have praised God in times of joy and sorrow in the major key and the minor. The Psalms also are the very words of God; in the first instance because the Holy Spirit breathed them, but also because Christ himself prayed them before us. Jesus did this as a practice of his personal prayer life, but also as the Savior of the world as he hung on the cross and he uttered lines from Psalm 22.

The Psalter thus understood also reiterates one of the themes we found central in the praying of the Lord's Prayer: the knowledge of self. Praying the Psalms, according to Luther, will help bring to light God, the church, the self, and creation.

> In a word, if you would see the holy Christian Church painted in living color and shape, comprehended in one little picture, then take up the Psalter. There you have a fine, bright, pure mirror that will show you what Christendom is. Indeed you will find in it also yourself and the true *gnothi seauton* (knowledge of the self), as well as God himself and all creatures.[106]

The self in its natural state is like a hermit thrush that desires to keep its nest unobserved. But the self in prayer takes a step out of the undergrowth of self-will into the light of day. The Psalms become the mirror into which we look, or perhaps better, the reflecting pond that catches a glimpse of the hiding self. In the act of prayer, with the lifting up of our heart to God, the self begins to take its first steps out into the open. We might say that the self moves away from the self, paradoxically speaking, in order to better know the God who made it and the world in which it moves. That is the power of the praise of God in the Psalms.

The Psalms teach us that the goodness of God is a true word that is worth repeating and praying. Take for example the comments on Psalm 118, Luther's favorite psalm, where it says in the opening line, "O give thanks to the Lord, for He is good; His steadfast love endures forever!" This wonderful refrain rejoices in all the daily kindnesses God unceasingly showers upon all living creatures.

> You must not read the words "good" and "His steadfast love" with dull indifference. Nor dare you skim over them "as the nuns read the Psalter," or as choirmasters and choristers bleat and bellow these fine words in the churches. No, you must bear in mind that these are vibrant, significant, and meaningful words; they express and emphasize one theme: God is good, but not as a human being is good; from the very bottom of His heart He is inclined to help and do good continually. He is not given to anger or inclined to punish except where necessary and where persistent, impenitent, and stubborn wickedness compels and drives Him to it. A human being would not delay punishment and restrain anger as God does; he would punish a hundred thousand times sooner and harder than God does.[107]

The delights that God showers unceasingly are of the best kind. God "is the Protector by day and night, and the Preserver of our lives. He causes the sun and the moon to shine on us, fire, air, water, and the heavens to serve us."[108] Out of the abundance of creation he causes the earth and sea to yield up a harvest of fruit, grain, wood, fish, and all necessities. He provides daily bread, house and family, neighbors and government. "In short, who can count it all?"[109]

Encouraged by such abundance and confronted with such astonishing benefits, who in their right mind would not be grateful? "What is all the money and wealth in the world compared with one sunlit day?"[110] Luther exults in drawing out the connection between the vision of the goodness of God and the only adequate response to that vision. Gratitude naturally flows out of the hearts of those who have received so many good and pleasing gifts. The goodness of God perceived cannot remain a thought hermetically sealed but calls forth a response in those who pray this truth.

The connection between intellect and affection—or to put it colloquially, head and heart—is fundamental. Perhaps we could say it is only by the response that we can be sure an individual has "got it."

> Therefore this verse should be in the heart and mouth of every man every day and every moment. Every time he eats or drinks, sees, hears, smells, walks, stands; every time he uses his limbs, his body, his possessions, or any creature, he should recall that if God did not give him all this for his use and preserve it for him despite the devil, he would not have it. He should be aroused and trained to thank God for His daily goodness with a joyful heart and cheerful faith and to say to Him: "Truly, Thou art a kind and benevolent God! For Thy kindness and goodness to me, an unworthy and ungrateful creature, are eternal, that is, unceasing. Praise and thanks are due Thee!"[111]

The evidence of a true understanding of this verse is witnessed by a mouth filled with praise. Praying this verse of Psalm 118, as we can see, is instruction with respect to the person of God, the unfolding of which leads to a self that has a new relationship. In relating with God in a new way, the self (confronted with its own ingratitude) learns to repent and is forever changed.

The Psalms do not speak only of the goodness of God but also of trouble and trial. In Psalm 118:5 we read, "Out of my distress I called on the LORD; the LORD answered me and set me free." Here, the psalmist speaks of real anxiety and many troubles. He does not explain his sufferings, but he speaks of them in general terms. As Luther explains, the Hebrew word for distress means "something narrow." It implies a process of squeezing, of clamping down, of pressing and narrowing. If we were to put it into psychological terms, we would speak of fear and pain, or turmoil and confusion. It might be a family matter or job related; it might be a chronic health issue, or persecution of one sort or another. The distress is real, but the Lord's response is real as well.

> Note the great art and wisdom of faith. It does not run to and fro in the face of trouble. It does not cry on everybody's shoulder, nor does it curse and scold its enemies. It does not murmur against God by asking: "Why does God do this

to me? Why not to others, who are worse than I am?" Faith does not despair of the God who sends trouble. Faith does not consider Him angry or an enemy, as the flesh, the world, and the devil strongly suggest. Faith rises above all this and sees God's fatherly heart behind His unfriendly exterior. Faith sees the sun shining through these thick, dark clouds and this gloomy weather. Faith has the courage to call with confidence to Him who smites it and looks at it with such a sour face.[112]

To be able to do this in the time of trial, Luther admits, is "skill above all skills." It is the work that only the Holy Spirit can accomplish in the life of the Christian. This is a work hidden from the eyes. When we do not doubt that God is not out to distress or destroy, then we can become a falcon and soar above distress. The falcon flies much higher than the hermit thrush.

Distress drives the believer to pray, implore, fight, exercise faith, and learn another aspect of God's person: the Lord desires for believers to pour out their troubles and prayers as a sacrifice. As Psalm 141:2 says, "Let my prayer be counted as incense before Thee, and the lifting up of my hands as an evening sacrifice!"

> It is important that you learn to praise also this point in this verse: "The Lord answered me and set me free." The psalmist declares that he prayed and cried out, and that he was certainly heard. If the devil puts it into your head that you lack the holiness, piety, and worthiness of David and for this reason cannot be sure that God will hear you, make the sign of the cross, and say to yourself: "Let those be pious and worthy who will! I know for a certainty that I am a creature of the same God who made David. And David, regardless of his holiness, has no better or greater God than I have." There is only one God, of saint and sinner, worthy and unworthy, great and small. Regardless of the inequalities among us, He is the one and equal God of us all, who wants to be honored, called on, and prayed to by all.[113]

We honor God best when in times of trial we offer prayers to the One who commanded we call on him by name. His name is hallowed in us when we kneel down, raise our eyes to heaven, and beg for comfort and help.

So far, we have heard very briefly about two themes in the Psalms: God's goodness and human distress. It is time to take up one more: thirsting after God. In Psalm 63:1, monks sang this sentiment each and every morning: "O God, you are my God; earnestly I seek you; my soul thirsts for you; my flesh faints for you, as in a dry and weary land where there is no water." It also appears in verses such as Psalm 143:6, "I stretch out my hands to you; my soul thirsts for you like a parched land." This theme is taken up in a popular booklet Luther wrote on the penitential psalms. In it, he makes the point that any work done without the grace of God is nothing. The proud in heart do not know this. They do not thirst for grace, and they do not stretch their hands to God. They consider their life entirely satisfactory.

But the one who is truly Christ-formed is

> inwardly disconsolate and of a contrite spirit and has a constant longing for God's grace and help. Yet when he tries to tell others of this cross and wants to teach them, he not only fails to find sympathy and a following but is repaid with ungratefulness and hatred. Thus he is inwardly and outwardly crucified with Christ. For the proud in heart stand boldly in their presumption that they are like those who are going to heaven. They do not have any fear of hell and thirst for grace.[114]

A thirst for God is one of the signs of faith. It is something we cannot take for granted; it is the object of prayer in the Psalter.

Prayer as a Mark of the Church

What marks out the church of Jesus Christ from other institutions that vie for that title? Where is the church? In moments of crisis this becomes an acute question. The early church faced just such a moment when the Gnostics denied that the creator God of the Old Testament was truly God, asserted secret knowledge about Jesus, and developed their own canon. In this way, the Gnostic church made a bid for its claim as the true church. Or again, the Donatists of the fourth century denied the validity of anyone (in their opinion) who apostatized as a result of persecution, and they claimed to be the true church. During this controversy, Augustine set out the view that the true church is shaped by four marks: oneness (*unitas*), holiness (*sanctitas*), catholicity (*catholicitas*), and apostolicity (*apostolicitas*), which is reflected in the Nicene Creed (AD 381), "We believe in one, holy, catholic and apostolic church."[115]

It comes as no surprise that when Luther takes up the marks of the church, he puts his own spin on them. In our context, we will find that Luther is convinced that "prayer" is one of the marks of the church. But his pathway to that conviction is a story worth telling. In article seven of the *Confessio Augustana* of 1530, it is stated: "The church is the assembly of saints in which the Gospel is taught purely and the sacraments are administered rightly."[116] This simple and ecumenical description of the church flows from the priority of the ministry of the word.

It is precisely this ministry of the word that Luther takes up in his treatise titled *On the Councils and the Church* (1539).[117] He wrote this "booklet" of approximately one hundred fifty pages in anticipation of a general church council to address the abuses and pressing needs of the church during the time of the Reformation. Pope Paul III, who held office from 1534 to 1549, had called for a general council to deal with the matter of reform, but he was as interested in finding the most advantageous moment for Rome as he was interested in just, biblical, and collaborative reform. This led to one postponement after another. Luther was quite open about his frustration with the cat-and-mouse game played by Rome in this regard.

Luther's *On the Councils and the Church* presents his negative critique of the Roman approach to papal and conciliar authority. In part one, he takes up the question of whether or not the church could be reformed and thus find its unity by agreeing on the decrees of the councils and the church fathers. As appealing as this idea may be, it is not workable given the fact that the councils are "not only unequal, but also contradictory."[118] To side with one council means to side against another, and to side with one church father means to side against another. Any attempt to find the unity or the marks of the church in this manner would result in endless haggling over which point of view to embrace.[119] Further, the church fathers themselves urge the primacy of Scripture over the opinion of any one individual, so to base unity on the councils and the fathers would be to establish the case using the very authority that rejects that approach.

Luther's extensive treatment of the history and theology of the early church allows for a more positive statement on the nature of the church. If the councils and the church fathers are not the key to unity or finding the true marks of the church, then how can we distinguish the true church from the false church? What is the continuity of the church that is a mark of its true character? Luther is unequivocal in his answer: "The holy Christian people are recognized by their possession of the holy word of God."[120] In fact, Luther insists that "even if there were no other sign than this alone, it would suffice to prove that a Christian, holy people must exist there, for God's word cannot be without God's people, and conversely, God's people cannot be without God's word."[121]

Two observations are in order. First, it should be noted that giving priority to the word of God is not something new to Luther in this treatise. The centrality of the gospel, the forgiveness of sins, and the work of the Holy Spirit are themes that appear elsewhere in his writings. The church is not tied to one place or another. Wherever the gospel is preached, there the church can be found. For example, he can say,

> In this Christian church, wherever it exists, is to be found the forgiveness of sins, that is, a kingdom of grace and of true pardon. For in it are found the Gospel, baptism, and the sacrament of the altar, in which the forgiveness of sins is offered, obtained, and received. Moreover, Christ and His Spirit are there. Outside this Christian church there is no salvation, or forgiveness of sins, but everlasting death and damnation.[122]

Second, in arguing in this way, Luther gives priority to a definition of the church that centers on "a Christian holy people" (*sancta et catholica ecclesia*) as recited in the Apostles' Creed. The church is not to be understood primarily in institutional terms with its hierarchy, laws, and customs as in much of Roman thinking. Neither is it to be seen as a Platonic ideal, where the church is hidden internally in the individual. The church is visible through its gospel ministry where Christ rules "*per redemptionem*, 'through grace and the remission of sin,' and the Holy Spirit, *per vivificationem et sanctificationem*, 'through daily purging of sin and renewal of life,' so that we do not remain in sin but are enabled and obliged to lead a new life, abounding in all kinds of good works, as the Ten Commandments or the two tables of Moses' law command, and not in old evil works."[123]

Even as *On the Councils and the Church* presents Luther's negative assessment, it also sets forward his positive description of the church. Here Luther enumerates seven marks of the church: (1) God's holy word; (2) the holy sacrament of baptism; (3) the holy sacrament of the altar; (4) the public office of the keys, or the forgiveness or retention of sins; (5) the calling and ordaining of bishops and pastors; (6) prayer, public praise, and thanksgiving to God; and (7) the sacred cross, or spiritual struggles or trial. Luther gives significant weight to the fact that it is the Holy Spirit who calls, gathers, and enlightens the church in holiness. "For Christian holiness, or the holiness common to Christendom, is found where the Holy Spirit gives people faith in Christ and thus sanctifies them."[124] He imparts true knowledge of God and faith according to the First Table of the law, and he sanctifies Christians in works according to the Second Table. In addition, Luther understands that "a Christian and holy people is to be and to remain on earth until the end of the world."[125]

Just a few years later, Luther gives another list of the marks of the church. This time Luther discusses ten: (1) Holy Baptism; (2) the Holy Sacrament of the Altar; (3) the keys; (4) the office of preaching and God's word; (5) the apostolic confession of faith; (6) the Our Father; (7) honor due the temporal power; (8) praise of the marriage estate; (9) the suffering of the true church; and (10) the renouncing of revenge for persecution.[126] The variation in these two lists shows the flexibility with which Luther can speak of the marks of the church. But the unwavering focus on the word of God as a means of grace is central: it is the creative and performative action of the word that brings the church into being.

For our purposes, it is key to note that prayer finds its way into both of these lists: in the first as "prayer, praise, and thanks to God"; and in the second as "the Our Father." Even though prayer appears later on in the list of those marks by which the church is recognized, it is nonetheless close to the heartbeat of the church. If we think back to the way in which the catechism consists of diagnosis (law), treatment (gospel), and medicine (prayer), then we see that prayer is the natural breathing in and out of the new life of faith. Through faith the believer is related to the world in a new way and is incorporated into the body of Christ, becoming a participant in Christ's benefits and a fellow citizen with other believers in the kingdom.

Luther is convinced that prayer is one of the marks of the church. What is striking is how broad this notion is in Luther's thinking. Regarding his point on the Lord's Prayer in his second list of the marks of the church, Luther says,

Sixth, the holy Christian people are externally recognized by prayer, public praise, and thanksgiving to God. Where you see and hear the Lord's Prayer prayed and taught; or psalms or other spiritual songs sung, in accordance with the word of God and the true faith; also the creed, the Ten Commandments, and the catechism used in public, you may rest assured that a holy Christian people of God are present. For prayer, too, is one of the precious holy possessions whereby everything is sanctified, as St. Paul says [1 Tim. 4:5]. The psalms too are nothing but prayers in which we praise, thank, and glorify God. The creed and the Ten Commandments are also God's word and belong to the holy possession, whereby the Holy Spirit sanctifies the holy people of Christ. However, we are now speaking of prayers and songs which are intelligible and from which we can learn and by means of which we can mend our ways. The clamor of monks and nuns and priests is not prayer, nor is it praise to God; for they do not understand it, nor do they learn anything from it; they do it like a donkey, only for the sake of the belly and not at all in quest of any reform or sanctification or of the will of God.[127]

Several observations apply to this dense paragraph. First, the formula of "prayer, praise, and thanksgiving" calls to mind the answer to the second commandment in the Small Catechism:

"You are not to misuse the name of God."

What is this? Answer:

We are to fear and love God, so that we do not curse, swear, practice magic, lie, or deceive using God's name, but instead use that very name in every time of need to call on, pray to, praise, and give thanks to God.[128]

The Small Catechism is known for its pairing of the concepts "fear" and "love." With each of the commandments, there are things we should not do; but Luther does not remain there as though the commandments are somehow only negative. When we love God, it causes us to spring into action on the positive side of things. "Prayer, praise, and thanksgiving" is the shorthand Luther uses for all the positive actions we undertake to honor the name of the Lord in a proper sense.

Second, as Luther presents prayer as a mark of the church, it is tied into his catechetical approach to the faith. Everything it takes to live as a Christian is contained in the catechism, especially as Luther restructures it. "Prayer," as Luther uses the term here, seems to embrace everything having to do with worship and what it takes to prepare the people to participate in it. For this reason, Luther includes the public use of the Psalms, the Ten Commandments, and the catechism as compatible elements with prayer as a recognizable mark of the church.

At this juncture, it is appropriate to call to mind Luther's advice in *A Simple Way to Pray* (1535). In that treatise Luther gives practical advice to his friend Peter Beskendorf to pray the Lord's Prayer. After first warming the heart through a recitation of the Ten Commandments and some words of Christ or of the apostle Paul, Luther urges that Beskendorf repeat the prayer word for word. After that, Luther advises him to take a portion of the prayer and meditate upon it, and to pray a prayer for each petition. This allows the Lord's Prayer to become the template for us to learn how to grow in the practice of prayer. Surprisingly, Luther even urges the praying of the Ten Commandments:

> If I have had time and opportunity to go through the Lord's Prayer, I do the same with the Ten Commandments. I take one part after another and free myself as much as possible from distractions in order to pray. I divide each commandment into four parts, thereby fashioning a garland of four strands. That is, I think of each commandment as, first, instruction, which is really what it is intended to be, and consider what the Lord God demands of me so earnestly. Second, I turn it into a thanksgiving; third, a confession; and fourth, a prayer.[129]

Luther has in mind the refining quality of this practice. The commandments are used in their fourfold aspect "as a school text, song book, penitential book, and prayer book. They are intended to help the heart come to itself and grow zealous in prayer."[130]

In addition, Luther instructs his friend in a simple exercise for contemplating the Apostles' Creed. Once again, the creed may be treated in the same manner to make it into a garland of four strands. This is how Luther contemplates the third article of the creed:

> "I believe in the Holy Spirit," etc.
>
> This is the third great light which teaches us where such a Creator and Redeemer may be found and plainly encountered in this world, and what this will all come to in the end. Much could be said about this, but here is the summary: Where the holy Christian church exists, there we can find God the Creator, God the Redeemer, God the Holy Spirit, that is, him who daily sanctifies us through the forgiveness of sins, etc. The church exists where the word of God concerning such faith is rightly preached and confessed.
>
> Again, you have occasion here to ponder long about everything that the Holy Spirit accomplishes in the church every day, etc.
>
> Therefore be thankful that you have been called and have come into such a church.
>
> Confess and lament your lack of faith and gratitude, that you have neglected all this, and pray for a true and steadfast faith that will remain and endure until you come to that place where all endures forever, that is, beyond the resurrection from the dead, in life eternal. Amen.[131]

Using these exact words is not advised as this would be what Luther calls "prattle." What is important is that the mind is allowed to meditate with the aid of the Spirit in quiet but directed reflection on the Triune God.

Prayer as a mark of the church is a concept that holds within it everything useful for instruction in the faith and in worship. Luther himself practices a total immersion in the elements of the catechism as a meditation of the human heart to grasp the treasures found therein with the aid of the Spirit. Where we find these practices, we find the church.

The Spirit and Prayer

The importance of Luther's view of the Spirit has not always been recognized. Bernhard Lohse, a respected Luther scholar, is correct when he says, "For Luther, there was not a single doctrine in all of theology where the activity of the Spirit would not be fundamental. The Spirit's activity may thus not be limited to the sphere of faith and the church."[132] The Spirit is present and at work in all of creation. The dynamic character of the ever-changing world is due to the Spirit. There is no human deed or natural occurrence that is not accompanied by the Spirit. In this sense, it is possible to say that when God engages the world and humankind, it takes place through the Spirit. Regarding Luther's position Lohse continues, "The Holy Spirit is among humans in a twofold way. First through a universal activity, by which he preserves them as well as God's other creatures. Second, the Holy Spirit is given from Christ to believers."[133]

Spirit is the connection between God, the world, and humanity. The work of the Spirit in this regard is expansive and cosmic in scope. And while prayer does involve thinking in terms of "faith and church," there is a sense in which prayer is precisely what links us for the first time to the Triune God, who draws us out of the isolation of our sinful bondage to a new relation with God, the world, and the community around us. This is the manner in which Luther speaks as he gives exposition of some key passages.

Luther continually returns to Romans 8:12–17 and Galatians 4:6, which speak of the Spirit. Whether in lectures delivered at the university or in various sermons preached at St. Mary's and later published, we find Luther taking delight in speaking about the role of the Holy Spirit in the life of the believer.

Paul writes in Romans 8:15, "For you did not receive the spirit of slavery to fall back into fear, but you have received the Spirit of adoption as sons, by whom we cry, 'Abba! Father!'" In commenting on this passage, Luther makes quite clear it is the Holy Spirit who makes possible the confession of faith, and it is the Spirit who intercedes for us. Thus the possibility and the beginning of prayer in the life of the believer are produced by God the Spirit.

Luther contrasts the spirit of fear and the spirit of adoption in the following way,

> For in the spirit of fear it is not possible to cry, for we can scarcely open our mouth or mumble. But faith expands the heart, the emotions, and the voice, but fear tightens up all these things and restricts them, as our own experience

amply testifies. Fear does not say Abba, but rather it hates and flees from the Father as from an enemy and mutters against Him as a tyrant. For those people who are in the spirit of fear and not in the spirit of adoption do not taste how sweet the Lord is (cf. Ps. 34:8; 1 Peter 2:3), but rather He appears to them as harsh and hard.[134]

Being gripped in the spirit of fear causes us to "shut down" or "clam up." Before faith, there is suspicion and wariness, enmity and hatred. God is not an object of understanding or devotion, but rather one of dread. But once faith comes, the heart opens wide and "releases feelings and speech." Corresponding to the *Deus Dixit*—the God who speaks—is the believer who has been given utterance for the first time. Luther's explanation in the Larger Catechism of the second commandment arrives at this same point: "Just as the First Commandment instructs the heart and teaches faith, so this commandment leads us outward and directs the lips and the tongue into a right relationship with God. For the first things that burst forth and emerge from the heart are words."[135]

Receiving the spirit of adoption makes it possible for us to cry, "Abba, Father." As Luther puts it,

> [Paul] is here describing the power of the kingdom of Christ, the proper work, and the truly high worship which the Holy Spirit works in believers, namely, the consolation through which the heart is released from the fright and fear of sin and set at peace. [He is describing] the sincere appeal which in faith expects a favorable hearing and help from God, which cannot at all happen through the Law or his own holiness.[136]

The two works of the Spirit, according to Luther, are comfort and supplication. In this way, the Spirit assures us we are God's children and desires that we cry out to him.

Luther says that the prayers of the believer are weak and begin in stammering, or at least in nursery syllables.

> The Hebrew word *Abba*, which means (as he himself explains) "dear Father," is what a young child who is the heir babbles with his father in simple, childlike confidence, and calls him *Ab, Ab*. It is the easiest word a child can learn to speak or, as the old German language said almost more easily: *Etha, Etha*. Faith also speaks such simple, childlike words to God through the Holy Spirit, but out of the depths of the heart and (as he says afterward [Rom. 8:26]) "with inexpressible sighing."[137]

We find an extended description of the cry of the Spirit in Luther's 1535 lectures on Galatians 4:6. Here he emphasizes that God has sent the Holy Spirit into our hearts not simply to pray but to cry out, "Abba, Father." This is due to the great need of believers who are weak and whose faith is correspondingly weak. Historical existence brings about real-life opposition. We do not find Luther pulling back from dealing with conflict in the Christian life. Instead he presents the work of the Spirit in the most realistic terms.

When trial and conflict commence, the conscience finds itself under attack. In such a circumstance, the certainty of God's good favor is lost. In place of the assurance of the forgiveness of sins, the accusation of the law insinuates itself, saying something like the following: "You are a despicable sinner and an offense against God. Therefore his wrath is directed against you and you will be cast into the outer darkness." Luther says,

> We have nothing to strengthen and sustain us against these great and unbearable cries except the bare Word, which sets Christ forth as the Victor over sin, death, and every evil. But it is effort and labor to cling firmly to this in the midst of trial and conflict, when Christ does not become visible to any of our senses. We do not see Him, and in the trial our heart does not feel His presence and help. In fact, Christ appears to be wrathful with us and to be deserting us at such a time.[138]

In addition, the power of sin, doubt, and the terrors of death press in with unbearable vividness. There appears to be nothing left except despair and eternal destruction.

It is in the midst of this very real attack that the Holy Spirit fights on behalf of the believer in a twofold manner. First, the Spirit bears witness that we are the children of God (Rom. 8:16), thus reasserting the true nature of Christ over against the unbelieving heart. Second, the Spirit helps us in our weakness by interceding for us with sighs too deep for words (Rom. 8:26). When we are weak and tempted the Spirit sets up the cry of intercession in our heart.

It is worth reflecting on the fact that the work of the Spirit is directed to the mind of the believer, as well as connecting the believer through prayer to the Father. We might well imagine that it would be enough to reassert Jesus as Savior over the images of Christ as judge that may be at work in the conscience—to convince the mind of the good favor of God once again should relieve the attack. However, that is not the whole story. The Spirit certainly speaks to the believer, but he simultaneously also reaches outside the believer to the Father with groanings too deep for words. It is as though a petition from the Spirit needs to penetrate the clouds to reach through to the Father. The very unity of the Triune identity is implicated here. Should the believer's intercession not reach its goal, then the one-sided view of the God of judgment and wrath would have to stand. As it is,

> No matter how great and terrible the cries are that the Law, sin, and the devil let loose against us, even though they seem to fill heaven and earth and to overcome the sighs of our hearts completely, still they cannot do us any harm. For the more these enemies press in upon us, accusing and vexing us with their cries, the more do we, sighing, take hold of Christ; with heart and lips we call upon Him, cling to Him, and believe that He was born under the Law for us, in

order that He might redeem us from the curse of the Law and destroy sin and death. When we have taken hold of Christ by faith this way, we cry through Him: "Abba! Father!" And this cry of ours far exceeds the cry of the devil.[139]

The Spirit cries in the believer when there is no strength to spare. Luther says that we have only the word, and in the heat of battle we sigh a little. We are barely aware that any sound is emitted at all.

> But "He who searches the hearts of men," Paul says (Rom. 8:27), "knows the mind of the Spirit." To Him who searches the hearts this sigh, which seems so meager to the flesh, is a loud cry and a sigh too deep for words, in comparison with which the great and horrible roars of the Law, sin, death, the devil, and hell are nothing at all and are inaudible. It is not without purpose, then, that Paul calls this sigh of the pious and afflicted heart the crying and indescribable sighing of the Spirit; for it fills all of heaven and earth and cries so loudly that the angels suppose that they cannot hear anything except this cry.[140]

The sighing of the Spirit is not something we can perceive through our senses. The work of the Spirit is not accomplished through the effort of the believer. In fact, one of the points of the passage is to show that the power of Christ is made perfect in weakness. Precisely when there is no energy and no will to dare even to mumble, the Spirit is granted to the afflicted, and he intercedes to reclaim his own.

CHAPTER 3

MEDITATION

The second rule for the correct way to study theology is *meditatio*, or meditation. Luther's description is energetic and detailed: he urges us to read and reread; we are encouraged to work with "diligent attention" and "diligent reflection." The meditation Luther is talking about is active indeed. This is how he explains it in the pertinent paragraph of the preface of his writings:

> Secondly, you should meditate, that is, not only in your heart, but also outwardly, by actually repeating and comparing oral speech and literal words of the book, reading and rereading them with diligent attention and reflection, so that you may see what the Holy Spirit means by them. And take care that you do not grow weary or think that you have done enough when you have read, heard, and spoken them once or twice, and that you then have complete understanding. You will never be a particularly good theologian if you do that, for you will be like untimely fruit which falls to the ground before it is half ripe.[1]

The meditation Luther is calling for is an engagement that demands concentration and focus. This is not like some of the more mystical kinds of meditation with which we have become familiar in our own time, especially within Eastern religions. This is not an escape from the space-time continuum; neither is it a matter of altering our consciousness or entering into a trancelike state. It is certainly not a matter of attaining the experience of *Gelassenheit* ("yieldedness" or "self-distraction") that the spiritual teachers of his time were urging.

Luther defines meditation not as an inward journey but as an outward-oriented concentration on the text of Scripture. Luther urges a reflective and deliberate reading and rereading of the words of the Bible. One cannot be satisfied to read a text once or twice, thinking that is enough. Only through diligent attention and reflection on the words themselves can meditation be fruitful. Meditation is a matter of concentrating on the word of God to release its essence, much like we rub an herb to release its aroma. The constant reading and rereading is ruminating on the word—repeatedly mulling over what the text says and what the Spirit means by it.

Luther's definition of meditation has a monastic origin, which should come as no surprise, insofar as he learned the practice of *meditatio* as an Augustinian friar. In monastic vocabulary, meditation means the slow, reflective, semiaudible recitation of Scripture texts. Some maintain that a more mental reading had replaced the semiaudible reading of the Middle Ages. In which case, Luther's assertion of the need to speak out loud may represent a return to the earlier tradition, or it may well be a technique Luther found especially helpful.[2] Here a premium is placed on the external speaking and hearing of the word, as well as the more internal meditation of the heart. The external affects the internal even as the internal touches on the external. The two dare not be parted. In an early treatise on prayer, Luther points out that spoken words are helpful in lifting the heart to God: "It is admittedly helpful to hear the words, for they stimulate thought and true prayer. As was said before, the spoken words have no other purpose than that of a trumpet, a drum, or an organ, or any other sound which will move the heart and lift it upward to God."[3] Without the external word, it is much easier for the devil to trick and smother the prayer or meditation in the heart. Therefore, we must not become tired of what we read or think that after one or two readings we have achieved something great. We cannot understand the depths of a matter without diligence over time. "The Spirit reserves much for Himself, so that we may always remain His pupils."[4]

In *The Love of Learning and the Desire for God: A Study of Monastic Culture*, Jean Leclercq, a twentieth-century French Benedictine monk, describes monastic theology for us. Through lectures given to young monks at the Institute of Monastic Studies in Rome, Leclercq outlined aspects of sacred learning that equipped the monks for a lifetime of service. Monastic theology focused on the grammar and vocabulary of Scripture in contrast to the Scholastics, who focused on deriving doctrine from the sacred text. The reading or *lectio* of Holy Scripture was therefore critical. The phrase *lectio divina* refers to the "the reading of Holy Scripture." It is interesting to note here that the phrase came to have slightly different meanings in Scholasticism and in monasticism. The Scholastic *lectio* is driven by questions and ensuing discussion. The monastic *lectio* is oriented toward *meditatio* and *oratio*, or meditation and prayer. "The objective of the first is science and knowledge; of the second, wisdom and appreciation."[5]

In the Middle Ages, the reader usually pronounced the words with the lips. With a low tone, the voice would repeat the sentence seen with the eyes. What results is more than a visual memory of the written words: there is a muscular memory of the text. The *meditatio* consists of monks concentrating on the act of taking the text into themselves. In *meditatio*, the text is slowly and carefully scrutinized and then taken into the mouth to be chewed. Just as a cow bites off grass and begins to chew, and then after a time chews again, so a monk ruminates on the text of Scripture as an act of devotion. More than once in Scripture, prophets of God are told to eat the scroll, the word of God (Ezek. 3; Rev. 10), which they find to be sweeter than honey. "Taste and see that the Lord is good" (Ps. 34:8) is something the monks took very seriously.

The act of *meditatio* is a means of assimilating the content of a text by prayerful reflection. The contemplation of Scripture provides the time necessary for the full flavor of a text to be released. In his comments on the book of Deuteronomy, Luther uses the language of rumination:

To chew the cud, however is to receive the word affectively (*cum affectu verbum suscipere*) and meditate with supreme diligence so that (according to the proverb) one does not permit it to go in one ear and out of the other, but holds it firmly in the heart, swallows it, and absorbs it into the intestines.[6]

Savor, not science, is the goal of the monastics. In other words, the assimilation of a text is not merely intellectual but includes the emotions as well. If a text is ultimately to change us, then it must occupy our minds and move our hearts. Indeed, the word of God changes minds and claims and rearranges affections. The grace of God shapes the person rather than some other perceived good. Thus the two components of the soul—the understanding (*intellectus*) of the mind (*mens*), and the emotions (*affectus*) of the heart (*cor*)—are involved in a complete meditation of a text. Both are necessary if we are to move from mere consideration of a text to the spiritual enjoyment and appropriation of the text.

Inner truth must be expressed with the external voice, in order to keep it from being subjective. The external repetition of Bible passages will make its way to the inner parts. To acknowledge this is to agree that the external word of God is what lends definition and forms the inner life of the subject, not the other way around. "Meditation therefore cannot retreat behind the text of Scripture, to become, as in Schleiermacher, a non-linguistic 'immediate existential relationship.' "[7] Luther asserts that the Spirit provides for us the words and mode of our expression, especially in the Psalter but throughout the entire text of Scripture. This assures us that in meditation we do not turn inward to ourselves but remain in the word.

This truth could be illustrated from a number of places in Luther's writings, but none are more pointed than his comments on John 15:7, "If you abide in me, and my words abide in you, ask whatever you wish, and it will be done for you." Here the essential relationship of Christ and the believer is set forward.

Christ adds this comment here: "Just pay attention to My Word; for everything depends on whether My Word remains in you, that is, whether you believe and confess the article taught in the children's Creed: 'I believe in Jesus Christ, our Lord, who was crucified for me, who died, rose again, and is seated at the right hand of the Father,' and whatever pertains to it. If you remain faithful to this and are ready to stake all on it, to forsake all rather than accept a different doctrine or works, if you thus remain in the Word, then I remain in you and you in Me. Then our roots are intertwined; then we are joined, so that My words and your heart have become one. Then you will not ask further how I abide in you or you in Me; for you will see this in yonder life. Now, however, you can grasp and comprehend it in no other way than that you have My Word, that you are washed in My blood by faith, and that you are anointed and sealed with My Spirit. Therefore your whole life and all your deeds are acceptable and nothing but good fruit."[8]

Remaining in Christ is a function of meditation as the way of theology. Our inner beings live in the outward reality of the word of God. The outward reality is what allows the inner reality of the heart to be joined to God the Son through the Spirit.

Luther's concept of meditation also evidences an anti-enthusiast edge. He asserts the absolute authority of the Scriptures against any illegitimate attempts to place human-received revelations or other spiritual insights in the center of Christian life. Increasingly, he had to contend with the propaganda of certain teachers who relied on inner illumination alone. Luther sought to assert that God does not give his Spirit without the external word found in Scripture.

> Thus you see in this same Psalm how David constantly boasts that he will talk, meditate, speak, sing, hear, read, by day and night and always, about nothing except God's Word and commandments. For God will not give you his Spirit without the external Word; so take your cue from that. His command to write, preach, read, hear, sing, speak, etc., outwardly was not given in vain.[9]

The external word and the Spirit are inseparable. As the critical passage above states, "God will not give you his Spirit without the external Word." At first blush, it may seem that this is a restrictive and exclusive statement privileging the external. But in reality, it is no more restrictive than saying that God reveals himself in Jesus Christ. It is thus not so much restrictive as it is programmatic in declaring where God is to be found.

Opposition to Luther's position on this point came early on in the Reformation. Already in 1521, the Zwickau prophets had disturbed many in Wittenberg during Luther's forced absence, while he was at Wartburg Castle for protection. They had stressed the inward and the spiritual to the highest possible degree. In this, Andreas Rudolf Bodenstein von Karlstadt (1486–1541) agreed.[10] The Spirit was set in opposition to the letters of Scripture, and the passage in 2 Corinthians 4 became something of a battle cry, "The letter kills, but the Spirit gives life." These sectarians had a radical notion of what that meant. The Spirit was considered able to dispense with all external aids, whether of art, images, music, or even of the sacraments as the outward channels of grace.

As a consequence of preaching these views, the separatists destroyed a great deal of church art (paintings and statues) in Wittenberg, forcing Luther to leave his Wartburg refuge to address the issue. First, he preached a series of sermons that quelled the immediate unrest.[11] A few years later, in 1525, Luther returned to the issue when he wrote a treatise titled *Against the Heavenly Prophets in the Matter of Images and Sacraments.*[12] In this work, Luther sets forward the proper relationship between the word and Spirit.

It is Luther's perception that Karlstadt reversed the order of the internal and external: "That which God made a matter of faith and spirit they convert into a human work." Karlstadt's theology apparently was based on concepts of mortification that would lead to the Spirit. Certain mystical steps, if followed, would result in the apprehension of God. If someone were to attain and remain in a state of "self-abstraction" or "yieldedness" (*Gelassenheit*), they could expect that a heavenly voice would come and God himself would speak. Karlstadt's advice represents a theology of glory—that is, a method by which the religious subject ascends to God.

Karlstadt proposes that the Spirit comes without external signs; he comes to those who seek him through ardent longing. The unmediated witness of the Spirit is the culmination or crown of this mystical way of seeking him. Seen in this light, the Spirit is the reward of those who strive and work, albeit spiritually, for God's favor. Karlstadt's desire to promote mortification of the flesh through seeking the Spirit in this way actually represents the turn to nomistic piety (that is, conforming to the moral law). "They place the mortification of the flesh prior to faith, even prior to the Word."[13] Luther was convinced that the attempt was being made to sanctify the old Adam through works of the law, and he sensed that Karlstadt was not content to perceive God in the lowliness of preaching or in the sufferings of Christ:

> Instead of the outward order of God in the material sign of baptism and the oral proclamation of the Word of God he wants to teach you, not how the Spirit comes to you but how you come to the Spirit. They would have you learn how to journey on the clouds and ride on the wind. They do not tell you how or when, whither or what, but you are to experience what they do.[14]

Luther saw this kind of spiritualizing as discarding all the means by which the Spirit might come to the believer. By placing the Spirit in sharp contrast to all things visible and external, the very means ordered by God for his coming were swept aside.

Over against Karlstadt's dualism that separates the spiritual from the physical, Luther argues their inseparability. Not only is it possible for the physical to be spiritual—for example, Christ's death on the cross—but it is assured by the acts of God in history. For Luther, God confronts women and men by his Spirit in the ordinary structures of human life. To despise that which is outward is to despise the God who has entered history. "God . . . sets before us no word or commandment without including with it something material and outward."[15] The entire biblical history gives evidence to that.[16] "The Spirit cannot be with us except in material and physical things such as the word, water, and Christ's body and in his saints on earth."[17]

The outwardness of the word is an important challenge to the piety, or to the way of speculation, that by works the believer wishes to reach God in his majesty. Opposed to this is the God who says, "Seek me where I may be found." The Christ of the stable and the cross is always an affront to human ideas concerning the way to God. Attempts to find God by speculation and works lead only to the unclothed God in his power, the *Deus Nudus* of the law; to meet God in this way leads to death. The way of the cross leads in another direction because the gospel is become deep in the flesh through the incarnation. The Son of God came to reclaim humanity and creation in suffering redemption. The signs of that redemption hold together the internal and the external and are the means through which God chooses to speak the promise yet again. That is why Luther places such an emphasis on preaching and the sacraments.

Luther's complaint against the "heavenly prophets" is that they take what is inward and turn it into outward self-contrived works. Even in the Lord's Supper, the recognition and remembrance of Christ is turned into a human work. Instead of a simple hearing in faith of the words "Given and shed for you for the forgiveness of sins," the efficacy of the Supper is hung on a proper remembrance full of "passionate ardor" of one sort or another.

> So, my brothers, cling firmly to the order of God. According to it the putting to death of the old man, wherein we follow the example of Christ, as Peter says [1 Pet. 2:21], does not come first, as this devil urges, but comes last. No one can mortify the flesh, bear the cross, and follow the example of Christ before he is a Christian and has Christ through faith in his heart as an eternal treasure. You don't put the old nature to death, as these prophets do, through works, but through the hearing of the gospel. Before all other works and acts you hear the Word of God, through which the Spirit convinces the world of its sin (John 16[:8]). When we acknowledge our sin, we hear of the grace of Christ. In this Word the Spirit comes and gives faith where and to whom he wills. Then you proceed to the mortification and the cross and the works of love.[18]

The Spirit comes in the word and brings faith. The external word gives the internal orientation of faith its proper object. Meditation as theology keeps this relationship between word and Spirit, outward and inward, intact, held within the reality of God's condescension to humankind in the incarnation of Christ.

Luther's Meditation on Romans 1

One of the most famous accounts of Luther's understanding of meditation on the word of God is found in his *Preface to the Latin Writings of 1545*. One year before his death, Luther looked back on some of the events central to the Reformation. In this historically rich passage, Luther rehearses his life, including the events surrounding the Indulgence Controversy and his unfolding work as lecturer on the Bible. Clearly, Luther uses this singular account of the preface to elucidate the tremendous theological changes in his thinking, especially those that led to his work as a reformer of the church. In addition to this explanation, his lively narrative depicts the accidental beginnings of what became a watershed movement in Western history.

Luther begins his account by begging his readers to be prudent and to exercise empathy. He asks for a judicious reading of the facts and a handling of the matter with great commiseration. As a young member of the Augustinian Order, he had been far from inciting a new beginning. As he points out,

> I was once a monk and a most enthusiastic papist when I began that cause. I was so drunk, yes, submerged in the pope's dogmas, that I would have been ready to murder all, if I could have, or to co-operate willingly with the murderers of all who would take but a syllable from obedience to the pope.[19]

At the start of these events, Luther conceded most everything to the pope, something he would never do as a mature theologian. But, as he admits, "At first I was all alone and certainly very inept and unskilled in conducting such great affairs. For I got into these turmoils by accident and not by will or intention."[20]

If we follow the story as Luther tells it, we see several times when events might have turned out differently. As Luther's narrative moves from the Indulgence Controversy and his posting of the Ninety-Five Theses to the Leipzig Debate of 1519 and beyond, the time seemed ripe for a paradigm shift. Popular piety had placed a crushing burden on the laity, which is why so many embraced Luther's evangelical interpretation of the gospel with such enthusiasm. Old ways of looking at religious questions had new answers based on the free grace of God shown in Jesus Christ.

"The Justice of God"

One critical turning point in Luther's reformation came from his meditation on the apostle Paul's idea of righteousness in the book of Romans. The justice of God, or *iustitia Dei* as the Latin Vulgate has it, presented an intractable obstacle to the struggling friar:

> Meanwhile, I had already during that year returned to interpret the Psalter anew. I had confidence in the fact that I was more skillful, after I had lectured in the university on St. Paul's epistles to the Romans, to the Galatians, and the one to the Hebrews. I had indeed been captivated with an extraordinary burning desire to understand Paul in the Epistle to the Romans. But up till then there had stood in my way not the cold blood about the heart, but a single word written in the first chapter, "In it the justice of God is revealed" (Rom. 1:17) because I hated that word "justice of God," which, according to the use and custom of all the teachers, I had been taught to understand philosophically regarding the formal or active justice, that is, justice by which God is just and punishes sinners and the unrighteous.
>
> Though I lived as a monk without reproach, I felt that I was a sinner before God with an extremely disturbed conscience. I could not be sure that my merit would assuage him. I did not love, no, rather I hated the just God who punishes sinners, and secretly, if not blasphemously, certainly murmuring greatly, I was angry with God, and said, "As if, indeed, it is not enough, that miser-

able sinners, eternally lost through original sin, are crushed by every kind of calamity by the Ten Commandments, without having God add pain to pain by the gospel and also by the gospel threatening us with his justice and wrath!" Thus I raged with a fierce and troubled conscience. Nevertheless, I continued to badger Paul about that spot in Romans 1 seeking anxiously to know what it meant.[21]

Luther had wrestled with Romans 1 years before he first entered the monastery. Then, one July afternoon in 1505 as he was returning to the university to continue his law studies, a thunderbolt threw him to the ground. Terrified of God, death, and damnation, he promised to become a monk if he survived the storm. He kept that vow and entered religious life inside the Black Cloister of Erfurt as an Augustinian monk.

But even then, as a young priest saying his first Mass, he was still terrified of God. In fact, he trembled so badly with fear at holding the Eucharist cup that he spilled a few drops from it. How could he possibly address the Divine Majesty? As Luther historian Roland Bainton describes it: "The horrors of Infinitude, smote him like a new lightning bolt, and only through a fearful restraint could he hold himself at the altar to the end."[22] Not only was he terrified of God, but he also viewed Jesus Christ as the "Just Judge" on the last day. At every turn, he saw only judgment and wrath.

It is no wonder, then, that the late medieval practice of devotion aimed at bringing about a more predictable judgment, an easing of the moment of death, and attracting a favorable divine disposition through the accumulation of pious works. In this passage on Romans 1 recorded for us by Luther, we see his uncertainty over his meritorious acts and his heightened sense of conscience as a result. Although Luther was a disciplined and scrupulous monk, he could find no peace or affirmation of his salvation in Christ.

For Luther, the problem was cumulative and systemic in nature. His thoughts of the severity of God and of Christ as judge were reinforced by his experiences in the cloister in Erfurt, where the stringent demands of the rigorist Augustinian Order and the goal of religious perfection loomed large. When boiled down, the church's advice came to the commonsense adage, "Do your best and God will do the rest." This, however, gave Luther no comfort, only vexation. The tendency to think of salvation increasingly in quantitative terms of the accumulation of virtue—along the Aristotelian construct that asserted we become good people by doing good deeds—pressed Luther to the breaking point.

As we have already seen, the central term that triggered Luther's deep spiritual trial was the "justice of God"—which he understood as the just God seeking out the lawbreaker with wrath and judgment. If this were true, Luther wondered, how was salvation possible? For Luther, justice (*iustitia*) was the problem, which could not be softened with other concepts such as the mercy (*misericordia*) or the goodness (*bonitas*) of God. While Luther knew that all medieval theologians had a doctrine of grace, such notions held little power for him when compared to the devastating bass notes of the ominous teachings about God's eternal providence and election. As he put it,

> As if, indeed, it is not enough, that miserable sinners, eternally lost through original sin, are crushed by every kind of calamity by the Ten Commandments, without having God add pain to pain by the gospel and also by the gospel threatening us with his justice and wrath!

Luther even sees the gospel as still another law to be met, rather than the word of promise that gives life. It is no wonder, then, that he accuses his monastic teachers of setting forward Christ exclusively as a judge to whom account had to be given.

The Grace of God

Johann von Staupitz (1465–1524) was the one exceptional religious figure in Luther's life who pointed him in another direction. When Luther came to his father confessor, complaining that the Lord God treats people too horribly, Staupitz did not try to mitigate the hard edge of human reality. There are indeed plagues for which there is no medical help, there are evidences of the devil's work, and there is the uncertainty of the moment of death and the afterlife. There is no way to warm up to the inscrutable God who determines all things. In his own nature, God is immense, incomprehensible, and infinite, and for that reason he is intolerable to human reason.

It is here where Staupitz, however, provides Luther with a new understanding of Christ. Drawing on a tradition from Augustine through monastic theology, Christ is depicted as the "sweetest Savior" instead of the angry judge.[23] Instead of seeking God in his majesty, Staupitz invited Luther to meditate on the wounds of Christ, much in the manner of Bernard of Clairvaux. To place ourselves within reach of the suffering of Christ, Staupitz told him, is to reject our attempt to know God as he is in heaven. Instead of Christ the "Just Judge," the witness of Scripture leads us to Christ, born of the virgin, as our Mediator and High Priest, the One in whom there is forgiveness of sin. This pastoral advice of Staupitz so impressed Luther that later on in his life he would say that his fellow friar was the one who started the new teaching.[24]

In light of Staupitz's liberating words, Luther can now return to his meditation on Romans 1 with a fresh approach:

> Night and day I meditated on those words until at last, by the mercy of God, I paid attention to their context: "The justice of God is revealed in it, as it is written: The just person will live by faith." Then I began to understand the justice of God by which the just person lives by a gift of God, that is by faith. And this is the meaning: the justice of God is revealed through the gospel, but it is a passive justice by which the merciful God justifies us by faith, as it is

written: "The just person lives by faith." All at once I had the feeling of being born again and entering into paradise itself through open gates. Immediately the whole of Scripture shone in a different light. I ran through the Scriptures from memory and found other terms also had analogous meanings: e.g. the power of God, by which God makes us powerful; the wisdom of God, by which he makes us wise; the strength of God, the salvation of God, the glory of God.

And I extolled my sweetest word—"justice of God"—with as much love as the hatred with which I had hated it. Thus that place in Paul was for me truly the gate to paradise. Later I read Augustine's *The Spirit and the Letter*, where contrary to hope I found that he, too, interpreted God's justice in a similar way, as the righteousness with which God clothes us when he justifies us.[25]

In what has become known as the "tower experience" (because he came to this new realization while reading Romans in the tower of the Black Cloister monastery), Luther realized that the person of faith lives by a gift of God—that is, by faith.[26] The "justice of God" is thus not the philosophical or the formal justice he had been taught, but rather it was a passive justice by which God comes to his own. Here, in great relief, Luther uses the language of "illumination" and speaks of being born again and entering into paradise as through open gates. He comes to a newfound certainty through his new apprehension of God's Holy Word as it shone out to him in a new light. From Luther's other statements, we know he was convinced that this revelation came through the power and the presence of the Holy Spirit. We now see Luther's former divided self—the one who hated God while feigning piety—replaced with the new man, captivated and convinced by the word.

It is tempting to read this "tower experience" account as a matter of personal conversion, marking the transformation of the pre-reformational Luther to the fully empowered Reformer. And indeed, this account has received an exceptional amount of scrutiny—not only because it is a powerful and memorable autobiographical statement, but also because it is connected with important issues regarding when Luther came to certain exegetical insights (that is, people are curious know when Luther had his big breakthrough).[27] As a result, the complex questions surrounding the historical data have led scholars to date this event anywhere from 1513 to 1519. This account of Luther's discovery has even been viewed as the center point of his theology, which guided the Reformer in his subsequent conflicts with Rome and the other reformers.[28] More recent scholarship, however, is less eager to make this move. Luther's theological development went through several stages, some of which were accompanied by moments of crisis followed by moments of relative quiet.

There is reason to believe that, in his usual dramatic fashion, Luther reduced years of spiritual struggle into a single "tower experience" (which makes for a much more exciting story). There are also those who believe that Luther wrote this as a rhetorical function of establishing his authority as a reformer of the church, presenting the content of his theology as assured by the Holy Spirit, rather than being merely a historical account.[29] Contrary to some opinions, there is no indication that Luther viewed his life prior to this event as pre-Christian.[30] With his concept of lifelong repentance, Luther simply does not fit well into the conversion model that stems from the Second Great Awakening—that is, that there is a dramatic moment of his "conversion" to which we can all point.

Meditation as Theology

Apart from trying to determine when Luther had his theological break-through on Romans 1, let's look again at his writing in the preface to see what it tells us about Luther's approach to meditation and the role it played in his critical transformation.

At the outset there are three features that draw our attention. First, this is a text about meditation, or *meditatio*, in the monastic sense of that term. As Luther put it, "Meditating night and day, I gave heed to the context of the words." It is clear that there is a real spirituality to Luther. When it comes to doctrine, we find Luther expressing it more as a theology oriented toward wisdom or experience—or, in this case, meditation.

Luther's understanding of theology as *meditation* takes into consideration the matter of time. There is a patient expectation that the word of God will constantly reveal and renew the believer. "Note well," says Luther, "that the power of Scripture is this: it will not be altered by the one who studies it; instead, it transforms the one who loves it. It draws the individual in—into itself—and into its own powers."[31] Meditation as theology proceeds from the human condition of not having, not seeing, and not knowing—and having to build from there. It was through his diligent meditation on Scripture that Luther came to this insight. Luther says that he is one "of those who, as Augustine says of himself, have become proficient by writing and teaching. I was not one of those who from nothing suddenly become the topmost, though they are nothing neither have labored, nor been tempted, nor become experienced, but have with one look at the Scriptures exhausted their entire spirit."[32]

Meditation as Memory

Second, Luther has a clearly monastic approach to memory, or *memoria*. "I ran through the Scriptures from memory and found other terms also had analogous meanings." Here we find Luther engaged in a monastic way of correlating texts of Scripture as well as important passages from Augustine. From the monastic point of view, it was memory that converted knowledge into useful experience, and thus memory cannot be separated from meditation and the process of creativity and composition.

In her work on memory in medieval culture, Mary Caruthers notes how different it is from modern society, which considers imagination—not memory—to be the highest human intellectual power. In our post-Freudian world, imagination has been linked with the dark and powerful forces of the unconscious. She writes: "Ancient and medieval people reserved their awe for memory. Their greatest geniuses they describe as people of superior memories, they boast unashamedly of their prowess in that faculty, and they regard it as a mark of superior moral character as well as intellect."[33]

Memory was an essential tool for storing and then retrieving words and facts necessary for the making of ideas. Thus monastic memory was not merely rote memorization, but also the means by which new ideas could be crafted. This kind of "memory" is not restricted to what we now call memory; it is a much more expansive concept that includes comparison, cognition, imagination, and invention. Not only was memory one of the five canons of ancient and medieval rhetoric, but it was also considered essential to the virtue of prudence—that which makes moral judgment possible.

For memory to be useful, it needs to be trained according to certain elementary techniques. In Book XI of *Institutio Oratoria*, Roman rhetorician Marcus Fabius Quintilianus (c. AD 35–100)—more commonly known as Quintilian—provides practical advice along these lines. After stating that "our whole education depends on memory,"[34] he then sets out specific ways of assisting and using memory. For one, "localities" are sharply impressed upon the mind; that is, when we are called upon to remember a passage verbatim, it is best for us to break up the text into several smaller passages. He likens the process to a spacious house divided into a number of rooms (hence the idea of "locality"): "The first thought is arranged in the forecourt; the second, let us say, in the living-room; the remainder are placed in due order all around the *impluvium* [an atrium light well in a Roman house]."[35] If a large amount of text needs to be remembered, it is helpful if certain portions are clustered and then linked to one another for easier retrieval. This locational model of memory allows us to "store" and "code" text in our mind. How we space and distinguish one image from another also establishes an architecture that helps with relationships and associations between thoughts. Seen in this light, it is clear that monastic memory includes creative thought. As Mary Caruthers writes,

> Medieval *memoria* was a universal thinking machine, *machinae memorialis*— both the mill that ground the grain of one's experiences (including all that one read) into mental flour with which one could make wholesome new bread, and also the hoist or windlass that every wise master-mason learned to make and to use in constructing new matters.[36]

In this view of meditation, the mind is free to roam its inventory, to cast its glance on words, facts, and relationships. In doing so, the real goal of reading is achieved and the possibility of baking nourishing bread, as Caruthers suggests above, is possible. Or, to change the imagery slightly, meditation as a craft of thinking allows us to sharpen our expression of God's truth and to prove ourselves as master builders using materials that will withstand fiery trials (1 Cor. 3:10–17).

All of this is to demonstrate that when Luther writes about running through the Scriptures by memory, he is referring to something very specific. As Quintilian suggests, Luther is regrouping images and words of Scripture from the storehouse of his memory into new "places," as his meditative mind draws them into altered patterns of relationships. Through his meditation on Romans 1, perhaps we can say that Luther was erasing the old labels in his mind regarding the "justice of God" and creating new ones that acknowledge the grace of God. Luther's discovery of the true meaning of *iustitia Dei* derived through meditation required a change in the way the idea was inventoried in the storehouse of his mind.

Meditation as Adoration

Third, we see an example, used by Saint Bernard of Clairvaux (1090–1153), of the way Luther meditated on the humanity and passion of Christ. As Luther says, "And I extolled my sweetest word—'justice of God'—with as much love as the hatred with which I had hated it." The transformation of Jesus as the "Just Judge" at the last day—Luther's "hatred" of God—into the sweet Savior comes directly out of what Luther learned from Staupitz and the tradition flowing from Saint Bernard.[37]

Saint Bernard is known for his explicit use of the "sweetness of Christ" (*Christi suavitas*) and the "sweetness of the Lord" (*dulcedo Domini*), which derive from the Vulgate translation of Psalm 33:9, "Taste and see that the Lord is sweet." Our English translations usually render the translation as "good." But this does not take into account the Latin term *suavis* (literally, "sweet") on which the monks meditated. Believers experience the sweetness of the Lord as they experience the forgiveness of sins when they are brought near to God through Christ.

It is important to note here that Luther is indebted to this monastic spiritual vocabulary, especially within the Bernardine tradition, focusing on the suffering Christ as the foundation and centerpiece of his theology. Through Luther's writing in his preface, we see that his theology is indeed a *sapientia experimentalis*—an experiential wisdom.[38]

A Meditation on Christ's Passion

Bernard Moeller, a church historian, makes the case that sixteenth-century Germany is marked by religious passion and fervor.[39] Against those who claim that the medieval church languished under the terrible weight of one misunderstanding after another, Moeller and others say that there was lively and excited lay participation in a great variety of devotional expressions. During this time of spiritual flowering, religious devotions flourished in unprecedented fashion: meditations on the Passion of Christ, veneration of relics, Marian devotions, pilgrimages, celebration of festival days, the veneration of the saints, and processions of various kinds. Eucharistic devotions, often associated with the feast of Corpus Christi, were held during the night as well as the day. Devotional literature was produced to fill the growing demand of the wealthy patrons. An abundance of types of religious writing became available, from lavishly ornamented books of hours and books of consolation to sermon manuals and missals. Spiritual publications comprised the greater portion of all books published during this time period.

Devotional art experienced a dramatic upsurge as well. Sculptures and paintings depicting the Madonna and child are ubiquitous, and the pietà as an art form emerged in part from the devotion directed toward the humanity of Christ.[40] Other themes—such as the image of the sacred heart and the man of sorrows—attained newfound popularity. Wood carvings for pieces used in Passion processions and the decoration of churches came in all ranges of ornate and subtle, as well as prosaic and crude. Carved devotional panels, small enough to fit in a person's pocket or purse, were created to aid in the pilgrim's meditations and devotion. Jewel-studded monstrances, used for holding the consecrated Host in processions, were created with special care and with the most expensive materials. Painted panel work, such as the Isenheim Altarpiece, portrays the death and resurrection of Jesus with breathtaking power. Depictions of the saints' lives, the legend of the Virgin Mary, and scenes from the life of Christ were favorite motifs found in devotional art of this period.

The burgeoning devotional religion of the laity demonstrates their desire to meet in tangible ways the transcendent reality of the God of the church. The privileged possession of the monastic orders, with its promise of eternal life to anyone taking holy orders, was giving way to a new framing of religious truth. The reform movements of the fifteenth century had created a new vigor and vitality within the monastic orders, and the treatises that had helped to spur these changes were helpful to the laity. Increased interest created the desire to implement what we might call a "lay monasticism." The concern of this movement was to bridge the gap between secular and monastic life by realizing some of the monastic ideals, including devotional practices, outside the walls of the monastery. The intensity of fifteenth-century religious expression was truly remarkable.

There are three treatises from Luther that each in its own way adds to our discussion on meditation. The first, *A Meditation on Christ's Passion*, was written by Luther in 1519 to address the devotional practices of the day. It is evangelical in tone but focuses on correcting the abuses of lay devotion. The second, *A Treatise on the New Testament, that is, the Holy Mass* (1520), sets forward Luther's evangelical understanding of the Lord's Supper, which is central to Christian worship. Third, he wrote *On the Freedom of a Christian* (1520) as a summary of his new evangelical thinking. Free of polemics and forward-looking, this treatise focuses on freedom in Christ. Because of the prominence it gives to the benefits that derive from the word of God and its focus on Christ, it is well worth our consideration.

Luther wrote *A Meditation on Christ's Passion* while in the midst of writing a treatise on the Lord's Prayer, a commentary on Galatians, and reading canon law in preparation for the upcoming Leipzig debate. So much for the quiet life of the academic! Luther's treatise touched a nerve, and by 1524 it had gone through twenty-four editions and had been printed in Wittenberg, Basel, Augsburg, Zurich, Erfurt, Munich, Nuremberg, and Strasbourg. An edition in Latin came out in 1521, which was later included in the Church Postil of 1525 as the "Sermon for Good Friday." There is no question that its clarity and profundity are carried along by its simplicity and brevity. The work's popularity, however, was soon overshadowed by the sales of Luther's larger writings.

The *Christ's Passion* treatise not only helps readers (or hearers) to orient their meditation on Christ in the proper way, but it also does so in memorable fashion. Paragraphs 1 through 3 set out improper ways of meditating on Christ's Passion. Luther advises that venting our anger against the Jews, entering into a contemplation to shield ourselves from suffering, or remaining in the pure enjoyment of the emotion of pity for Christ are not ultimately fruitful manners of meditation. Paragraphs 4 through 11 turn to what constitutes a proper meditation on the Passion of Christ—namely, an unflinching regard for "the stern wrath and the unchanging earnestness with which God looks upon sin and sinners, so much that he was unwilling to release sinners even for his only and dearest Son without his payment of the severest penalty for them."[41] Paragraphs 12 through 15 move from the Passion of Christ (Good Friday) to his resurrection (Easter), when the forgiveness of sin takes center stage and the heart becomes firm in Christ. After receiving Christ as a gift, the believer is urged to use Christ's Passion as a pattern for life as they follow after him.

Under the first three points of his Good Friday sermon, Luther denounces the false use of the Passion of Christ. The first aberration he identifies is characterized by a focus on Judas and the Jews. Those who allow themselves to be carried away by their emotion to focus on "wretched Judas" (*armer Judas*) do not use the Passion of Christ rightly.[42] "That is not meditating on the suffering of Christ, but upon the wickedness of Judas and the Jews."[43] Another approach is characterized more by sentimentalism than by anger. For these individuals, the Passion of Christ takes second place to the exercise of their own religious feeling. The Passion of Christ is appropriated through faith, not the production of sentimental feelings. Even Jesus sought to stop the tears of this kind of mourner, saying, "Daughters of Jerusalem, do not weep for me" (Luke 23:28). In like manner Luther delivers his assessment by declaring, "They are the kind of people who go far afield in their meditation on the passion."[44] Finally, Luther mentions the misuse of those who carry pictures, booklets, letters, and crosses on their person as amulets to ward off peril of one sort or another. They do not reap the fruit of Christ's Passion, "for in so doing they are seeking their own advantage."[45] Thus Luther says that it is useless to meditate on the Passion of Christ through the venting of anger, exercising sentimental feelings, or using amulets to ward off harm. These human emotions or attempts to modify outcomes do not reach the human heart and do not transform it.

Luther does not confine himself to criticizing only the false ways of meditation on the Passion of Christ. Something more is at stake. His sermon can be summarized under the following three headings: (1) Coming to the Cross, paragraphs 4–11; (2) Death and Resurrection, paragraphs 12–14; and (3) Taking on Christ's Life and Name as Our Own, paragraph 15.[46] By setting it out in this way, I hope to emphasize the fact that the rational and emotional aspects of a proper meditation of Christ go together.

Coming to the Cross

Luther's bold line of thinking here begins with a positive declaration:

> They contemplate Christ's passion aright who view it with a terror-stricken heart and a despairing conscience. . . . Thus he says in Isaiah 53[:8], "I have chastised him for the transgressions of my people." If the dearest child is punished thus, what will be the fate of sinners? It must be an inexpressible and unbearable earnestness that forces such a great and infinite person to suffer and die to appease it. And if you seriously consider that it is God's very own Son, the eternal wisdom of the Father, who suffers, you will be terrified indeed. The more you think about it, the more intensely will you be frightened.[47]

Luther's presentation is striking not simply for the forcefulness with which he sets out, but because of the form of meditation he implies. A terror-stricken heart and despairing conscience are at the center of activity. A proper meditation on the Passion of Christ is not the activity of an aloof observer but the soul-wrenching experience of one who is held in the grip of an event made present. Luther was convinced that the power of Scripture brings the one who meditates on its pages into the presence of the Lord.

An Enlightenment approach to knowledge presupposes an observer who has a greater or lesser degree of distance from the object of inquiry. Data is gathered and analyzed from a perspective of suspended judgment or objectivity. The relation of subject and object is determined only later as a result of "objective" analysis. Key in this approach is the separation of intellect from affections and the priority of rationality. This is not the approach we find in Luther. As with others in his time period, the Reformer was convinced that true wisdom has a way of embracing both reason and emotions with equal power.[48] This leads to two quick observations.

First, notice the language of feeling, or affection, given a prominent place in this passage. As Luther says, "This terror must be felt." He does not use the language of "knowing" (*Wissen*) or "understanding" (*Verstand*) but of "feeling"

(*Gefühl*). Luther encourages us to seek after knowledge that includes both the intellect and affections. Why is that? It might well be answered that any true meditation on the Passion of Christ requires some reckoning along the lines that we read in Scripture, "Who do men say that the Son of God is? . . . But who do you say that I am?"[49]

Second, Luther lives in the world of the Bible and is able to hold together disparate elements of history in the present. His approach to Scripture does not emphasize a historical gap between himself and the events of the Bible. In one breath, Luther can use the names of Moses, Anselm, Paul, Adam, and Eve as though they are contemporaneous.[50] As Mary Caruthers writes, "Few features of medieval scholarship are so distinctive as an utter indifference to the pastness of the past, to its uniqueness and its integrity 'on its own term,' as we would say."[51] Luther scholarship is now coming to recognize this aspect of his approach to Scripture.[52]

In Luther's world of thought, a proper meditation of Christ's Passion brings the cross into the present. The mental image produced by calling to mind and remembering (*reminiscentia*) is vivid and compelling, making it real to the intellect and the emotions and thus placing us into the middle of the action as we meditate on it. The external events of the crucifixion are plain to see and are filled with meaning as explained by various Scriptures. "You must get this thought through your head and not doubt that you are the one who is torturing Christ thus, for your sins have surely wrought this."[53] The experience of the cross with its external demand becomes personalized and evokes an internal response.

Luther is convinced that the main benefit of Christ's Passion is realized during meditation when we see into our true selves and are "terrified and crushed by this." Unless we acquire that knowledge "we do not derive much benefit from Christ's passion."[54] Being conformed to Christ is the fruit of this meditation on his sufferings. This does not happen because of the depth of feeling, or because of the strength of human will, but it is accomplished by God through His Spirit.

Death and Resurrection

When Christ's Passion does its work, there is a death and a resurrection. As Luther puts it,

> This meditation changes man's being and, almost like baptism, gives him a new birth. Here the passion of Christ performs its natural and noble work, strangling the old Adam and banishing all joy, delight, and confidence which man could derive from other creatures, even as Christ was forsaken by all, even by God.[55]

An evangelical meditation on Christ results in God's alien work (*opus alienum*), paving the way for his proper work (*opus propter*). The "natural and noble work" of the Passion of Christ strangles the "old Adam and "banishes all joy and delight." Consequently, there is an undermining of any human confidence derived from friendships or associations, or any moral or religious actions. Our experience of God-forsakenness, after the pattern of Christ from the cross, becomes the fruit of this meditation.

A person who meditates on Christ sojourns in Passion Week and rightly celebrates Good Friday but must pass on to the day of Easter. After our sin is brought into the light and we are terrified in heart, the risen Christ takes away the affliction of our conscience. "Just as [our knowledge of] sin flowed from Christ and was acknowledged by us, so we must pour this sin back on him and free our conscience of it."[56] To feel guilty after receiving forgiveness is to fall prey to self-torture or the false notion that we can rid ourselves of sin by means of good works, indulgences, or pilgrimages. The false joy and delight of the old Adam is exchanged for the true joy and delight of the new creation.

Taking on Christ's Life and Name as Our Own

In the last paragraph of his sermon, Luther briefly touches on the consequences of the meditation of Christ. "After your heart has thus become firm in Christ, and love, not fear of pain, has made you a foe of sin, then Christ's passion must from that day on become a pattern for your entire life."[57] Luther explains that up until this point the Passion has come to us and has been used as a gift while we are passive. From now on, however, "we can draw strength and encouragement from Christ against every vice and failing."[58]

Luther's advice on the meditation of the Passion of Jesus Christ is not meant to be practiced once with all benefit derived. The meditation on the Passion of Christ is the way of the true penitent, or true pilgrim. This is said, not to take away anything from the fact that sin has been swallowed up once and for all by the resurrection of Christ, but rather to refer to the fact that the strangling of the old Adam does not take place all at once. Thus meditation on the Passion of Christ becomes a lifelong pattern for the believer.

A Treatise on the New Testament, that is, the Holy Mass (1520)

The sacraments are also occasions for Luther's meditation on Christ. Beginning in 1520, we see a concerted effort on his part to free the sacraments from the tyranny and exactions of canon law. He writes a series of treatises that deal with the sacraments; some are more devotional while others are more polemical, but all drive home the centrality of Christ who comes to us through promise. The following comments are based on *A Treatise on the New Testament, that is, the Holy Mass* (1520), a devotional piece from which Luther quotes in his more famous polemical writing, *Babylonian Captivity of the Church* (1520).

First, Luther gives the Words of Institution a central position in understanding the Lord's Supper:

> If we desire to observe mass properly and to understand it, then we must sur-
> render everything that the eyes behold and that the senses suggest . . . until we
> first grasp and thoroughly ponder the words of Christ by which he performed
> and instituted the mass and commanded us to perform it. For therein lies the
> whole mass, its nature, work, profit, and benefit. Without the words nothing
> is derived from the mass.[59]

The Words of Institution become the fixed starting point for all expositions and
criticisms for the Lord's Supper. Luther's meditation on Christ is not contrary
to or outside of Scripture but rather flows out of serious engagement with the
text itself.

Luther held this position in opposition to customary practice. At that time,
the church used the canon of the Mass to give definition to the Mass, without
any recourse to the Words of Institution. Luther was concerned that, as a result,
there was a great deal of idolatry in Christendom due to the faulty and impious
practice of the Mass. He complained that nothing was heard about the feeding
and the strengthening of faith. The words of the testament were not spoken out
loud to the people; as a result the proclamation nature of the sacrament was
lost. Further, suffering consciences failed to hear the words that might have
comforted them. "But would to God that we Germans could say mass in German and sing these 'most secret' words loudest of all!"[60]

Luther says that God's promise of salvation through Christ is the beginning, the foundation, and the rock upon which all works, words, and thoughts
of human beings should be based. Action does not originate from the human
side of things, but rather it is God who establishes his promise. The nature of a
promise is that it can be received in only one way: through faith. Trust and faith
are thus the beginning, the middle, and the end of the matter. "God does not
deal, nor has he ever dealt, with man otherwise than through a word of promise,
as I have said. We in turn cannot deal with God otherwise than through faith
in the Word of his promise."[61]

Luther rehearses for his readers some of the promises God has extended
throughout history. A promise was given to Adam after the Fall when God
spoke to the serpent, "I will put enmity between you and the woman, and between your offspring and her offspring; he shall bruise your head, and you shall
bruise his heel" (Gen. 3:15). This promise sustained Adam and his descendants
until the time of Noah. In similar fashion, God gave a promise to Noah until the
time of Abraham. Then came Moses, who declared the promise under various
figures under the law: God promised the people of Israel the land of Canaan;
they believed the promise and were sustained and led into the land.

In the New Testament, Christ likewise gives a promise and solemn vow,
which is contained in the Words of Institution: "Take and eat, this is my body,
which is given for you. Take and drink of it, all of you, this is the cup of the new
and eternal testament in my blood, which is poured out for you and for many
for the forgiveness of sins."[62] This promise stands out and is different from the

previous promises of God. As Luther says, "Not every vow is called a testament, but only a last irrevocable will of one who is about to die, whereby he bequeaths his goods, allotted and assigned to be distributed to whom he will."[63]

Luther points out that Christ, the true paschal lamb (1 Cor. 5:7), is an eternal divine Person who ratifies a *new* testament. Therefore, all previous promises are surpassed, rendered obsolete, and no longer in effect. This eternal testament is not temporal like the covenant with Moses (with its temporal promises of land), but it has eternal promises so that the old is consigned to the past and the new action of God becomes central and preeminent. What is this testament? What is bequeathed to the beneficiaries? Precisely what the words indicate: "Given and shed for you for the forgiveness of sins." The sacrament of the altar grants a great, eternal, and unspeakable treasure.

> It is as if Christ were saying, "See here, man, in these words I promise and bequeath to you forgiveness of all your sins and the life eternal. In order that you may be certain and know that such a promise remains irrevocably yours, I will die for it, and will give my body and blood for it, and will leave them both to you as a sign and seal, that by them you may remember me."[64]

Christ does this, not for himself, but for his children who in this life need the aid the testament brings. The world is arrayed against the believer, and the devil seeks to seduce unsuspecting believers with joys and sorrows, extinguishing their love for Christ. This is why the sacrament is urgently needed, so that faith might gain new strength for life's journey.

By returning to the words of Scripture, Luther is able to cast the Lord's Supper in its proper light. It is a last will and testament of the very Son of God who lays down his life for the redemption of the world. As the testator, Jesus sets down the terms of the will and stipulates the heirs. He is also the one who guarantees with his very presence the reliability and the blessing that comes in and with the sacrament.

Luther loves to speak about this gift in terms of an inheritance; he says this shows us how we should think about the Supper and observe it. We should conduct ourselves toward the Supper as we would act if a friend or a relative were to leave a large sum in a will with our name on it. Who would remain cold and apathetic in the face of this news and reality? Approaching the Supper with anticipation and a hunger for the great treasure about to be received is the proper preparation. This is especially the case, since there is no condition for us other than to remember the testator and give him praise and thanks.

Luther urges those who participate in the Supper to heed the words of Christ, "This cup that is poured out for you is the new covenant in my blood" (Luke 22:20). What is offered is nothing less than the forgiveness of sin and the invitation into God's eternal kingdom. We give God his due when we believe these words and keep them in our hearts. In fact, the one and only way in which the sacrament can be received is through faith. A gift is received; it cannot be worked for or earned. In this way, we see that the sacrament understood as a testament places faith and works in their proper relation. We receive the grace of God, and as our hearts are changed we go out to serve the greater good through our vocation and care for the other.

There are two particular abuses Luther addresses before concluding this treatise. The first is the widespread opinion that participating in the Supper is considered to be a good work or a merit. Luther argues that to think in these terms denies the gift character of the sacrament. "Who has ever heard that he who receives an inheritance has done a good work?"[65] In the Mass we give nothing to Christ, but we humbly receive in faith that which is stipulated in the testament. As Luther goes on to point out, the concept of a meritorious good work is excluded in baptism and the sermon as well. In light of this, Luther reminds us that we receive the sacrament (testament) to nourish and strengthen our faith, we offer our prayer in one accord, and we distribute alms for the poor, according to ancient custom.

The second abuse has to do with the concept of sacrifice that had become central in the liturgical structuring of the canon of the Mass. Luther rejects the idea that there is anything in the Mass to give it the name of a sacrifice.[66] However, Luther does not jettison all elements of sacrifice; but instead of thinking that the sacrament is essentially a bloodless reenactment or sacrifice of Christ, Luther speaks of the sacrifice that every Christian makes. Each Christian offers himself or herself as a sacrifice along with Christ. "That is, we lay ourselves on Christ by a firm faith in his testament and do not otherwise appear before God with our prayer, praise, and sacrifice except through Christ and his mediation."[67] As we lay our lives "on Christ," so Christ in his turn advocates for us and brings us before the Father.

Luther's meditation on Christ leads him from Scripture to the Lord's Supper and then back again. He uses biblical passages in such a way that Christ is seen clearly once more and the freedom of the gospel is retained: "Christ has gathered up the whole gospel in a short summary with the words of this testament or sacrament. For the gospel is nothing but a proclamation of God's grace and of the forgiveness of all sins, granted through the sufferings of Christ."[68]

On the Freedom of the Christian (1520)

In 1520, Luther wrote *On the Freedom of a Christian*, which was part of a last-gasp effort to defuse mounting tensions between himself and his supporters and the papal court and its defenders. Karl von Miltitz (c. 1490–1529)—a high-ranking church official who had been working behind the scenes to avoid or mitigate the condemnation and impending judgment at the imperial diet (that is, a formal assembly) that met in Worms in April 1521—convinced Luther to write a letter of reconciliation to Pope Leo (1475–1521). As a result, Luther composed a letter in meticulous rhetorical style, appending to it a treatise that described the very heart of his beliefs.

The treatise has a complicated printing history, in part due to the fact that Luther wrote both a German and a Latin version.[69] The Latin version was directed to theologians, clerics, and church leaders, while the German version was addressed to the German-speaking public including the nobility, townsfolk, the lesser clergy, and those who could read or have Luther's writings read to them. Between 1520 and 1526, there were no less than thirty printings of this work. *On the Freedom of a Christian* was one of the best sellers that established Luther as the most published author of the sixteenth century.[70]

In this treatise, we meet a confident and bold Luther who has developed beyond his early writings. While not completely overturning his mystical roots, Luther brings all the tools of biblical humanism to set forward his evangelical theology.[71] This is shown in the highly structured treatise that follows the rules of rhetoric as laid down by Cicero and Quintilian. Luther's body of the work sets out the idea that freedom and servitude cohere in the Christian life. The life of the Christian—in both external and internal connections—is made free not by works but only through God's word received in faith. The bond of faith between believers and Christ creates a new reality, puts us in right relationship to God, and sets us free to care for our neighbor in love.

Luther launches into the exposition of his theme by saying that Christian freedom is made possible by nothing external. Do good health and a great exercise program help the soul and make it blessed? Do bad health, a lack of sanitation, and bad neighbors harm the soul? Is the soul adversely affected by the body wearing everyday clothes, or is it aided by wearing sacred robes set apart for the clergy? Luther concludes that nothing external—including doing spiritual exercises of whatever sort—has any benefit. This is how Luther makes his emphatic point:

> One thing and one thing alone is necessary for the Christian life, righteousness, and freedom, and that one thing is the most holy word of God, the gospel of Christ. As John 11[:25] states, "I am the resurrection and the life, whoever believes in me will never die." And John 8[:36]: "If the Son makes you free, you will be free indeed." And Matt. 4[:4]: "One does not live by bread alone but by every word that comes from the mouth of God." Therefore, we may consider it certain and firmly established, that the soul can lack everything except the word of God. Without it absolutely nothing else satisfies the soul. But when the soul has the word, it is rich and needs nothing else, because the word of God is the word of life, truth, light, peace, righteousness, salvation, joy, freedom, wisdom, power, grace, glory, and every imaginable blessing.[72]

It is worth noting that for Luther the "word of God" is not synonymous with the Bible as it is in much of conservative American Christianity. His focus is exclusively concentrated on the gospel of Christ. It is not an accident that the examples given are those of the spoken word. The Scriptures cited are examples of New Testament preaching. Elsewhere in his writings, Luther makes the point that the gospel, strictly speaking, is a spoken word.

In this regard, Luther follows the apostles and Paul, who refer to the Old Testament as Scripture. For the first few centuries of the Christian era, the New Testament was not spoken of as Scripture in the same sense as the Old Testament, but instead as teaching based on those prior documents. That is the position of the early church father Irenaeus (c. 130–202), who designates the Old Testament as Scripture and the New Testament as the preaching of the apostles.[73] Along these lines, Luther points out that the Old Testament

> alone bears the name of Holy Scripture. And the gospel should really not be something written, but a spoken word which brought forth the Scriptures, as Christ and the apostles have done. This is why Christ himself did not write anything but only spoke. He called his teaching not Scripture but gospel, meaning good news or a proclamation that is spread not by pen but by word of mouth.[74]

Luther moves from a description of what the gospel is to its preaching. In the course of doing so, he points out that the word of God is spoken in law and gospel (commands and promises), and the effect is nothing short of a death and a resurrection. Believers are first humbled through the law and shown that there is nothing in them that could lead to salvation. Being brought low like this brings an end to the old self. But then the gospel proclaims the word of what God has done in Christ to redeem humanity and the world. This word raises up through faith those who have been struck down through the law. This law-gospel approach guides preaching to produce faith, and it is a key insight into how Luther carries out his meditation on the word of God.

Faith, for Luther and the New Testament, is neither the product of the human will nor a theological virtue, as it was with Aristotle. "Faith comes from hearing, and hearing through the word of Christ" (Rom. 10:17). Luther's reflections in this passage focus on Christ, who alone can produce faith. Faith is thus not a condition to obtain the treasure (Christ); it is a result of believers hearing the gospel and being swept up in it.

After setting forward the gift of faith, Luther discusses the three powers of faith. He asserts that the soul that has been grasped by the promise is saturated and intoxicated by its power (or benefit). The first power of faith is that the word of God has the power to form the soul. The second power of faith consists in giving God his due. Faith "honors the one in whom it trusts with the most reverent and highest regard possible for this reason: Faith holds the one in who it trusts to be truthful and deserving."[75] Faith puts to an end the rebellion of the old creature against God. Envy, pride, falsehood, and setting up idols in our hearts are swept aside in the intoxicating moment of being forgiven by the touch of Christ. The universal Christian experience recognizes that we owe all to Jesus. "But when God sees that we ascribe truthfulness to him and by our heart's faith honor him as is his due, then in return God honors us, ascribing to us truthfulness and righteousness on account of this faith."[76] Regarding the third power of faith, Luther writes:

The third incomparable benefit of faith is this: that it unites the soul with Christ, like a bride with a bridegroom. By this "mystery" (as Paul teaches) Christ and the soul are made one flesh. For if they are one flesh and if a true marriage—indeed by far the most perfect marriage of all—is culminated between them (since human marriages are but weak shadows of this one), then it follows that they come to hold all things, good and bad, in common. Accordingly, the faithful soul can both assume as its own whatever Christ has and glory in it, and whatever is the soul's Christ claims for himself as his own.[77]

This beautiful metaphor is referred to as the joyous exchange (*fröhliche Wechsel*) between Christ and the soul, which highlights the intimate connection between Christ and the soul that holds all things in common. As faith intervenes, the sin, death, and hell belonging to the soul now are Christ's and the grace, life, and salvation of Christ belong to the soul. This is a joyous exchange where the pain and misery of sinfulness is overcome in the self-giving love of God in Jesus Christ.

It has been pointed out that Roman marriage law distinguished between property (what one owned) and possession (what one had use of). In marriage, the property of the one spouse became the possession of the other spouse and vice versa.[78] This makes for a compelling vision of the nature of justification by faith. It has also been pointed out that the language of the uniting of Christ and the soul as bride and bridegroom has deep roots in the mystical tradition and is found in Staupitz and Bernard of Clairvaux, among others.[79] For Luther, the uniting of the bride and groom is through faith, not an affective relationship of love as it would be in mysticism. As Luther moves to a theology of the word, it is important to note that he does not merely repeat the concepts of the mystics but rather gives them new meaning. Yet that does not erase the fact that there are still structural affinities to mysticism that continue throughout his writings.[80]

In reflecting on the fruit of effective preaching, Luther almost breaks out in song as he speaks of the joy, confidence, and love that attend proclamation of the word of God:

What person's heart upon hearing these things would not rejoice from its very core and upon accepting such consolation would not melt in love with Christ—something completely unattainable with laws and works? Who could possibly harm or frighten such a heart? If awareness of sin or dread of death overwhelms it, it is ready to hope in the Lord. It neither fears hearing about these evils nor is moved by them, until it finally despises its enemies. For it believes that Christ's righteousness is its own and that its sin is now not its own but Christ's. More than that, the presence of Christ's righteousness swallows up every sin. As noted above, this is a necessary consequence of faith in Christ. So the heart learns with the Apostle to scoff at death and sin and to say: "Where, O death, is your victory? Where, O death, is your sting? The sting of death is sin, and the power of sin is the law. But thanks be to God, who gives us the victory through our Lord Jesus Christ." For death is swallowed up in victory—not only

Christ's but ours—because through faith it becomes our victory and is in us and we are conquerors.[81]

From this position of forgiveness, certainty, and joy, the remainder of the treatise deals with the natural consequence of the life of faith. Works flow naturally from it, like a master woodworker crafting custom cabinets, or a bishop dedicating a new church building or confirming children. These people do the works they do because that is who they are. In a manner of speaking, justification by faith puts us back into paradise, where works were freely done. They were not done to make a person acceptable or to obtain righteousness, as was the case with Adam and Eve.

The freedom that comes in the gospel transforms all of life, and discipline is necessary because the flesh is opposed to the spirit. But with faith toward God, we can now show love toward our neighbor.

> Look at what love and joy in the Lord flow from faith! Moreover, from love proceeds a joyful, gladsome, and free soul, prepared for willing service to the neighbor, which takes no account of gratitude or ingratitude, praise or blame, profit or loss. For such a soul does not do this so that people may be obligated to it, nor does it distinguish between friends and enemies, nor does it anticipate thankfulness or ingratitude. Instead, it expends itself and what it has in a completely free and happy manner, whether squandering these things on the ungrateful or on the deserving.[82]

Even as the Father has supported us freely in Christ, so Luther urges us to freely support our neighbors. We are, as he says, "to become to the other a kind of Christ, so that we may be Christs to one another and be the same Christ in all, that is, truly Christians!"[83]

Summary of Luther's Meditation on Christ's Passion

In this section, we looked at *A Meditation on the Passion of Christ* (1519), which emphasizes death and resurrection. Instead of talking about what the text says and adjusting what he might say "about" Christ, Luther gets busy and lets the reality of the word have its say. He is not looking for the meaning behind the Passion of Christ as much as he is allowing the word to recreate Christ's Passion in time and space, doing its work of accusing and comforting.

In *A Treatise on the New Testament, that is, the Holy Mass* (1520), we saw how Luther meditates on Christ by bringing us back to the Words of Institution. In this sacrament of the word of God, Christ promises to be present for the strengthening of faith and the granting of forgiveness. Luther says that the Lord's Supper is a summary of the gospel.

In *On the Freedom of a Christian* (1520), we looked at Luther's method of meditation as he set out the proper distinction of law and gospel—through which we sense the reverberating joy as the wedding ring of faith joins bride and bridegroom. Luther speaks with such conviction and metaphorical power, we can almost hear the music emanating from the wedding feast!

Meditation on the Text of Scripture

Even as there can be a false meditation on the Passion of Christ, there can also be a false meditation on the text of Scripture. Luther takes pains to craft simple and direct advice for the laity precisely on this matter. After his highly publicized encounter with the emperor at the imperial diet in 1521, Luther was ushered into the protection of the Wartburg Castle. During this time he was without his library, but he did not want to be sidelined from the important matters of the day. He therefore threw himself into writing a series of sermons that would become known as the "Wartburg Postil." As an introduction he wrote *A Brief Instruction on What to Look for and Expect in the Gospels* (1521), in which he sets forward a set of observations meant to help the laity in their meditation on Scripture.

Luther was convinced that a number of obstacles had been put in the way of the average layperson in this regard. The first obstacle was the practice of speaking of four Gospels. This can lead to the mistaken idea that the Epistles of Paul and Peter are about something altogether different than the Gospels of Matthew, Mark, Luke, and John. Luther found the notion problematic that the books of the Bible might be at odds with one another. The second obstacle was much worse in that it regarded the Gospels and Epistles as law books that show us all the works we are to do. It took the works of Christ and made them a list of examples; in other words, it reduced Christianity to moralism. "Now where these two erroneous notions remain in the heart, there neither the gospels nor the epistles may be read in a profitable or Christian manner, and [people] remain as pagan as ever."[84]

Luther takes pains to point out that there is only one gospel, although many apostles describe it. Matthew, Mark, Luke, and John do it in their way; Paul does it in his abbreviated way in his Epistles, as does Peter in his. Some are longer than others, and some concentrate on the words and works of Jesus, whereas Paul does not. Yet still the *gospel* is set forward, although in various ways. "Thus the gospel is and should be nothing else than a chronicle, a story, a narrative about Christ, telling who he is, what he did, said, and suffered—a subject which one describes briefly, another more fully, one this way, another that way."[85]

Luther here assures the laity that there is one gospel and not four. Paul and Peter set forward Christ just as surely as the four Gospels do. As Luther puts it, "Just as there is no more than one Christ, so there is and may be no more than one gospel."[86] This fact clears the way for a productive reading of the Epistles alongside the Gospels. They are not at odds, nor are the Epistles to be understood as merely ancillary to the Gospel writers, nor are they so much "color commentary." Paul and Peter do their work to teach Christ, and "so their epistles can be nothing but the gospel."[87]

The Old Testament points to Christ in a similar manner. For example, Isaiah the prophet says that Christ is the one who will take upon himself our infirmities and will carry our sorrows (Isa. 53). Because he bore the sins of many, his punishment will bring us peace. The prophet thus sets out Christ as the pure gospel and, along with the rest of Scripture, focuses on him. As Jesus says in John 5, "You search the Scriptures because you think that in them you have eternal life; and it is they that bear witness about me." The single focus of Scripture—or what Luther and the biblical humanists would call the *scopus* of the Bible—is Jesus, the Son of God. Luther asserts that having this foundation places us in a position to be illuminated by the Scriptures. This is how he answers the first obstacle to the reading of Holy Scripture.

The second obstacle he approaches in a slightly different manner. It is one thing to recognize that Jesus Christ is the object of all of Scripture. Although it is critical for us to come to this position, it is still possible to see Christ in the text and get things wrong. Luther therefore moves to a distinction that defines his approach more completely, which he introduces with a memorable bit of advice: "Be sure, moreover, that you do not make Christ into a Moses, as if Christ did nothing more than teach and provide examples as the other saints do, as if the gospel were simply a textbook of teachings or laws."[88] There is a distinction between the laws and the promises of God. If believers looked at Christ in the same way they looked at Moses, then they would be turning Jesus into a lawgiver—which Luther urges strongly against.

For Luther, the way to distinguish between law and gospel in regard to Christology is by looking at the distinction of Christ as gift (*donum*) and Christ as example (*exemplum*). Luther sets out this distinction, first used by Augustine, for a twofold purpose. In the first instance, the distinction is meant as a criticism against those who would reduce the life of Christ to a set of works to be emulated. Christ is indeed a pattern for the life of the believer, but that is not the sum total of the faith, and we cannot access the saving work of Christ by mere repetition of a set of good works. In the second instance, and more positively, the distinction is meant to show how good works take form within faith. As Luther points out, Christ as gift precedes in importance Christ as example. Receiving Christ as gift sets faith in motion and begins to produce works of obedience as a result:

> Therefore, make note of this, that Christ as a gift nourishes your faith and makes you a Christian. But Christ as an example exercises your works. These do not make you a Christian. Actually they come forth from you because you have already been made a Christian. As widely as a gift differs from an example, so widely does faith differ from works, for faith possesses nothing of its own, only the deeds and life of Christ. Works have something of your own in them, yet they should not belong to you but to your neighbor.[89]

Grasping Christ at the highest level is to have him as the foundation and chief blessing of salvation. This is to receive Christ as gift. From this the other part follows, where Christ as example shapes the actions of our lives. Once this union is achieved, Luther emphasizes that faith and love move forward, the commandments of God begin to be fulfilled, and there is a fearless joy willing to embrace suffering, if that is what service to our neighbor requires.

In the following extended quotation, Luther shows that he sees this distinction between example and gift coming out of Scripture itself.

> Therefore, you should grasp Christ, his words, works, and sufferings, in a two-fold manner. First as an example that is presented to you, which you should follow and imitate. As St. Peter says in I Peter 4, "Christ suffered for us, thereby leaving us an example." Thus when you see how he prays, fasts, helps people, and shows them love, so also you should do, both for yourself and for your neighbor. However this is the smallest part of the gospel, on the basis of which it cannot yet even be called gospel. For on this level Christ is of no more help to you than some other saint. His life remains his own and does not as yet contribute anything to you. In short this mode [of understanding Christ as simply an example] does not make Christians but only hypocrites. You must grasp Christ at a much higher level. Even though this higher level has for a long time been the very best, the preaching of it has been something rare. The chief article and foundation of the gospel is that before you take Christ as an example, you accept and recognize him as a gift, as a present that God has given you and that is your own. This means that when you see or hear of Christ doing or suffering something, you do not doubt that Christ himself, with his deeds and suffering, belongs to you. On this you may depend as surely as if you had done it yourself; indeed as if you were Christ himself. See, this is what it means to have a proper grasp of the gospel, that is, of the over-whelming goodness of God, which neither prophet, nor apostle, nor angel was ever able fully to express, and which no heart could adequately fathom or marvel at. This is the great fire of the love of God for us, whereby the heart and conscience become happy, secure, and content. This is what preaching the Christian faith means.[90]

The joyful, good, and comforting message of being joined to the living Christ through faith is the essence of the gospel. Receiving Christ as gift is what makes possible and properly orders the new life of the Christian as we follow after Christ as example.

Luther's singular approach warrants two observations. First, Holy Scripture is to be viewed in a particular manner. Holy Scripture is not to be viewed as a book of laws or commandments. It is not a fixed repository of unchanging eternal truths by which the believer and the world is to be measured. Rather, the purpose of Scripture is to convey the chronicle, the story, the narrative about Christ. Seen in this light, Scripture is "a book of divine promises in which God promises, offers, and gives us all his possessions and benefits in Christ."[91] The fact that Christ and the apostles provide much good teaching about God's law is a great benefit, but the purpose of the text is to witness to Christ.

Holy Scripture is authoritative precisely because it sets before us Christ. The material content of Scripture is the source of its singular standing among all other books. Because Christ is true and Scripture tells us about the redeeming work of Christ, it alone among all other books is a book of wisdom. Its authority is thus a derived authority. We do not believe in Christ because the Bible is true; we know the Bible to be true because it sets forward Christ, who is himself the truth. Luther is uninterested in establishing a formal theory of authority that is grounded in some source outside of Christ. To try to do so would be to rely on an external criterion for truth apart from the actual and compelling witness to Christ that produces faith.

Second, the gospel is our guide to the Holy Scriptures. Since the text of Scripture is written to present the living Christ—who he is, for what purpose he has been given, and how he is promised—it is the gospel that guides us in reading the Scriptures. For example, Paul speaks of how the gospel was promised beforehand by the prophets in Holy Scripture (Rom. 1:1–2). Again, Peter mentions the prophets who prophesied about the grace that would come through the preaching of the Holy Spirit (1 Pet. 1:10–12). In the Acts of the Apostles, Luke records: "And all the prophets who have spoken, from Samuel and those who came after him, also proclaimed these days" (Acts 3:24). Luther contends that it makes no sense to read the Scriptures from any other vantage point than that of the gospel. The proper reading of Scripture recognizes the One who helps us, and it is careful not to turn him into a taskmaster.

For Luther to assert that the gospel is our guide to Holy Scripture is in reality to affirm what the church has contended for since the earliest questioning of the biblical canon (that is, the books that make up the Bible). Scripture and the Apostles' Creed go together. The creed is a summary of the content of Scripture that is Trinitarian in shape and gospel-centered in focus. It is a statement as to how the church has read its Scriptures. So, for Luther to say that the gospel is our guide to the Scriptures is also to say that Scripture and the creed are like two interlocking pieces of the same puzzle. To read the Bible apart from the gospel-purpose of Scripture is to deviate from a church-oriented appropriation of the text.

This presentation of Christ as gift and Christ as example provides the background necessary to give greater attention to the distinction between law and gospel. While the rather complex topic can be—and has been—approached in a number of different ways, I would like to look at it simply from three angles: Christology, Scripture, and experience. But first, let's consider a few general statements of the centrality of this distinction.

As we have seen, Luther assigns the highest importance to the distinction between law and gospel. In 1521 he wrote, "Almost all Scripture and the understanding of all theology hangs on the proper understanding of law and gospel."[92] In a sermon from 1532, he states that rightly dividing the word of truth (2 Tim. 2:15) depends upon it:

For this distinction between law and gospel is the highest art in Christendom, which all who boast of the name "Christian," or assume it as a name, can and ought to know. For wherever there is confusion about this matter, one cannot recognize how a Christian is different from a heathen . . . this is how vitally important it is to make this distinction.[93]

In his lectures on Galatians he says, "Whoever knows well how to distinguish the Gospel from the law should give thanks to God and know that he is a real theologian."[94]

Christ as gift and Christ as example is the christological basis for the distinction between law and gospel, a formula that by all accounts is at the heart of Luther's theology. It is perhaps the most fundamental way to speak of the distinction and provides a way of discerning whether or not Christian freedom is being hindered. As we have already noted, Luther sees that Christ as gift is the source and fountain of faith and establishes and nourishes the new creation. Christ as example promotes works. These works do not make someone a Christian; they proceed from those who already have faith. As long as the distinction is maintained, then moralism is avoided.

Conversely, when the distinction is not upheld, the gospel becomes law and faith tries to justify itself before God with works. While we might think that this is not very likely, there are a plentiful number of Christians today who imagine that moralism—that is, avoiding wrongdoing of every kind—is what Christianity is all about. In the words of ethicist Jacques Ellul, "In the eyes of most of our contemporaries, Christianity is a morality first of all. And have not many epochs of Christian history been characterized by the church's insistence upon actions and conduct?"[95]

Luther also describes the law/gospel distinction with respect to Scripture. We have already quoted his comments from *On the Freedom of a Christian* (1520) about two doctrines in Scripture: the laws and the promises. The law demands but does not give the power for a person to comply; the promise is given and obtains through faith what the law demands. Or, in the words of the Heidelberg Disputation, "The law says, 'do this,' and it is never done. Grace says, 'believe this,' and everything is already done."[96] The distinction between law and gospel is to be applied to the reading of Scripture and beyond that to the critical matter of preaching.

The problem in Luther's time was that the preaching in the church, for a number of reasons, was horribly wrong. The dominance and, as Luther saw it, the tyranny of the papal decrees led the laity away from Christ. Believers were told that if they prized their salvation, then they had to submit to rules regarding abstaining from meat on certain days, masses for the dead, receiving the sacrament in only one kind, and a host of other laws.

And whoever is not obedient to the pope and the bishops is not obedient to the Christian Church; and he who disobeys the church, disobeys the Holy Spirit.

Thus they have deluded the simple folk with such braying; they have intimidated and cowed all the world; and no one has dared raise his voice in protest.[97]

It is no wonder that preaching in the church in Luther's day was characterized by a number of problems. In *On the Freedom of a Christian*, Luther lists three issues in descending order from least to worst. First is preaching Christ in his works, life, and words as historical facts for their moral example apart from their saving significance. According to Luther, this was what some of the "best preachers" of his day were doing. Second, and far less sufficient, are those who say nothing at all about Christ and preach human laws and the decrees of the church fathers. Third are those who manipulate emotions and through sympathy with Christ influence their audience to be angry toward the Jews.

Law and gospel rightly discerned and applied to the text and the sermon are meant as a remedy for these various forms of "deadly preaching."

> Rather ought Christ to be preached to the end that faith in him may be established that he may not only be Christ but be Christ for you and me, and that what is said of him and is denoted in his name may be effectual in us. Such faith is produced and preserved in us by preaching why Christ came, what he brought and bestowed, what benefit it is to us to accept him. This is done when that Christian liberty which he bestows is rightly taught and we are told in what way we Christians are all kings and priests and therefore lords of all and may firmly believe that whatever we have done is pleasing and acceptable in the sight of God. As I have already said.[98]

Law and gospel seek to clear away the clutter that might get in the way of the grace and mercy of God in Christ. It is an approach to preaching that eschews emotional manipulation used so often by preachers, pushing away other distractions to the clear and life-giving preaching of Christ.

Luther can also speak about the distinction of law and gospel in experience. The following is a lively illustration of the point.

> It's the supreme art of the devil that he can make the law out of the gospel. If I can hold on to the distinction between law and gospel I can say to him any and every time that he should kiss my backside. Even if I sinned I would say, "Should I deny the gospel on this account?" It hasn't come to that yet. Once I debate about what I have done and left undone, I am finished. But if I reply on the basis of the gospel, "The forgiveness of sins covers it all," I have won.[99]

As this account shows, holding on to the distinction between law and gospel allows the person suffering under an accusation the ability to stand firm. In the following passage, Luther clarifies how law and gospel apply to the Christian experience:

> The devil turns the Word upside down. If one sticks to the law, one is lost. A good conscience won't set one free, but the distinction [between law and gos-

pel] will. So you should say, "The Word is twofold, on the one hand terrifying and on the other hand comforting." Here Satan objects, "But God says you are damned because you don't keep the law." I respond, "God also says that I shall live." His mercy is greater than sin, and life is stronger than death. Hence if I have left this or that undone, our Lord God will tread it underfoot with his grace.[100]

Luther's Prefaces to the Books of the Bible

In addition to teaching Christ as gift and example in *What to Look for and Expect in the Gospels*, and the distinction between law and gospel as outlined in *On the Freedom of a Christian*, and speaking about law and gospel in experience, Luther also provides some help by writing prefaces to the books of the Bible. The first prefaces appeared with the publication of his German translation of the New Testament in 1522. The rest of his translation of the Bible came out in installments until its completion in 1534. These prefaces were published with all the editions of the Luther Bible until the seventeenth century, when they were removed. Their longevity is a testament to their significance and contribution.

Luther had full confidence in the power of the Bible to tell its own story. At the same time, however, he felt the need to provide some guidance to the theologically uneducated people who craved access to Holy Scripture. In the preface to the completed work, he suggests that it would be right and proper for the Bible to be published without any introduction. But due to the fact that there had been so many misleading ideas commonly held, and so many unwarranted positions asserted, that some corrective work was imperative.

> Necessity demands, therefore, that there should be a notice or preface, by which the ordinary man can be rescued from his former delusions, set on the right track, and taught what he is to look for in this book, so that he may not seek laws and commandments where he ought to be seeking the gospel and promises of God.[101]

The New Testament is a book that needs a proper translation since it needs a proper reading. Luther completed the translation while in hiding at the Wartburg, and he intended on making a contribution to a proper reading with his prefaces. Further, although Luther knew that the New Testament had been handed down in an ecclesiastical context, he also knew that the ecclesiastical tradition had misread the New Testament in a few decisive points. He was therefore convinced that some aid should be given to help free readers from that misleading tradition.

It might be said that attaching these prefaces to his new translation of the New Testament was prejudicial, as they suggest a particular approach to the text and thus the reader is not altogether free in the interpretation of the text. These complaints are born more from our own time period than that of Luther.

The idea that "personal autonomy" is the highest ideal in the reading of the text of Scripture is a modern notion. Luther is completely uninterested in personal freedom in that sense. And the accusation that he is using an outside criterion to evaluate Scripture would also strike him as odd. This goes against the tradition of reading Scripture in light of the Apostles' Creed and understanding the Apostles' Creed in light of Scripture.

In its struggle with Gnosticism, the early church was faced with some serious decisions. When Marcion established a canon of Scripture that eliminated the Old Testament and seriously truncated the New Testament, the church was forced to respond. On the one hand, the church chided Marcion, saying in effect, "These are not your scriptures, they belong to the church." This was to assert that the self-identity of the church could be accounted for on the basis of apostolic teaching. On the other hand, the church developed the creed as the critical criterion or the rule by which Scripture is read. That is to say, the church recognized those elements essential to a Christian appropriation of Scripture, which is Trinitarian in shape and redemptive in outcome.[102]

This takes us back to the reformulation of the catechism Luther undertook. For Luther, as we have seen, the catechism is a matter of diagnosis (law), treatment (gospel), and medicine (prayer). The creed points us to the grace of God the Father, the mercy of Christ the Son, and the enabling power of the Holy Spirit. It gives what the law requires through faith, thus creating a believing heart out of unfaith. It is no surprise, then, when we find Luther giving high priority to the place of the gospel in his work on the prefaces. Only by reading the Scripture in light of the gospel do we receive its benefits. Any other way of reading the text mixes law and gospel, and in the end this robs the believer of the glad news and turns Christ into a law-giving Moses.

In his prefaces, Luther provided helpful discussions of the books of the Bible. Of special note is his preface to the book of Romans. It is the longest of the prefaces, which is commensurate with Luther's estimation of its importance. It begins with definitions of key terms, such as "law," "sin," "faith," "righteousness," and "flesh and spirit." These definitions, even after almost five hundred years, are still wonderfully clear and helpful. After that, he proceeds chapter by chapter, giving an account of the contents of the book. It contains moving passages such as the following that contrasts the human notion of faith with true faith:

> Faith, however, is a divine work in us which changes us and makes us to be born anew of God, John 1[:12–13]. It kills the old Adam and makes us altogether different, in heart and spirit and mind and powers; and it brings with it the Holy Spirit. O it is a living, busy, active, mighty thing, this faith. It is impossible for it not to be doing good works incessantly. It does not ask whether good works are to be done, but before the question is asked, it has already done them, and is constantly doing them. Whoever does not do such works, however, is an unbeliever. He gropes and looks around for faith and good works, but knows

neither what faith is nor what good words are. Yet he talks and talks, with many words, about faith and good works.[103]

It may be this precise passage that has a historical connection worth mentioning. On May 24, 1738, just three days after his brother Charles had come to faith and about two hundred years after Luther wrote this preface to Romans, John Wesley had his famous conversion experience. He puts it this way in his journal,

> In the evening I went very unwillingly to a society in Aldersgate Street, where one was reading Luther's preface to the Epistle to the Romans. About a quarter before nine, while he was describing the change which God works in the heart through faith in Christ, I felt my heart strangely warmed. I felt I did trust in Christ, Christ alone for salvation; and an assurance was given to me that he had taken away *my* sins, even *mine*, and saved *me* from the law of sin and death.[104]

It would seem Luther's prefaces have been of help to more than just Lutherans!

It should be clear at this point that Luther is committed to the gospel, even in his prefaces. As he writes,

> Thus, this gospel of God or New Testament is a good story and report sounded forth into all the world by the apostles, telling of a true David who strove with sin, death and the devil, and overcame them, and thereby rescued all those who were captive in sin, afflicted with death, and overpowered by the devil. Without any merit of their own he made them righteous, gave them life, and saved them, so that they were given peace and brought back to God. For this they sing, and thank and praise God, and are glad forever, if only they believe firmly and remain steadfast in faith.[105]

What is fascinating about Luther's view is the dynamic inherent in the both the preached word and the written word. Sin is laid bare, forgiveness conveyed, captives released, sinners made righteous, and those far off are brought back to God. The joyful response comes in song, thanksgiving, and praise, and those who receive the gospel are glad forever. Luther is confident that the word of God has the power to create faith. Believers know that the verbal and the written word are authoritative when Jesus Christ is present with the Holy Spirit in those transformative moments. As Scripture is read, as the sermon is preached, as the sacraments of baptism and the Lord's Supper are administered, new life is created.

> All the genuine holy books agree in this, that all of them preach and drive home Christ. And that is the true test by which to judge all books, when we see whether or not they promote Christ. For all the Scriptures show us Christ, Romans 3[:21]; and St. Paul will know nothing but Christ, I Corinthians 2[:2]. Whatever does not teach Christ is not yet apostolic, even though St. Peter or St. Paul does the teaching. Again, whatever preaches Christ would be apostolic, even if Judas, Annas, Pilate, and Herod were doing it.[106]

This is an astounding statement that dismisses any attempt at placing the authority of Scripture in a formal theory secured outside of Christ. Luther and early Lutheranism operated in this understanding. Incidentally, it means that Luther, while interested in questions having to do with authorship of the biblical books, does not see those issues as significantly affecting authority. More importantly, it reaffirms the fact that the gospel is our guide in understanding the Holy Scriptures. Christ as the center point of Scripture is the abiding source of scriptural authority. Through this content, Holy Scripture authenticates itself. As Christians we do not believe in Christ because the Bible is true in some abstract way, but we affirm the truthfulness and reliability of Scripture because Christ speaks to us out of its pages in a way that produces faith. The wonder of Holy Scripture is its continuing ability to change and transform lives and bring women and men back to God.

Luther uses Scripture's capacity to create faith to critique the Roman Catholic thesis that the church established the canon and thus is the guarantor of scriptural authority. Since the church dictated which books would be included in the canon, it was reasoned that the church was prior to the Scripture and therefore stood above Scripture. Luther points out that this makes little sense. It would be like saying John the Baptist is greater than Christ because he pointed to him at the Jordan River. And on the basis of what Paul says in Galatians 1:9, Luther further argues that Holy Scripture is the queen who rules, and everyone—including the pope, Luther, Augustine, Paul, or an angel from heaven—must be subject to her and be witnesses, disciples, and confessors of Scripture.[107] This is a rather powerful way of saying that no one is in a position to validate Scripture; it is Scripture that validates itself. The church's attitude toward Scripture can only be that of placing itself in a position of obedient listening and recognition of the witness Scripture bears to itself as God's word.

Luther's critique also applies to Bible fundamentalism, which seeks to ensure the authority of Scripture on formal grounds—that is, on a theory of the nature of Scripture established prior to the material witness of Scripture. The problem with this approach is that it tends to identify the word of God with the written text alone. It collapses the reciprocal relationship between the verbal word and the written word. In so doing, it denies the self-authenticating nature of Scripture and seeks to assure the authority of the text against the corrosive criticisms of modernity by hiding behind an unassailable claim of truth. Having thus lost the vitality of the law/gospel distinction, there is also the tendency to view Scripture as a book of laws and commandments.

For some time Luther scholarship has been leaning in the direction of saying that Luther gave priority to the word of God in its preached form. And there is really no question that the living voice—the *viva vox*—plays an essential role in Luther's theology. The word of God given and received from one living person to another better reflects the God who created heaven and earth by his word, and who shares himself eternally through the Word made flesh than holding out for a form of written propositional truth that stands as a bulwark against the corrosive forces of modernity. Yet, Oswald Bayer is correct to point out that a one-sided emphasis on what is spoken would overlook the high value Luther gives to the written word as the source and root of the spoken word. In this fact, Luther simply mirrors the mode of thinking found in Paul who, in presenting the resurrection, first sets out the evidence of the eyewitnesses and then adduces the witness of Scripture.[108]

It is important to see that there is a reciprocal relationship between the preached word and the written word. The preached word, certainly in the case of the New Testament, brought forth the Scriptures. The written word of God has its source in the oral proclamation. Over time, the Scriptures were written down so that the apostolic witness would be properly remembered and read in public worship. In this way, Scripture has become the indispensable source for Christian preaching and Christian worship. Written Scripture is necessary as the external means by which the ongoing preaching of its ministers can be measured against the normative apostolic message. This gives congregations the standard by which to ensure their teachers do not become false teachers.

It is the word of God that creates the church, and it is in the church that the word of God has pride of place. As Holy Scripture is read and preached within the communion of those who believe, we find ourselves in the midst of those stories. As the word discloses itself in law and gospel, our own lives are interpreted, bringing about the true self-knowledge that only God through his word can provide. This meditation on the word of God is the pathway of faith, the context in which theology is carried out. Oswald Bayer says it well, "In brief, we can sum up Luther's remarks as follows: a theologian is a person who is interpreted by Holy Scripture, who lets himself or herself be interpreted by it and who, having been interpreted by it, interprets it for other troubled and afflicted people."[109]

The Spirit and Meditation

Meditation, as the second rule for the correct study of theology, cannot be undertaken successfully without the Spirit. Whether we are meditating on the Psalter, the Passion of Christ, the gift of Holy Communion, the catechism, or a passage from the New Testament, the Spirit is key. The role of the Spirit is to bring the disciple of Christ into all truth (John 16:13). The Spirit shows that the teaching of Christ can be trusted, and gives us the strength to believe and the discernment to avoid deception and to judge false spirits. The Spirit is able to break through the pride and self-seeking of the heart turned back on itself (*cor curvum in se*); the Spirit is able to reveal the truth of God where human perception is powerless, and apart from the Holy Spirit no one can say, "Jesus is Lord" (1 Cor. 12:3).

Let's turn now to a discussion of a few of the connections between word and Spirit, which can be organized under three headings: the Holy Spirit as the

Spirit of truth, the Holy Spirit as preacher, and the Holy Spirit as participant in the divine essence with the Father and the Son.[110]

The Holy Spirit as the Spirit of Truth

In his exposition on John 16:13, "When the Spirit of truth comes, he will guide you into all the truth," Luther speaks of the power and presence of the Spirit. Reason and the human heart could never achieve an accurate perspective on Christ. Neither could they persist in a confession of faith in light of the opposition and trials that seem to attend Christians in this life. Luther points out that Jesus' disciples found out in their own experience how difficult it is to remain faithful under adverse circumstances. During Christ's arrest, trial, and suffering, the disciples abandoned him in ignominious fashion. They could not reconcile his cruel death with his positive teaching about the kingdom of God. Whatever remained of faith in their hearts was almost extinguished by the mocking of the devil.

> "Behold," he said, "where is your Christ now? What a fine king He has become! How well He has liberated Israel! How you have been put to shame! How miserably you have let yourselves be deceived!" The true Christians always have discovered and still do, that this truth, that is, faith which should hold firmly to the articles concerning Christ and His kingdom, cannot be retained by human reason or power, but that the Holy Spirit Himself must accomplish this. And it is a sure sign of the presence of the Holy Spirit and of His power when faith is preserved and is victorious in real battle and trial. But why should I say a great deal? All experience and the work itself show daily that in Christendom the Holy Spirit Himself must do everything that pertains to the real guidance of Christendom. For without Him we would not baptize or preach very long, nor would we retain the name of Christ. In one hour the devil would have dispossessed us of everything and would have destroyed it.[111]

The Holy Spirit is the Spirit of truth precisely in that he connects believers with the truth about Christ and seals this within our hearts, something human reason could never do. The task of the Spirit is to teach Jesus' disciples and show them that everything that Christ told them is the truth. The Spirit confirms the truth in our hearts and makes us sure and certain of it.

The role of the Holy Spirit is to bring to mind those things that Christ has spoken (John 14:26). The task of the Holy Spirit is to point to Jesus Christ, who is the truth. The connection between Christology and pneumatology is thus quite striking. It is the Spirit who brings us to Christ. How does this take place, given the fact that the saving work of Christ, his crucifixion and resurrection, took place in and around Jerusalem over two thousand years ago? How is it that something that happened so long ago has application today? In his Large Catechism, Luther provides the answers:

Neither you nor I could ever know anything of Christ, or believe in him and receive him as Lord, unless these were offered to us and bestowed on our hearts through the preaching of the Gospel by the Holy Spirit. The work is finished and completed; Christ has acquired and won the treasure for us by his sufferings, death, and resurrection, etc. But if the work remained hidden so that no one knew of it, it would have been all in vain, all lost. In order that this treasure might not remain buried but put to use and enjoyed, God has caused the Word to be published and proclaimed, in which he has given the Holy Spirit to offer and apply to us this treasure, this redemption. Therefore being made holy is nothing else than bringing us to the Lord Christ to receive this blessing, to which we could not have come by ourselves.[112]

Through the preaching of the Holy Spirit, the truth of Christ is made present. The distance between his saving benefits achieved in the past and the present is bridged in the action of the Holy Spirit. Christ is present with the believer together with the forgiveness of sin won through the cross and the resurrection. The divide separating past and present is overcome in the action of the Spirit. Or, to put it in other words, the objective work of Christ is subjectively applied to the life of the believer by means of the Spirit of truth in the here and now. This is achieved as Christ is made contemporaneous with the believer.

As we have seen, the centrality and the preeminence of Christ are present throughout Luther's work. The *solus Christus* of Luther means, in the first instance, that it is Christ alone who reveals God. To attempt to grasp God apart from Christ and his work is folly. In this regard, the interesting suggestion of Bernard Lohse is that we should add a corresponding *solo Spiritu Sancto*, even though Luther never coined that exact phrase.[113] Lohse highlights this precisely because the work of the Spirit is to promote and point to Christ without bringing attention to himself. Further, as the quotation above indicates, the Spirit is given as a gift in and with the word to apply to us the treasure of salvation.

Luther's view of the Holy Spirit as the Spirit of truth can also be seen in his dispute with Erasmus of Rotterdam, the most famous humanist of his day. Although Luther recognized him as a man of great and unusual ability, Erasmus approached Scripture with skepticism. He was of the conviction that there was much in Scripture that was hidden and dark. What constitutes proper doctrine thus had to be yielded up to the senate of learned men for dispassionate discussion. He shied away from assertions preferring the distance of uncommitted reason, what the rhetoricians of the time referred to as *collatio*, the collation of texts often left unresolved.[114]

This approach was something Luther could not abide. Against the skepticism of Erasmus, he hurled the following remark,

By such tactics you only succeed in showing that you foster in your heart a Lucian, or some other pig from Epicurus' sty who, having no belief in God himself, secretly ridicules all who have a belief and confess it. Permit us to be assertors, to be devoted to assertions and delight in them, while you stick to

> your Skeptics and Academics till Christ calls you too. The Holy Spirit is no
> Skeptic, and it is not doubts or mere opinions that he has written on our hearts,
> but assertions more sure and certain than life itself and all experience.[115]

Luther holds fast to the fact that Scripture is meant to preach and drive home
Christ for the sake of producing a change in the human heart that is willing to
say, "I believe, and so I spoke" (2 Cor. 4:13). The text itself is clear for anyone
who will read, and it has one meaning for those passages decisive in determining doctrine. Even though some dark passages linger, the essential characteristic of clarity remains because Christ is the *scopus* or center point for Scripture.

Luther speaks of a twofold clarity of Scripture.[116] First, the external clarity
of Scripture is sufficient to instruct any reader of the text; the storyline of God's
dealings with the nation of Israel and the revealing of Christ as the center point
of Scripture is evident. Second, the internal clarity of Scripture has to do with
the working of the Holy Spirit, the addition of divine activity that awakens the
human heart. The Holy Spirit uses the external word to bring about a changed
reality in the inner being of the reader. The light that the Holy Spirit brings
makes it possible for the one who previously denied God to acknowledge God
in thanksgiving and praise. This is the ultimate clarity that allows the promise
that comes in Christ to reshape and remold life in the image of God.

The Holy Spirit as the Spirit of truth provides aid to the believer in a number
of ways. For Jesus' fearful disciples, the Holy Spirit supplied the power to retain
the truth of Christ and his kingdom where human reason was not enough. The
Spirit also brings the finished work of Christ into the present, bridging the
distance between past and present. When it comes to Scripture, the Holy Spirit
illumines the mind and grants the internal clarity necessary to grasp the things
of God. And all of this allows the believer to embrace the truth of God in Christ
with bold certainty over against a cold and bloodless skepticism.

The Holy Spirit as Preacher

"For he will not speak on his own authority, but whatever he hears he will
speak" (John 16:13). Luther states it boldly, "Here Christ makes the Holy Spirit
a preacher."[117] We have already seen how the preaching of the gospel by the Holy
Spirit makes known the finished work of Christ and brings it into the present.
But there are more ways to describe the preaching office of the Holy Spirit.

First, the Holy Spirit preaches comfort. Luther loves to depict the Holy
Spirit as a Comforter against the evil spirit that rules in the world. The devil
desires to assault Christians with knowledge of their sins. He renders the heart
despondent and unable to answer.

> He not only cites the sins which you yourself must confess, such as murder
> and adultery, and blows them up with his fiery breath to such proportions
> that your heart melts like salt in water; but he can also transform your good

conduct and your best works into many kinds of sin and shame, so that you do not keep even a speck of them.[118]

Luther continues, "He makes things so hot and horrible that man considers heaven and earth too cramped and wants to hurl himself into fire from fright."[119]

In order to counteract this spirit of terror, Christians are given "a Comforter, who, as God Himself, is much stronger with His comfort than the devil is with his terror."[120] And when the devil does his best to dislodge the truth of the gospel from the Christian and shatter every semblance of faith,

> The Holy Spirit, on the other hand, will come and whisper consolingly to your heart: "Be of good cheer and unafraid. Go, preach, do what you have been commanded to do; and do not fear the terrors of sin, death, or the devil, even if the terrors present themselves in the name of God. God does not want to be angry with you, nor does He want to reject you; for Christ, God's Son, died for you."[121]

The preaching of the Holy Spirit is a preaching that inspires confidence and gives consolation to stricken hearts.

> In brief, I will fear nothing, even if lightning were to strike this moment and throw everything into confusion. For Christ is mine with His suffering, death, and life; the Holy Spirit, with His comfort; and the Father Himself, with all His grace. He sends the Holy Spirit to preach Christ into my heart and to fill it with His consolation. This is the main glory and prerogative of the Holy Spirit.[122]

In the view of Luther, the main glory and prerogative of the Holy Spirit is the preaching of Christ.

Second, the preaching of the Holy Spirit preserves us from false teachers and false arguments. In this regard, Luther has in mind the enthusiasts who believed it was possible to attain the Spirit apart from the word of God. In his *Sermons on John*, Luther refers to the fluttering spirits and enthusiasts who gape after God as he is in heaven. In the pattern of the theology of the cross, Luther explains that the Holy Spirit has been given to us as a preacher to pull us down from heaven and speak to us here on earth through the word. "He wants us to adhere solely to the Word and to regard it as the only truth. And through this Word alone He governs the Christian Church to the end."[123]

Luther further explains that there are teachers who speak on their own authority, evolving their message from their own reason and religious zeal. In a quote that applies to both the enthusiasts and the Roman Catholic leaders of his day, Luther says, "That is just what the old devil did and the ancient serpent did, who also made Adam and Eve into Enthusiasts, leading them away from the eternal word of God to spiritualizing and to what comes from one's own imagination."[124] To position ourselves above the word is to find ourselves outside the word and the authoritative message of the Spirit as received from the Father and the Son. Therefore, we ought to—and must—persevere in this:

that God does not seek to deal with us human beings apart from the external word and sacrament. Everything that is praised concerning the Spirit, apart from word and sacrament, is of the devil.[125]

The Holy Spirit uses external means, because that is where the promise of God is to be found. To seek God outside of the prescribed means of baptism, the Lord's Supper, and the preaching of the gospel leads to uncertainty and deception. The inseparability of the word and the Spirit stresses that God's reliable promise is present where he says he will be present. Anything that happens by the Spirit will conform to the bounds of his ministry—namely, Christ and his word. In this way, there is a sure guide and touchstone for judging false spirits. The fanatics and the papacy in departing from this understanding undermine the ability to discern false spirits. "The Holy Spirit, however, is the sort of teacher who is sure and makes men sure, and does not let them toss and dangle, for in Christ it is not yes and no, but yes and amen."[126]

Third, the Holy Spirit will impel the Christian to become a witness to Christ. Even as the Holy Spirit witnesses to Christ, in like manner the Christian follows suit. Once our hearts have been emboldened by the gospel, and our minds and understanding have been confirmed in the truth, the Spirit impels us to testify to what has occurred. The Spirit first witnesses internally in our lives and then externally through confession, preaching, and carrying out our vocation.

The Holy Spirit as Participant in the Divine Essence with the Father and the Son

Luther often speaks of the Holy Spirit in order to outline and describe the work or the office of the Spirit. He is keen on presenting in powerful terms the role the Holy Spirit plays in our daily struggle. But from time to time, even in his sermons, Luther did allude to the relations within the Trinity and the Person of the Holy Spirit. In his sermon on John 16:13, we find just this kind of instance. After spending most of his exposition explaining how it is that the Holy Spirit is the Spirit of truth in contrast with the spirit of lies, Luther makes a segue with the following words: "This is the plain and simple meaning of this text concerning the office of the Holy Spirit. But here there is more to say about the Person of the Holy Spirit, about how it is distinct from that of both the Father and the Son."[127]

Luther proceeds to build his reflections beginning with the words of Jesus, as he says: "When the Helper comes" (John 15:26), "Whatever He hears He will speak" (John 16:13), and "He will glorify Me, for He will take what is mine" (John 16:14). The Holy Spirit is shown to be a true being and distinct from Father and Son. These texts refer to the "Comforter who will come," and the One who can be described as "Whatever He hears He will speak." As Luther reasons, "Now He surely is not the Father, since the Father does not come and is not sent. Nor is He the Son, who has already come and now returns to the Father, and of whom the Holy Spirit will preach and whom He will glorify."[128]

By highlighting the distinct personhood of the Spirit and his particular attribute, Luther demonstrates the Spirit's divine essence together with the Father and the Son:

> For here Christ refers to a conversation carried on in the Godhead, a conversation in which no creatures participate. He sets up a pulpit both for the speaker and the listener. He makes the Father the preacher and the Holy Spirit the Listener.[129]

In conformity with the word, "Whatever He hears He will speak," the Spirit participates in the divine dialogue. The Father is the preacher, the Son is the Word spoken, and the Holy Spirit the listener. This is not a physical preaching or hearing, but one inherent in the essence of the Godhead. Luther describes it in the following manner:

> Here it is relevant to state that Scripture calls our Lord Christ—according to His divine nature—a "Word" (John 1:1) which the Father speaks with and in Himself. Thus this Word has a true, divine nature from the Father. It is not a word spoken by the Father, as a physical, natural word spoken by a human being is a voice or a breath that does not remain in him but comes out of him and remains outside him. No, this Word remains in the Father forever. Thus these are two distinct Persons: He who speaks and the Word that is spoken, that is, the Father and the Son. Here, however, we find the third Person following these two, namely, the One who hears both the Speaker and the spoken Word. For it stands to reason that there must also be a listener where a speaker and a word are found. But all this speaking, being spoken, and listening takes place within the divine nature and also remains there, where no creature is or can be. All three—Speaker, Word, and Listener—must be God Himself; all three must be coeternal and in a single undivided majesty. For there is no difference or inequality in the divine essence, neither a beginning nor an end. Therefore one cannot say that the Listener is something outside God, or that there was a time when He began to be a Listener; but just as the Father is a Speaker from eternity, and just as the Son is spoken from eternity, so the Holy Spirit is the Listener from eternity.[130]

This striking meditation on the Person of the Holy Spirit and the Trinitarian relations bases the unity or unifying of God on the basis of *communio*, an eternal sharing or eternal conversation. While this is not the only manner in which Luther can reflect on the Trinity, it does depart from the well-known Augustinian tradition that bases the unity in *caritas*, in which the Holy Spirit is a kind of inexpressible communion or fellowship of Father and Son.[131] Luther's meditation on these texts works well with his Reformation theology that emphasizes the *Deus dixit*—the God who speaks.

Luther's theology gives faith a central position. He does this because this is what he sees Paul doing. "So faith comes from hearing, and hearing through the word of Christ" (Rom. 10:17). So it is no surprise to find passages in Luther that reflect this fact. "Therefore a man becomes a Christian, not by working but by listening. And so anyone who wants to exert himself toward righteousness must first exert himself in listening to the Gospel."[132] In another place he says, "There is nothing to be done here but to hear."[133] It is clear that for Luther it is the ear that is the organ that makes a Christian, not the hands (works) or the eyes (beatific vision).

This marks a decisive shift in Christian theology that since the days of Augustine had been oriented toward the beatific vision. Neoplatonic thought insisted that the soul had an inherent ability to see. In order to attain to the divine, it was necessary for the soul to shed itself of all physical images to see things on a higher plane of existence. Discipline and effort are required to achieve this highest form of contemplation. This kind of Platonic vision is something Augustine himself reports having in his *Confessions* (7.23). In his later years, he did not say anything to discount the experience or to indicate it was anything less than authentic. Through Augustine and other variations, this form of mysticism played its role in the life of the church so that the beatific vision was an accepted and even expected form of thought.

Luther's meditation on the Person of the Holy Spirit highlights an innovation embedded in his theology. Robert Jenson makes the case that Luther's insights lead to a radical reversal of the Greek philosophers' approach to ontology and epistemology:

> In their doctrine, the specific character of personal beings, "souls" is that their being is determined by what they, as perfect eyes, *see*. Luther switched that; for him the specific character of personal being is that we are what we as perfect ears *hear*. Moreover, if for the Greeks "to be" generally is to perdure, to hang on to oneself, for Luther "to be" is to share oneself by speaking: thus for Christ "to be" is to share himself in his Word.[134]

Luther's meditation on the Trinitarian relations, although brief, seems to have consequence that provides resource for pastoral theology. As a teacher in the church, he recognizes that the work he does is for others and for their edification and welfare. The work of meditating on the text, with the aid of the Holy Spirit, is done for the sake of the community. Speech about the Trinity has its uses and is not in itself a speculative venture to be avoided. This is all the more reason to meditate on Scripture while listening to the Holy Spirit.

CHAPTER 4

SPIRITUAL TRIAL

The third and last rule for the right study of theology is spiritual trial, or *tentatio*. In German, the term is *Anfechtung* (or in the plural, *Anfechtungen*). This is a term for which there is no adequate English equivalent. In the opinion of Roland Bainton, this is a German word that has as much right to be carried over untranslated into English as other words, such as *blitzkrieg* (which literally means "lightning war"). Bainton explains the difficulty of trying to translate *Anfechtung* with only one meaning: "It may be a trial sent by God to test man, or an assault by the Devil to destroy man. It is all the doubt, turmoil, pang, tremor, panic, despair, desolation, and desperation which invade the spirit of man."[1] In more recent accounts of Luther's theology, this word has been translated as "agonizing struggles" or "spiritual trial."[2]

We turn once again to the paragraph in Luther's *Preface to German Writings*:

> Thirdly, there is *tentatio, Anfechtung*. This is the touchstone which teaches you not only to know and understand, but also to experience how right, how true, how sweet, how lovely, how mighty, how comforting God's Word is, wisdom beyond all wisdom. Thus you see how David, in the Psalm mentioned, complains so often about all kinds of enemies, arrogant princes or tyrants, false spirits and factions, whom he must tolerate because he meditates, that is, because he is occupied with God's Word (as has been said) in all manner of ways. For as soon as God's Word takes root and grows in you, the devil will harry you, and will make a real doctor of you, and by his assaults will teach you to seek and love God's Word. I myself (if you will permit me, mere mouse-dirt, to be mingled with pepper) am deeply indebted to my papists that through the devil's raging they have beaten, oppressed, and distressed me so much. That is to say, they have made a fairly good theologian of me, which I would not have become otherwise. And I heartily grant them what they have won in return for making this of me, honor, victory, and triumph, for that's the way they wanted it.[3]

Luther mentions "enemies, arrogant princes, false spirits and factions," along with assaults, the "devil's raging," oppression, and distress. This is indeed a full lineup of human and spiritual adversaries! When confronted in such a way, the believer feels great opposition and even despair.

In an often quoted passage from *Explanations of the Ninety-Five Theses* (1518), Luther describes in graphic terms the intensity of the affliction he experienced through agonizing struggles. He says that to suffer under these punishments for half an hour, or even one-tenth of an hour, would reduce the sufferer to ashes. "At such a time God seems terribly angry, and with him the whole creation. At such a time there is no flight, no comfort, within or without, but all things accuse. At such a time as that the Psalmist mourns, 'I am cut off from thy sight' [Ps. 31:22]." In this poignant isolation, Luther explains that the soul cannot believe it will ever receive forgiveness, and it does not know where to turn for help. "In this instance the person is stretched out with Christ so that all his bones may be counted, and every corner of the soul is filled with the greatest bitterness, dread, trembling, and sorrow in such a manner that all these last forever."[4] It is as though Luther has experienced the crucifixion of Christ in his own person.

It is one thing to have theological knowledge, a good education, and an excellent grasp of human religion, but it is quite another to be challenged to the core in our inner being and to have nowhere to turn except to the word of God. Only along this path is it possible to experience, and not just to know or to understand, "how right, how true, how sweet, how lovely, how mighty, how comforting God's Word is, wisdom beyond all wisdom."

Not all may experience trials with the intensity that Luther the Augustinian friar did in the monastery.[5] But trials will come to all Christians; all Christians will experience the suffering that comes under various labels—trial, *tentatio*, struggle, tribulation, inner conflict, *Anfechtung*. Christians are destined for affliction (1 Thess. 3:3–4). Jesus himself says, "In the world you will have tribulation. But take heart; I have overcome the world" (John 16:33). The apostle Peter directed his letters to Christians undergoing persecution, and the great *cantus firmus* ("fixed song") in the Apocalypse is for "those who overcome."

What does Luther mean by "experience"? This is one question that arises in our attempt to understand the Reformer on the matter of *tentatio*. We would run into a serious misconception here if we were to proceed on the basis of an Enlightenment view of experience. In this viewpoint, the German philosopher, Immanuel Kant, contrasts reason with experience. In his attempt to secure a sure basis for metaphysics through the assertion of the autonomy of reason, he was able to express himself in the following way, "Nothing, indeed, can be more injurious or more unworthy of a philosopher, than the vulgar appeal to so-called adverse experience."[6] Experience, according to Kant, can have nothing to add to the understanding of the intelligible world—that is, the world of ideas. On this point, Kant is not in harmony with Luther.

This is not the place to rehearse the history of the concept of human experience. The contributions to the field by William James and Rudolf Otto, to name just two, are not insignificant but do not give us direct help in understanding our topic.[7] Even the discussions in earlier Luther scholarship on the Reformer's view of experience have not always given us the best information.

At the beginning of the twentieth century in Luther scholarship, there was some discussion of the subject of "faith and experience." But as Regin Prenter has pointed out, this introduced an attitude foreign to Luther. For example, Reinhold Seeberg makes Luther responsible for a "religious transcendentalism," and Emil

Brunner sees in Luther a dialectical anti-psychological attitude.[8] Over against these theories, Prenter urges a different understanding of Luther's conceptuality—one that emphasizes Luther's close relationship to biblical realism.

For Luther, the experience of faith stands as a singular event that places the listening human subject up against the word of God. In the first instance, believers come to faith by agreeing with the judgment of God against human sin, in such a way that we understand ourselves to be sinful. This is not an experience that has its starting point in the human spirit, or in the ability of the human to perceive the good and to affirm it, as outlined in Scholastic theology. It is the word and the word alone that has the power to make such things known. In the second instance, we experience faith by being joined to Christ as a bride to her bridegroom. The wedding ring of faith binds him to us and us to him. In this union, there is what Luther calls the "happy exchange": he takes our sickness, sin, and death, and he gives us his health, his righteousness, and his salvation.

The experience of faith is a real experience that by its very nature is in opposition to all other experience. This helps to explain why the comments of the young Luther on experience and inner conflict are so closely correlated. As Luther comments in the Heidelberg Disputation, "It is certain that man must utterly despair of his own ability before he is prepared to receive the grace of Christ."[9] Indeed, inner conflict signifies the crisis for all natural experience. The self-will of the heart turned in on itself (*cor curvum in se*) clouds human judgment and natural experience. As this comes under attack (*Anfechtung/tentatio*) and inner conflict increases, the question of what is real and what is only imagined is raised as an existential reality.

For Luther, experience means that the intercession of the Holy Spirit for us in the muck and the mire of the agonizing struggles proves to us that Christ, in whom we take our refuge and with whom we are conformed, is a reality and not a dream. The exegetical background for this realization comes in the eighth chapter of Romans. There, the apostle speaks of the Spirit interceding for us with "groanings too deep for words" (Rom. 8:26). This word about the Holy Spirit as our comforter and intercessor is connected with *Anfechtung*, the inner conflict. Romans 8:26 is the testimony about the work of the Holy Spirit that shows the true love from and toward God. When the conscience is weighed down and the soul is convinced that no help is at hand, then trembling, anguish, and despair set in. In this narrow strait from which there seems no release, the sinner has no strength to stand and takes no comfort. Even an effective fight is rendered impossible. All that is left are the listless groans of someone in *extremis*. It is in that moment, when all strength is gone, that the Holy Spirit comes to our aid and groans to God in the midst of our human death and hell. It is not the last gasp of human effort that achieves an upward call; it is Christ's own Spirit in the midst of human turmoil who cries out to God. It is the Holy Spirit himself who, as our helper and comforter, groans in us and for us.

So it is that Luther can call *Anfechtung* or *tentatio* "the touchstone which teaches you not only to know and understand, but also to experience how right, how true, how sweet, how lovely, how mighty, how comforting God's Word is, wisdom beyond all wisdom." *Anfechtung, tentatio,* or inner conflict is a true experience with God, but this experience does not stand alone. God himself intercedes with groans that cannot be uttered to enable the man, woman, boy, or girl to acknowledge Christ and to give God his due.

But even as the Holy Spirit witnesses to Christ, so also the Holy Scriptures witness to Christ. In Scripture, we have the witness or testimony of those who have sojourned in the reality of faith. Their witness speaks to and reiterates the inner witness and testimony of the Holy Spirit. That is the connection between our inner conflict and the Scriptures. It is not enough to have a historical knowledge of Christ and his work. For that to be applied to your life, it takes more: it takes experience. The specific understanding Luther has of experience now comes to light. This experience is a legitimate form of knowledge, distinguishing the vain imaginings of the mind from reality. When Christ, by the witness of the Spirit, is proven to be a reality separate from a mere thought or fancy, then this is the experience of faith. As such, it appears in contrast to other forms of experience. And since the revelation of God is in hiddenness, the witness of God's Spirit struggles with our own reason and senses. But the experience of faith is a real experience of a reality that stands over and above all other realities.

This agonizing struggle drives the believer to experience what is true by the intercession of the Holy Spirit. But this is not Luther's last word on the matter. The experience of *Anfechtung* has the helpful effect of giving us a new appreciation and a new appropriation of the sacred text. The Holy Scriptures are vindicated in the trial and now are shown to be the height of wisdom. The experience of inner conflict is not a general, diffuse, or open-ended experience, but it is an experience authenticated in the inscripturated word of God. The real point of Luther's famous statement "*sola experientia facit theologum*" ("only experience makes a theologian") is misapplied when it has no recourse to Holy Scripture.

Luther's Own Spiritual Trial

Throughout his life, Luther was subject to struggles of various kinds. His time in the monastery and his work as a lecturer on the Bible; his role later as husband and father; and his activity as a reformer, with its demands to establish sustainable structures, pressed in upon him. These *Anfechtungen* fenced Luther in, confronting him with the mysteries of a terrible world as well as the inner turmoil of his own soul. Luther research has shown that Luther's inner, personal experiences are the context of his formation and cannot be separated from his theological perceptions, his scholarly work, or especially his study of the Bible. "I didn't learn my theology all at once," Luther said. "I had to ponder over it ever more deeply, and my spiritual trials [*Anfechtungen/tentationes*] were of help to me in this for one does not learn anything without practice. This is what the spiritualists and sects lack. They don't have the right adversary, the devil. He would teach them well."[10]

In previous pages, we have highlighted moments of Luther's struggle—for example, his battle for Melanchthon's recovery through prayer and his struggle to break through to a proper understanding of the righteousness of God. At this point in our study, we highlight briefly two more moments in Luther's life: his *Anfechtung* during a critical turning point in his life, and his struggle at the death of his daughter Magdalene.

The ten years that followed Luther's posting of the Ninety-Five Theses had been full and demanding. During this time, Luther produced an amazing array of treatises on astoundingly diverse topics—from a critique of monasticism to a devotional piece written for the elector, from a treatise on good works to technical discussions of the doctrine of the Lord's Supper. In 1525, Luther wrote a full-length reply to Erasmus of Rotterdam on the subject of the bound will. And just as certain aspects of his publications against Rome were winding down, another conflict emerged: this time with Karlstadt and the Swiss, who challenged his view of the Lord's Supper.

Luther began 1527 with the heavy weight on his shoulders of having to answer these rivals. Luther familiarized himself with their writings and worked hard from January to mid-March on completing his book before the spring book fair, a large gathering of publishers and booksellers where the latest publications were on display. Luther was of the opinion that it was the devil's stratagems that had caused this struggle over the sacrament: "Satan is infuriated and perhaps feels that the day of Christ is at hand. That is why he raves so fiercely and tries through the enthusiasts to rob us of the Savior, Jesus Christ."[11]

The years of being the leader of a movement, however, had taken their toll on Luther, and his earlier years of physical deprivation in the cloister had permanently damaged his health. By 1527, these factors started to affect Luther in concentrated ways. On April 22, he had to suspend his preaching because of a dizzy spell, which became so severe that for several weeks he was unable to read or work. During these days when he was turned inward, it was hard for him in his mind not to constantly rehearse the insults of his opponents and the flagrant twisting of his words. His life's work slandered, his faith mocked, and his own struggles minimized—these were dangerous things to stew over.

Personal troubles were also close at hand. Maintaining a household was expensive, and Luther in his generosity had stood as surety for several loans. When they went unpaid, Luther was responsible and had to pawn three silver goblets to make things right. His cash was so short, he complained he could not loan the previous prior of the cloister even as little as eight guldens.

On July 6, he suffered a severe fainting spell that caused everyone great concern. Early that Saturday morning, Luther had asked for his pastor, Johannes Bugenhagen, to hear his confession and absolve him in anticipation of receiving the sacrament on Sunday.[12] In that interview, Luther confided in his pastor about the deep spiritual *Anfechtung* he was experiencing because of the uproar in the world and its ingratitude for the word of salvation that God offered through him. It may well be that Luther felt the sting of the rejection he was receiving at the hands of Karlstadt, Zwingli, and the others, which may have triggered questions surrounding his calling. He accepted the invitation from some nobles to join them at an inn later that morning, but he ate little. Afterward, he spent an extended period of time with Justus Jonas, a Lutheran theologian and friend, discussing these same issues and sharing his heart. As he left, he invited Jonas and his wife to supper.

That evening with Jonas and his wife, Luther was troubled with a severe buzzing in the ear and wanted to lie down. But he grew worse rapidly and asked Jonas for water. He became cold and thought his last hour had come. He cried out in a loud prayer, surrendering to God's will, and then prayed the Lord's Prayer and recited two penitential psalms: "O Lord, rebuke me not in your anger" (Ps. 6), and "Have mercy on me, O God, according to your steadfast love" (Ps. 51).

He was put to bed, where he continued to pray and make his personal preparations for death. He regretted that God had not allowed him to be a martyr for the faith. No doubt he had in mind a few of his students who had been honored with that privilege. Alternately, Luther decried the enthusiasts and speculated about how they would carry on after his death. He said that, if it were possible, he would like to live a bit longer and use the gifts God had given him for the sake of the people. He urged those who were gathered around his bedside to bear witness that he remained true to the end and did not revoke what he had written against the pope about repentance and justification—that he had held fast to the gospel and to the truth of God. Then he asked about his son, little Hans, who was only a year old at the time. He commended the child and Katie to God's will. Katie was also convinced that, in addition to herself and the child, there were many Christians who still needed Luther.

After all this, the treatment administered by the doctor, Augustine Schurf, proved successful. Luther's strength returned and he was able to rise for supper the next day, but his head refused to let him work for a time. Although he had wrestled with death, he slowly recovered physically. Spiritually, however, Luther continued to be buffeted by doubts and despairing anxiety. Those around him prayed, and by that means, he sensed that God began to have some mercy upon him to rescue him from the depths of hell.

In late July, an epidemic of the plague began in Wittenberg that lasted for months. For health reasons, the university had been moved to Jena, and the elector wanted Luther to go there too. But, contrary to that advice, Luther remained in Wittenberg to lecture to those students who had remained. After the plague claimed some of its first victims in Wittenberg, a cloud of fear spread throughout the town. In addition to this, Luther's spiritual trials continued, and he recognized that he could not endure on his own. In a letter to his friend Justus Menius, he asks him to pray for him in this special time of need. He recognized that Satan and his angels had made him sick, not only in body but especially in spirit. Luther, however, was confident that Menius's prayers would be heard and honored by God so that Satan would be trodden underfoot.[13] Fear of the plague continued to spread, and it was for this reason that Luther claimed the need to remain at his post, as an example to the common people. He stood at his post with the pastor, Bugenhagen, and the chaplains, George Rörer and Johannes Mantel. When the wife of Tilo Dene, the burgomaster, died in Luther's arms, this was the first death in the center of town. The fisherman's quarter was hit hardest.[14]

A clergyman in Breslau asked Luther to give his opinion on whether or not it was proper for Christians to flee in the face of danger such as the plague. After being delayed due to his own health issues, Luther published an open letter in response. The final product was a short pamphlet titled *Whether One May Flee from a Deadly Plague*, which was widely circulated in nineteen editions.[15] While he thought it was laudable to say believers should not run away from their duty in the face of such danger, he did not impose this as a law on the weak. Since only a few Christians were strong and so many were weak, he said, he simply could not place the same burden on all. But those who were engaged in a spiritual ministry, or those who had responsibility for government and the welfare of the community, had an obligation to remain at their posts. Luther said that it was natural and permissible for believers to save their lives, but only if they did not endanger their neighbor by doing so.

Luther also emphasized the need to think about others in the midst of such a crisis. In the same way we owe it to our neighbor to help put out the flames of a fire, so we have the duty to help in a time of plague: use proper medicines, fumigate your house and yard, and do not expose your neighbor needlessly to the sickness. Luther suggested that piety and decency should induce the community to provide a public burying ground outside the town. In short, the best practices for handling the disease should be used.

In addition, Luther was concerned to say that the spiritual side of this kind of event is even more important. After all, it is the devil who stands behind these events, with the permission of God. Fear of the devil should be rejected, however, and people should take up their responsibilities in a manner that would spite him. This can be done in a twofold manner. First, caring for our neighbor is a work that is pleasing to God, so to engage in this activity is divine service. It should be gladly undertaken, especially as it cuts the nerve of the devil's terror. Second, God comforts the poor and the needy: "Blessed is the one who considers the poor! In the day of trouble the Lord delivers him" (Ps. 41:1). Luther believed that those who nurse the sick with love, devotion, and sincerity are generally protected—that God himself would be their physician and attendant. Therefore, caregivers should not fear boils and infections. "In someone who is sick we meet no one but Christ; this thought from *Freedom of a Christian* finds its specific, ultimate application here."[16]

Infirmities and *Anfechtungen* continued to afflict Luther into October and November. Self-doubts remained, and it was all he could do to console himself with the thought that he had purely preached the gospel; beyond that, he had to hope for a gracious God. He put on his best face to others, but the fact was that Luther's house had become a hospital. Special care had to be taken against infection, and the several who were ill were quarantined as well as the various rooms in the Black Cloister (which had become Luther's house) would allow. Augustine Schurf's wife and Margaretha von Mochau had their own rooms. Little Hans was also ill and had not eaten anything for three days. Luther was concerned for his pregnant wife Katie, especially because Hanna Rörer, the wife of Georg Rörer, was in an advanced stage of pregnancy and had been infected by the plague. Despite all this, Luther still managed to acknowledge the tenth anniversary of his posting of the Ninety-Five Theses, even raising a toast to his friend Amsdorf, who was safely away in Magdeburg.

The death of Hanna Rörer, shortly after giving birth to a stillborn child, deeply affected Luther and the entire household. And because the plague also brought a tremendous sense of isolation, Bugenhagen and his wife moved into the Black Cloister to give mutual aid to Martin and Katie. As a result of all these struggles, Luther was in such desperate straits that he had lost the ability to console himself with the gospel. Fortunately, Bugenhagen was there to preach a word into his ear. Following is a sample Luther recorded of Bugenhagen's encouragement to him:

> Right here at this table, when the rest of you were in Jena, Pomeranus [this was Luther's name for Bugenhagen because he was born in eastern Pomerania] sometimes consoled me when I was sad by saying, "No doubt God is thinking: What more can I do with this man? I have given him so many excellent gifts, and yet he despairs of my grace!" These words were a great comfort to me. As a voice from heaven they struck me in my heart, although I think Pomeranus did not realize at the time what he had said and that it was so well said.[17]

In late November, the epidemic finally began to abate. In a letter to Justus Jonas, Luther related that the physician's wife had recovered and that Margaretha, against all expectations, had escaped death. Also, Katie had given birth to a healthy baby girl. The only added loss was five pigs, which were struck down by the plague. Of these, Luther wished that the plague would be content with this as a tribute and would be done.[18]

By the end of December, Luther was still not free from his *Anfechtung*, and he describes his relationship to Christ as hanging by a thread—Satan had bound him with an anchor and chains that were pulling him down. Only the weak Christ, through the intercessions of his friends, had the upper hand until now. Luther thus urges his friends to strengthen Christ through their prayers so that with his weakness he might break the power of the devil.[19] Luther's emphasis on the "weak Christ" may sound strange to our ears. But a theologian of the cross recognizes that God in Christ exercises his power in this world under the form of the opposite. It is the self-giving Christ who overcomes the greed and the envy of the devil to make room for faith.

Late in the next year, Luther finally recovered from his spiritual trial, breaking through once again to a gracious God. His struggles with *Anfechtung* during this time period were as intense as those he had earlier experienced in the monastery—which may help to explain the argument he carried on with monasticism in his publications of this time, in parallel to his conflict with the enthusiasts. In both cases, these approaches to Christianity had begun to rely on something more than Jesus Christ, who is present in the external word.

We also see that Luther was at his weakest in his struggles with his calling and in light of the defection of many of his followers. But precisely because he was too weak to bear up and overcome his own struggles, he had to rely all the more on Christ. The grace of Christ was manifest in Luther's weakness that brought to nothing any victory of the devil. For Luther, God—who hides himself in the incarnation and under the form of the opposite—seeks to break that which is whole and make whole what is broken.[20]

Luther and Family

We turn now from the very personal spiritual struggle of Luther to one in the center of family life. Luther's large family was a source of great joy to him. His union with Katarina (Katie) von Bora produced six children: Hans (June 7, 1526), Elizabeth (December 10, 1527), Magdalene (May 4, 1529), Martin (November 9, 1531), Paul (January 29, 1533), and Margaretha (December 17, 1539). By all accounts, this was a household that was both lively and happy.

When viewed from a particular vantage point, we could say that this family was something of a miracle: he was an Augustinian friar who had made a vow of celibacy; she was a nun who escaped from a Cistercian monastery among the herring barrels! Reformation teachings had called into question the value and the role of monastic vows within the church. The practical effect of this saw many, like Katie, exiting the cloistered life. On the positive side, it also meant that a new model for married clergy was emerging in the young evangelical movement.

In 1525, Luther shocked the world and caught his closest colleagues off guard by marrying an ex-nun. At a time when the success of the Reformation cause was being strained, this seems to be a most inauspicious moment for such a personal action. Most thought this was an impetuous deed because it left him open to the charge that he had started the Reformation just so that he could get married—a charge that has lingered to this day![21]

Why did Luther do it? What motivated him to choose the married life instead of the spiritual rigors of the monastery and the prospect of perfection? The theological reasoning behind this move is as important as it is interesting. Believing that the end of the world was at hand, Luther reasoned that a man ought to be found living as God had intended him to live on earth. In this instance, trading in his cowl for a wedding ring was the best way to pray that section of the Our Father, "Thy will be done on *earth* as it is in heaven." It is

Luther's commitment to the theology of the cross that leads him to embrace life on earth, as a human being, doing human activities, and caring for the earth that God created.

The usual religious answer given to the challenge of the nearness of the end would be to leave off doing "earthly" things to instead do "spiritual" things, however that may be defined. Since much spirituality—certainly that of the sixteenth century—seeks to escape the hindrance of the temporal body and sees salvation as an escape from the earth, it is no surprise that Luther's earth-affirming move was a shock to so many. Luther felt that completing the move from the monastery to the world God had created was the natural step implied by the gospel. The gospel is the antidote to the problem of sin that twists human nature, causing it to want to be a god. The proclamation of the gospel, and its reception in faith, releases the believer from that bondage to embrace once again what it means to be truly human.

Because of his faith in the goodness of creation, Luther was persuaded not to leave this world or to despise it, but to enter into it all the more fully, taking up its concerns and tasks all the more seriously. This is what we find Luther doing as he becomes a husband and a father. Making a home with Katie would be his greatest joy, but it would also bring some of the greatest challenges he would face.

The demands of the household were nothing short of immense. In addition to his children, the family helped to raise eight orphaned nieces and nephews. Katie's aunt Lena also lived with them for many years. In addition, they provided lodging for various tutors, exiled clergymen, escaped nuns, government officials, visitors, and students. There were many occasions when there were as many as twenty-five for meals! The responsibility for running such a large operation fell to Katie—who had a good head for numbers and a license to brew beer, and whose management of the garden, animals, and fish pond helped them through good times as well as bad.

Luther and Katie were attentive parents who created an atmosphere of respect and discipline. While Luther may have been a bit stricter with Hans, his oldest, he does seem to have taken great delight in being a father and interacting with his children. Childrearing provided more than one illustration of the faith for him. "The doctor took his son on his lap, and the child befouled him. Thereupon he [Martin Luther] said, 'How our Lord God has to put up with many a murmur and stink from us, worse than a mother must endure from her child!"[22] On another occasion it was recorded,

> When his infant son Martin was being suckled at his mother's breast, the doctor said, "The pope, the bishops, Duke George, Ferdinand, and all the demons hate this child, yet the little child isn't afraid of all of them put together. He sucks with pleasure at those breasts, is cheerful, is unconcerned about all his enemies, and lets them rage as long as they wish. Christ said truly, 'Unless you become like children,' etc." [Matt. 18:3].[23]

But for all the joy the couple derived from their children, there was also heartache and struggle. Elizabeth, their oldest daughter and second child, died as an infant merely seven months after she was born. And Magdalene, a young girl of thirteen, fell ill in the fall of 1542. The situation was dire enough to call Hans, her older brother with whom she was especially close, to come home from his schooling in Torgau.

As her illness became graver, Luther attended the bedside of his daughter. There he entreated the Lord, yielding himself to his will. Afterward he said to his daughter, "Dear Magdalene, my little daughter, you would be glad to stay here with me, your father. Are you also glad to go to your Father in heaven?" The sick girl replied, "Yes dear Father, as God wills."[24] In this tragic moment, Luther reminded himself that God had given to no bishop such great gifts as he had been given in a little one such as his "Lenchen."

When the agony of death was upon her, Luther fell on his knees before the bed and cried out to God. She breathed her last in the arms of her father. He was crushed. When she died he said, "I am joyful in spirit but I am sad according to the flesh. The flesh doesn't take kindly to this. The separation troubles me above measure. It's strange to know that she is surely at peace and that she is well off there, very well off, and yet to grieve so much!"[25] Although Katie was in the room, she stood away from the bed on account of her grief. This was a painful parting indeed.

The funeral was held the same day. The university took part in it, for the Luther family belonged to that level of society. When they placed the body in the coffin, Luther was overcome with sobbing; but collecting himself, he looked at her and said, "Ah dear child, to think that you will be raised up and will shine like the stars, yes, like the sun!"[26] At the service, the university rector spoke of her blessed end and affirmed again the resurrection of the dead. The inscription on her coffin read: "The child sleeps here in the earth as one born to die and someone lost because of sin, but thanks to Christ's blood and death she lives."[27]

In his grief over Magdalene's death, Luther once again longed for his own death. The pain of the separation was hard to shake for both Katie and Luther. In spite of thankfulness of her peaceful falling asleep in the Lord and the strength of her faith, there was a sadness that took some time to lift.

Luther and the Devil

In our own day, there is not much talk of a personal devil. Since the Enlightenment and the advent of modern science, the concept of the devil has decreased. There are a few notable exceptions such in as the Pentecostal movement and some independent Bible churches, but even there the devil is usually remote and removed from the world. This, however, was not the case with Luther, who was always convinced of the reality and the everyday meddling of the devil.

Luther came to this belief in his childhood, although we know little about Luther's upbringing except for a few brief anecdotes. But we do know that at the time of Luther's entrance into the monastery, his father—unhappy with Luther's decision—reminded his son of the command, "Honor your Father and your Mother," and then suggested the possibility that the devil might have fooled him into his rash action.[28] Luther's mother, we are told, had to carefully placate her neighbor, who was a witch actively perpetrating mayhem among her children and the community.[29] This may tell us something about the atmosphere in which Luther was raised and the worldview he received.

Luther operated in a manner wholly consistent with what he had learned. The devil remained a companion during his life to such a degree that he could describe with precision the moments of their meetings. In the liminal zone between sleep and consciousness was when Luther could expect to be bothered by the devil. "For it is like this with me. When I am awaking, the devil quickly comes and disputes against me, until I admonish him: Lick my ass!"[30]

Luther did not have qualms about using vulgar language, especially when it had to do with the devil. As Heiko Oberman has shown, there is a strong connection between the two.[31] There are woodcuts that depict the emergence of the antichrist from the backside of the devil. But what is more important is the word of God in defeating the devil in these exchanges. To quote the Bible to the devil is ineffectual; he might just quote Scripture right back at you. What is at issue is to have the right word at the right time:

> For when Satan disputes with me whether God is gracious to me, I dare not quote the passage, "He who loves God will inherit the kingdom of God," because Satan will at once object, "But you have not loved God!" Nor can I oppose this on the ground that I am a diligent reader [of the Scriptures] and a preacher. The shoe doesn't fit. I should say rather, that Jesus Christ died for me and should cite the article [of the creed] concerning forgiveness of sin. That will do it![32]

The point here is to see that the conflict is not merely between the believer—Luther in this case—and the devil; the real battle rages between God and the devil. The life of the human stands under the shadow of this great conflict in which the devil assaults Christ and persecutes him in his church.

The devil's opposition to God is complete and his offenses can be seen in a number of ways in this world. Not only does he bring about sadness and melancholy, but also suicides, wars, provocation to sedition, and pestilence all derive from his unholy will. God is the author of life. But death came into the world through the devil's envy, and on this account the devil is called the author of death.[33] One day, Luther and Katie were almost crushed by a collapsing wall. Luther knew it was the devil and his deadly intentions that stood behind this missed opportunity.[34]

For the Reformer, it was not only diseases that were caused by the devil but also bad weather. Luther recounts how a furious storm fell upon the city of

Nürnberg during the night of February 18, 1533. The wind raged so violently that over four thousand trees were damaged, and it ripped away almost half the roof of the castle. The lightning strikes and accompanying thunder caused some to think the last day was at hand. This was all provoked by the devil! Luther says that while the devil produces bad weather, angels provide good and salubrious winds.[35] The devil can also employ sorceresses to create tempests.[36] This added dimension of sorcery and witchcraft was also an element of Luther's thought world that was discussed around his table at night. On one occasion, a local pastor came to Luther vexed because he had been dealing for some time with poltergeists breaking dishes in his home and wanted relief for his wife and children from this unwanted intrusion. Luther related some personal experiences of his own, gave the pastor some direct advice, and sent him on his way.

These kinds of fascinating, and for some disconcerting, stories of Luther's vivid grasp of the supernatural could be multiplied. At the very least, they reveal two important facts. In the first instance, they show that Luther shared the convictions and worldview of his time. To keep in mind the otherness of Luther, or his strangeness, from our own day is a healthy historical discipline. If we can do this, then it is less likely we will appropriate Luther to our modern ideas and sensibilities. Observing this distance is the best way we have of allowing Luther to speak in his own distinctive voice and thus for us to be in a position to hear him in fresh ways.

In the second place, we should see that his concerns run counter to our scientific age, which is occupied with rational explanations and empirical data. Our age has done its work well, and as a result the devil has in large measure been exorcised by attractive ideologies. But that very success has blinded our era to insights into the spiritual world, which is not the world of causal effects, but the conflict between God and the devil. Although Luther had occasional interest in mathematics and the arts physicians used to heal their patients, his abiding interest was in the God of creation who revealed himself in the suffering of the cross to forgive sin and lead us to freedom.

Luther saw that the devil stands in the way of this freedom and uses methods to block the human race from allowing God to be God. The two things with which he goes about his work are murder and falsehood.[37] John 8:44 identifies the devil as a murderer from the beginning and as a liar and the father of lies. It is this specific biblical word that directs Luther's doctrine about the matter, but it is also the word that confirms the reality of his own personal experience. Luther knew firsthand that the devil was out to kill him, and that he would speak falsely in order to redirect him from a gracious God and his son Jesus Christ, who is the embodiment of that grace.

Luther was also well aware of the fact that the devil is agile and he knows more than we do. He has been at his craft for several thousand years, taking hold of and shaking the patriarchs, the prophets, and even Christ himself. He is, after all, the "ruler of this world" (John 12:31; 14:30) and the "god of this world" (2 Cor. 4:4).[38] He is able to quote Scripture, use syllogisms, and through his own alchemy makes even our good works appear to be evil.[39] This is "an art in which he is a master and an excellent theologian."[40]

The method of the devil works in two directions: toward the smug and satisfied, he extends their presumption, keeping them separated from a true knowledge of God; and toward those of faith, he afflicts, bullies, accuses, and drives to despair. In order to get the upper hand, the devil might take up a sin or a particular propensity, as in the case of Jerome Weller, who tended toward bouts of depression. Or, in the case of Luther, he might sling an arrow such as this, "Do you claim to be the only one who has the true Word of God and no one else has it?"[41] At all costs it is the article of faith in Christ, the main article of the faith, which the devil derides and attempts to replace with his own wisdom.[42]

What kind of advice does Luther give for handling these kinds of circumstances? How can we counter the devil's attacks? Murmuring against God can be induced by the following syllogism from the devil, "You have sinned, God is angry with sinners, therefore despair!"[43] In the event of this kind of spiritual depression, Luther recommends that we proceed from the law to the gospel so that the article concerning the forgiveness of sins is firmly in our grasp. Beyond that, seeking out company, playing games, laughing, and making merry should be the order of the day. On the basis of Christ's victory, a Christian has reason to be cheerful. When we are driven away from this joy for too long, we can expect the devil stands behind it.

The strongest defense against the methods of the devil is the word of God, for by it alone is the devil overcome. Luther especially remarks on the power of the oral word: "To think that Satan, that proud spirit, may be put to flight and thrown into confusion by such a frail word on human lips!"[44] When the devil insinuates a word in our ear, saying that we have not been living right and on that account we are doomed to hell, the Christian can respond,

> No, that is not the will of God. Begone, devil, you and the evil world; for my Lord Christ says no to you, He tells me that the Father is not angry with me but will give me the Comforter, who will come to me an answer to His prayer. They concur in this, that they do not want me to be frightened and sad, much less rejected and condemned, but comforted and happy.[45]

The word of God comes in oral form and is preserved by the proper distinction of law and gospel. All is lost if we get into an argument with the devil about the law and how well, or how badly, we have fulfilled its demands. But if on the basis of the word of God we are able to move from law to gospel, then our defense is sure.

In addition, the word of God that comes in the sacrament is also a defense against demonic attack. When the Christian is brought under accusation and the gracious will of God is doubted, Luther encourages the believer to utter these words, "I have been baptized."[46] Affirming our baptism is to recall the sure word of God given in the sacrament: "Whoever believes and is baptized will be saved" (Mark 16:16). The Lord's Supper also reveals in tangible form the gracious will of God, serving as a bulwark against the devil that seeks to trap and destroy the unsuspecting. Satan resists the holy ministry in its forms of word and sacrament with their external character. For that reason, Luther is convinced that the devil is the one who stirred up all those theologians who also disparage the external word.

Even in this brief accounting of Luther and the devil, we can see it would be impossible to take the devil out of Luther's theology without losing major insights of his system of thought and thus distorting its structure. To summarize this structure we could say that Luther meets the devil in the very place where he meets Jesus Christ—in between God and humanity. In his role as mediator, Jesus is the one who brings about unity and salvation with God. The devil, however, strives to displace Christ from that position to take it for his own. The devil seeks to break the connection with the Father, and as the originator of the first great falling away, he wants to eliminate altogether the true mediator.

If we think of God above, Christ or the devil in the middle, and humans below, it might help make Luther's position easier to visualize.[47] As long as Christ is not grasped in faith he does not stand in the middle, but rather the devil stands in his place. God looking down sees a human race subservient to the devil, bound in servitude and sin. The human race looking out sees little evidence of the divine, due to the fact that the devil hides God and muffles his voice. All that is apparent is the random violence of the world or, to put it in religious terms, a wrathful God.

In this situation, it is clear that both the human race and the devil seek to distance themselves from God and continue in their rebellion. As long as Christ does not stand in between, there is no way to differentiate between God and the devil. So when the difficulties of life arise, it is quite impossible to know for sure whether we are suffering at the hands of God or if demons are putting us to the test. The actions of God and the actions of the devil are just too similar to tell apart.

The example of Job serves as illustration. It can be said that Satan attacked Job's life in both body and soul. What happened to Job was Satan's work. And yet, Scripture also attributes this activity to God (Job 2:3). This is an instance where what God does seems identical to what the devil does. We can make the distinction that the devil pursues his work of destroying Job willingly, while God merely gives permission. But the outcome is the same. When asked if the devil uses his power at God's command, Luther responded, "Good gracious no! But our Lord God doesn't stop him. He looks through his fingers. It's as if a great lord saw that somebody set his barn on fire, did nothing to prevent it, but merely winked at it. This is what God does to the devil."[48]

Another way of saying the same thing is that God uses means or instruments to accomplish his ends.[49] Luther asserts that God uses Satan as an instrument to kill and the law as a means to accuse us and condemn us of our sin, so that we might be humbled and learn to live by grace alone and by the kindness of God. But the question naturally arises, "Why are these things attributed to God, when he does not do them Himself but uses means?" Luther answers that it must be so to retain the unity of the faith and the belief in one God. The Manicheans explained the difficulties of the world by referring to two principles: one good, the other bad. The good was naturally attributed to one god and evil attributed to another god. "But God wants us, whether in pleasant or adverse circumstances, to have confidence in Him alone. He does not want us to be among those of who Isaiah says (Isa. 9:13): 'The people did not turn to Him who smote them.'"[50]

In the matter of death and afflictions, the human race deals only with God. Yet, at the same time, Satan and the law still remain instruments at work as well. It is necessary to see the work of God and Satan's work as one. The question is how we can differentiate them. It would seem, however, that the overlap between them is too complete to discern any difference. Here we are cast back on the revelation of God in Christ; we return to a theology of the cross in which God is revealed under the sign of the opposite. It is only in Jesus Christ—as he says, "If you have seen me you have seen the Father"—that we can know that the raw power standing behind this universe with its devastating force and its ability to graciously renew life is "for us." Only then is it possible to say that although God and Satan are involved in what happens to someone like Job, in effecting the same action they have different intentions. The wrath of God is expressed in the penalty for sin, and Satan magnifies that sin for an individual so that the person can do nothing but despair.[51] Both assault the individual in a strong manner. God, however, does it to save us from the prideful attempt to be a god, and to set free those who would believe and direct them into his loving arms. Satan does it in order to rip us finally and completely away from God. These are two different things. One acts in order to save; the other acts in order to destroy.

We see then the great importance of the word of Christ. Since the Fall, the human race has ascribed devilish traits to God and godly traits to the devil. In this situation, God and the devil are confused with one another. But once he is grasped in the gospel, Jesus Christ allows the eyes of faith to recognize that God is God and the devil is the devil. The ability to distinguish God from the devil is made possible only in Jesus Christ. His cross is the final victory over sin, death, and the devil. It can be described as Christ bearing the sin of the world in order to uphold the righteousness of God. It can also be described as a victory over the principalities and powers. But in the end, Jesus is the last man standing on the field of battle.

It is a fact that the devil has a role in the theology of Luther as one who stands against Christ, the word, and against the working of his word. He attempts to hinder and disallow the word of Christ in every way possible. But everything said about God and the defeated Satan really serves only to magnify the account of Christ. The good news is that the One who conquered through his cross and resurrection promises the forgiveness of sin and eternal life. This word is a powerful weapon in the fight with the devil. Through it he is overcome and our consciences can find consolation in Christ. As Luther writes in the third stanza of "Our God He Is a Castle Strong," later known as "A Mighty Fortress Is Our God":

> And did the world with devils swarm,
> All gaping to devour us,
> We fear not the smallest harm,
> Success is yet before us.
> This world's prince accurst,
> Let him rage his worst,
> No hurt brings about;
> His doom is gone out,
> One little word can overturn him.[52]

Spiritual Trial in Luther's Sermons

It is not possible or even desirable to be comprehensive in showing all the instances in which Luther spoke about struggle in the Christian life. It is enough, however, to move the thesis of this book forward to highlight a few examples of how Luther taught the laity to deal with trial. The following selections are taken from early to late periods in Luther's preaching corpus to show that this is a consistent approach. They are a small sample of the kinds of advice Luther directed toward the laity.

A Sermon on Preparing to Die

First for consideration is "A Sermon on Preparing to Die" from 1519, a sermon that deals with the ultimate struggle.[53] The advice Luther gives in this piece struck a popular chord, indicated by the fact that the treatise went through no less than twenty-two editions in the first three years of its publication, followed by two more in 1523 and 1525! The sermon has a pragmatic and direct feel about it, dealing with temporal ordering of the dying person's possessions as well as touching on what it means to take leave spiritually—all the while containing a sympathetic understanding of the customs and strictures surrounding death practices of the time. With that, Luther exercises his pastoral office to help his hearers wrestle through the trial that stands out before everyone in light of Christ.

The editions were adorned with woodcuts depicting various scenes appropriate to the subject. One might have a picture of a newly departed being lamented by family members, with an elderly man with walking stick and wayfarer's garb looking on. Another might have a three-paneled woodcut depicting a person on their deathbed with their spirit exiting their mouth into the arms of an awaiting angel, a saint in the wilderness contemplating death, and a figure of death hoisting a coffin on one shoulder. The artistic representations say much about the closeness and force of death in the popular imagination at that time.

Set out in twenty paragraphs, the sermon begins with advice on how to dispose of earthly possessions and the need to focus on the spiritual aspects of dying. Since everyone must depart this life, Luther urges his hearers, saying, "We must turn our eyes to God, to whom the path of death leads and directs us."[54] We are to set aside the idea that this life is expansive and that the next life is confined. Rather, we are to joyfully venture out in anticipation of what will be. "The death of the dear saints is called a new birth, and their feast day is known in Latin as *natale*, that is, the day of their birth."[55] We must be willing to bear the anguish of death, knowing that joy and fulfillment far outweigh the momentary pain. The vastness of the life to come calls us, and preparation for this journey begins with a proper use of the sacraments.[56] Receiving what the sacraments signify through faith places us in the company of Mary, who said, "Let it be to me according to your words" (Luke 1:38).

After this opening, Luther identifies the evils that the believer faces. Three evils threaten to undo us—the image of death, the image of sin, and the image of hell and eternal damnation.

> Death looms so large and is terrifying because our foolish and fainthearted nature has etched its image too vividly within itself and constantly fixes its gaze on it. Moreover, the devil presses man to look closely at the gruesome mien and image of death to add to his worry, timidity, and despair. Indeed, he conjures up before men's eyes all the kinds of sudden and terrible death ever seen, heard, or read by man. And then he also slyly suggests the wrath of God with which he [the devil] in days past now and then tormented and destroyed sinners. In that way he fills our foolish human nature with the dread of death while cultivating a love and concern for life, so that burdened with such thoughts man forgets God, flees and abhors death, and thus, in the end, is and remains disobedient to God.[57]

The threat Luther speaks about here is no joke. Sin, death, and the terror of eternal damnation have power in their ability to separate the believer from the one true God. When the conscience broods over these matters, God turns into an enemy and the believing soul flees and forgets God.

So what are we to do in the face of these terrible threats? How can we stand and fight against them, driving them out for good? Luther gives a terse response: "The one and only approach is to drop them entirely and have nothing to do with them."[58] This sounds simple enough, but how can we do that? The thoughts of sin, death, and eternal damnation come easily enough and oftentimes without bidding. How do we banish the evil inherent to death? Again, Luther provides the answer:

It is done in this way: You must look at death while you are alive and see sin in the light of grace and hell in the light of heaven, permitting nothing to divert you from that view. Adhere to that even if all angels, all creatures yes, even your own thoughts, depict God in a different light—something these will not do.[59]

Luther understands that the power of death is primordial and cannot be overcome by human willpower or mere methodology. That is why he urges the believer to ponder death, not in the weakness of human nature, but in view of Christ and his saints.

Viewing Christ and his saints over against the picture of death is the only way to allow death to be what it is. When death is seen in the light of Christ, we can "leave it alone" and it will not appear gruesome and terrible.

For Christ is nothing other than sheer life, as his saints are likewise. The more profoundly you impress that image upon your heart and gaze upon it, the more the image of death will pale and vanish of itself without struggle or battle. Thus your heart will be at peace and you will be able to die calmly in Christ and with Christ, as we read in Revelation [14:13], "Blessed are they who die in the Lord Christ." This was foreshown in Exodus 21 [Num. 21:6–9], where we hear that when the children of Israel were bitten by fiery serpents they did not struggle with these serpents, but merely had to raise their eyes to the dead bronze serpent and the living ones dropped from them by themselves and perished. Thus you must concern yourself solely with the death of Christ and then you will find life. But if you look at death in any other way, it will kill you with great anxiety and anguish.[60]

Luther urges his hearers to look away from the image of death to Christ and his saints. In like manner, we must not look at sin in sinners, or sin in our conscience, but we must engrave the image of Christ and his grace and keep it before our eyes. Further, we must not regard hell and eternal damnation in themselves or in those who seem to be overwhelmed in their path. Against that reality, we must gaze at the heavenly picture of Christ who died on the cross and descended into hell on behalf of his own. "In that picture your hell is defeated and your uncertain election is made sure."[61]

It is along these lines that Luther offers his advice to the laity as they face the temptations presented in sin, death, and hell. Luther's pastoral theology is sensitive to the experienced reality of his hearers. To that circumstance, he sets forward a picture of Christ as the mediator between God and humanity. His presentation cuts through the ambiguity of lay practice, proving that he is the dearest Son, who gives salvation to us all if we but believe. Luther's gospel insight was won in the crucible of his personal *Anfechtungen* and now with his advice to the laity seeks to aid them break through their *Anfechtungen* to true theological existence.

Luther's concerted effort was directed against the tortuous works that many were taught to engage in at the last hour.[62] For example, the laity was instructed to give a complete confession on their deathbed to a priest. Only that would assure the peaceful conscience necessary for entering death. There were additional sets of spiritual exercises to be accomplished as well. But all these actions could be viewed only as something that would distract the person in need from the word of the gospel—the one thing necessary—in that moment. "Luther's sermon stands in an old tradition, but he opens it out onto a decisive position even as he compresses it into one point: only faith in the cross of Christ helps in the last distress."[63]

Sermons on 1 Corinthians 15

Our next example comes from a series of sermons preached over a decade later. The year 1532 was eventful for the Reformation cause and for Luther personally. Only two years had passed since the dramatic confrontation between Catholic and evangelical theologians at the Diet of Augsburg. Luther continued his church visitations, and he addressed the need for improvement in priest and parish. Further, the death of elector John the Steadfast on August 16 meant a change in government over which Luther was somewhat uncertain. If that were not enough, Luther's recurring poor health created many interruptions in his preaching schedule. For weeks at a time, he was unable to work. In June 1532, he sent a letter to Nicolas von Amsdorf, stating that he had recovered his natural strength and was able to resume normal activities.[64]

On August 11, 1532, Luther began a series of seventeen sermons on 1 Corinthians 15. The series was preached mostly on Sunday afternoons and, with a few interruptions, ended on April 27, 1533. The sermon series serves as a running commentary on the entire chapter. George Rörer preserved both the sermons and the dates on which they were given. The volume was edited by Caspar Cruciger, published in German, and offered to the public with a dedication to the new elector, John Frederick.

This pivotal chapter in the Pauline corpus is a sustained argument for the resurrection of Jesus Christ and its central role in Christian existence. Paul begins by asserting the gospel tradition as handed down. He moves on to address those in Corinth, who were asserting that there is no resurrection of the dead, and over against their skepticism sets out a theological discussion of Christ as the firstfruits from among those who sleep. He goes on to counter mistaken ideas of resurrection and ends by explicating and extolling the mystery and victory of Christ's work achieved on the cross and vindicated in his resurrection on the third day.

Luther dives into his task with the ease of one who lives in the world of the Bible and who is intimately familiar with Paul's writings. In the preface, he sets out the problem as Paul had to face it: "A number of factious spirits had arisen who were ruining their faith and teaching that the resurrection of the dead is nothing."[65] Whether they did so by saying the resurrection already took place, or whether they simply asserted that Christ had not been raised from the dead at all, they were trying to overturn the gospel. In Luther's view, this resonated with his present reality:

> Unfortunately today we have again arrived at the point where many, both peasants and townspeople, and particularly Junker Hans of the nobility, prate so absurdly, shamelessly, and heathenishly about this when they presume to be so smart and stick their nose into the Scriptures. For now they have become so learned through us that they are all our teachers and each one claims to know everything.[66]

What Paul knew of rival teachers, Luther also experienced.

The undermining of the doctrine of the resurrection is nothing short of a calamity. "For where this article is surrendered, all the others are gone too; and the chief article and the entire Christ are lost or preached entirely in vain."[67] The point of Paul's argument and Luther's sermons is to set the resurrection of Christ in its central position, and subsequently to hold out the hope of the resurrection of the dead at the end of time as the Apostles' Creed asserts. "For after all, that is the goal of our faith in Christ, of Baptism, of sermon, and of sacrament, that we hope for a new life, that we come to Christ, that we rule eternally with Him, delivered from sin, devil, and death, and every evil."[68] With these kinds of comments, Luther sets out the summary of his argument.

The force with which Luther argues his case causes him to identify this article in the creed on the resurrection as the chief article of Christian doctrine.[69] It is a linchpin in Paul's argument as well: "And if Christ has not been raised, your faith is futile and you are still in your sins" (1 Cor. 15:17). But it should be pointed out that Luther has a penchant for using that phrase, "chief article." At various times in his writings, he adduces the "chief article" label in connection with the doctrine of justification, the doctrine of Christ, and the doctrine of the Trinity.

Luther's sermons on 1 Corinthians 15 are lyrical in places and in others reverberate with all the mythological and primordial drama of the struggle between Christ and the devil. They are important for this study primarily for two reasons. First, because the article on the resurrection is established by faith and not human reason, all the tension between human logic and the revelation of God in Christ is at work. On this point where there is doubt and struggle, Luther adduces a twofold remedy: the witness of Scripture, and the work of the Holy Spirit as confirmed in the experience of the human heart. Second, in this series of sermons the concepts of the defiance of death and the defiance of the devil play a prominent role. Unlike "A Sermon on the Preparation for Dying," which focused on the art of dying, Luther's sermons on 1 Corinthians 15 revel in the realism of Christ's victory.[70] Their focus is not so much on death as on the work of Christ in the ongoing life struggle of the Christian.

In the first four sermons, Luther follows the preaching and logic of the great apostle. Paul took pains to offer two kinds of proof for Christ's resurrection.

First, he points out that his proclamation is based on the sure testimony of Scripture. That is why he repeats the phrase "according to the Scriptures." Thus the teaching he sets out is based on Christ's self-understanding and the prophecy of the Old Testament. Second, he bases his preaching on the accounts of the eyewitnesses of the resurrected Christ. Peter and then the other apostles reported seeing Christ alive. After that, he was seen by more than five hundred. Paul's preaching is thus based on reliable Scripture and reliable experience.

Luther points out that "Paul does this in order to resist the temptation to take counsel with reason in this and other articles of faith, or to listen how the world with its wisdom presumes subtly to argue and to speculate about this."[71] For even though Paul's preaching has basis, has produced faith, and represents Christ and his work fairly, questions still arise. When human reason comes into contact with this article of faith, it is simply at a loss. The observation of reason is that the world has stood a long time, one person dies after another, they all decompose in the ground and from this fate no one has returned. In light of these facts, it is absurd to assert resurrection. So it is that the experience of faith comes into conflict with human reason.

Teaching about the person and work of Christ cannot be penetrated by human wisdom. As Luther points out, "Reason cannot and will not remain within the Word or be captive to it, but it must also give its cleverness a voice, and this insists on understanding and mastering everything."[72] The end result is that faith no longer has any room but must give way to reason and perish.

> But over against all that reason suggests or tries to fathom and explore, yes, against everything that all senses feel and comprehend, we must learn to adhere to the Word and simply to judge according to it, even though our eyes behold how man is interred, furthermore, that he decays and is consumed by worms and finally crumbles into dust. Likewise, even though I feel sin oppressing me so sorely and my conscience smiting me, so that I cannot ignore these, yet faith must conclude the opposite and hold firmly to the Word in both these instances.[73]

The language of faith existing under the form of the opposite recalls the theology of cross. As a knowledge that comes through revelation, it is sometimes counterpoised with the kind of knowledge that comes through human reason. And even as reason cannot remain within the bounds of the word, so faith cannot remain within the bounds of human reason. The knowledge and wisdom of faith thus supersedes the wisdom of the world. It is only in this way that we can be helped.

As Paul preached, and Luther after him: "Christ has been raised from the dead, the firstfruits of those who have fallen asleep. For as by a man came death, by a man has come also the resurrection of the dead" (1 Cor. 15:20–21). Luther continues to teach in this same line as he explains that Christ died and was buried, just like other people. "But He came forth alive from the grave in which He lay and destroyed and consumed both devil and death, who had devoured Him. He tore the devil's belly and hell's jaws asunder and ascended into heaven, where He is now seated in eternal life and glory."[74] After him, we are called "Christians," we receive baptism, and we hear and profess the word. The attacks of the devil are not aimed at us but are really aimed at Christ and his kingdom, for the devil is his enemy. But the devil does harass and weary believers with dogged pursuit so that they might forsake Christ.

> But we will confront him confidently and say: "No, you despicable, vile devil, you will not bring matters to such a pass that I surrender Baptism and the name of my Lord for your sake. If you can defiantly rely on and make an uproar with your death, fire, water, pestilence, and hell, we can defiantly rely on this Lord Jesus Christ, who has vanquished you. He can again destroy you and cast you into hell eternally—as He in fact will do—and wrest us alive from your jaws. Therefore devour us if you can, or hurl us into the jaws of death, you will soon see and feel what you have done. We, in turn, will cause such a great disturbance in your belly and make an egress through your ribs that you wish you had rather devoured a tower, yes, an entire forest. For you previously consumed a Person and put Him under the ground, but He was too strong for you. To your great disgrace you had to return Him although you blasphemed defiantly: 'He saved others; He cannot save Himself, etc.' (Matt. 27:42). But now He defies you in return; He has become your death and hell. And soon He will overthrow you completely through us on the Day of Judgment."[75]

Although Christ was devoured, he now devours the Devourer; Christ experienced death but now his death is the death of Death. Even as the resurrected Jesus tore a hole in the "belly" of the devil, so believers will make a great disturbance in the devil's belly and make a mighty egress through his ribs to freedom in the eternal kingdom. Luther takes great delight in the imagery so loved by the early church fathers, who depicted the victory of Christ as a victory over sin, death, and the devil.[76]

The ability of the believer to remain in holy defiance of the devil is an exercise of faith that places our entire trust in the victory of Christ and his promise—for Christ did not die for himself, but that we might follow after him. The victory of Christ places its claim on the present as well as on the future, and that is what makes the believer bold in the face of opposition. The defiance of the believer is a reflection of the defiance Christ showed in his conflict with the devil, and it aids the believer in embracing the doctrine of the resurrection.

Sermons on the Gospel of John

According to Luther, spiritual trial is an integral part of Christian existence and an essential element in theological formation. But how do we deal with this? Throughout his sermons on the Gospel of John, Luther gives advice and even scripts for believers struggling in various kinds of temptation and degrees of hardship.

Luther began his sermons on the Gospel of John (chapters 14–16) in March 1537, just after his harrowing near-death experience in Schmalkalden. For over three days, Luther was so sick that he was unable to attend the meetings set to receive and discuss the documents outlining the Lutheran faith for the upcoming general council called by Pope Paul III. Since it was thought that Luther was at the end of his life, preparations were being made. As he puts it in a letter to his wife Katie, "I was dead; I commended you, together with the little ones, to God and to my gracious Lord, since I thought that I would never again see you in this mortal life. I felt great pity for you yet had resigned myself to the grave."[77] Miraculously, Luther's health returned and sometime around the month of June, he was back in Wittenberg and preaching through John 14, where we read the words, "Let not your hearts be troubled." In this exposition we find the following comment by Luther:

> It is indeed a real Christian art to distinguish in the heat of battle between the suggestions of Christ and those of the devil. Only one who is experienced will realize the difficulty. For, as I have said, the devil can so clothe and adorn himself with Christ's name and works and can pose and act in such a way, that one could swear a thousand oaths that it is truly Christ, although in reality it is the arch-enemy and the true Arch-antichrist. Therefore if you are a Christian you must learn to conclude from this that anyone who wants to terrify and dishearten you is surely the devil's messenger. For whenever Christ frightens someone away from unbelief and a sinful life into penitence and conversion it is of short duration. Thus He frightened Paul before his conversion, and thus St. Paul, in the name of Christ, frightened the Corinthians and the Galatians. For it is not Christ's purpose to keep you sad; no, in a short time He frees you from sadness and comforts you. The devil does not do this. He does not let a single proud and impenitent person despair or when such a person finally does lapse into terror and fear, as happens in the end to all such, then he deserts him. Even then he does not put an end to his terrorizing but oppresses and distresses him so severely that he must despair eternally unless he is restored by Christ.[78]

In this striking quotation, we find Luther urging upon Christians a particular skill touching upon human experience and the appropriation of the gospel of promise. Discerning between the suggestions of Christ and the devil is at issue. It brings to mind the well-known title in Luther studies, *Luther: Man between God and the Devil*. In his sermons on John we find Luther, on the basis of his personal struggle and experience, instructing believers in how to negotiate the difficult waters of terror, despondency, and temptation.

Luther points out that the opening passage of John 14 shows Christ looking after his disciples. The Lord is concerned with what will happen to them when he is gone. Suffering and the cross will separate them, and the disciples will be left in "peril, fear and terror." Before, they had the comfort and assurance of the Lord's presence. But moving forward, this would not be the case. "Thus Christ, as One well aware of the situation they were to face, wants to fortify and preserve them."[79] Christ's sermon in John 14–16 "contains the most precious and cheering consolation, the sweetest words of Christ."[80]

Although Christ admonished and consoled his disciples, Luther points out, "These words were recorded, not for their sakes, but for ours that we might also learn to apply this comfort to both present and future need."[81] Every believer, when baptized and dedicated to Christ, must expect encounters with terror and anxiety—the kind that make the heart afraid and dejected. As Luther warns, "Therefore if you want to be a Christian like the apostles and all the saints, arm yourself, and be assured that the hour will come when your heart will be terrified and despondent."[82]

The consolation that Christ prepares is on offer to all his disciples in those moments of struggle and trial. Here, Luther places into Christ's mouth the following words for that moment of testing:

> "What are you doing? You surely will not be scared to death and quail because of this! Be of good cheer, and take heart. Even if the devil, the world, or your own conscience plague and frighten you, and even if you do not feel My presence, do you not recall that I foretold this long ago and left this comfort with you to strengthen and to preserve you?"[83]

In this way, Luther wants to build up within believers the ability to apply the consolation of Christ in times of trouble. The Christian needs to understand that "mourning and a faint and fearful heart do not come from Christ."[84]

Luther's argument to this point could be summarized by the well-rehearsed adage, "Preach in such a way as to comfort the afflicted and to afflict the comfortable." Preaching must be tailored to the situation, and the situation varies from person to person. There is a sense in which Luther's teaching on this point focuses on how the words of Christ are actually heard and taken into our consciousness. The smug do not feel terror, for they believe that all is well and that they are righteous. Conversation with God is at a minimum and is decidedly one-sided, reconfirming a static and supposedly benign state of affairs. On the other hand, those who strive to lead a pious Christian life seek to live in such a way that does not bring dishonor to the gospel; they eschew greed, robbery, theft, deceit, and lies. Consequently, they are the ones who can be driven by the wheedling deception of the devil. The threatening and terrifying words of the Deceiver afflict the conscience of the tenderhearted in an attempt to dislodge them from faith. Luther says,

> Now if one could learn to differentiate, then each side would be fairly treated. Christ would comfort those whom the devil wants to frighten and dishearten, and, on the other hand, He would intimidate those whom the devil makes smug and presumptuous. After all, these two must always contend against each other. What the devil ruins and destroys, Christ must build up and restore; and

what the devil establishes, Christ destroys, as we read in I John 3:8: "The reason the Son of God appeared was to destroy the works of the devil."[85]

Another aspect to Luther's argument is how we become skilled artists, able to distinguish between the voice of Christ and the voice of the devil. This is Luther's concern, especially in light of his statement that in the heat of battle there is a real difficulty in distinguishing the one from the other.

In what circumstance is this true? How does Luther describe this battle? Luther is fond of pointing out that Satan is able to disguise himself as an angel of light (2 Cor. 11:14). Three times in rapid succession Luther makes reference to this fact. With his usual flair for description, Luther puts it this way,

> For, as I have said, the devil can so clothe and adorn himself with Christ's name and works, and can pose and act in such a way that one could swear a thousand oaths that it is truly Christ Himself, although in reality it is the archenemy and the true Arch-antichrist.[86]

In such a moment, we are faced with an ambiguity of ominous proportions. Who exactly is speaking, and how can we distinguish the voice of the devil from the voice of Christ? While it is true that Christ uses words of comfort, he also speaks some harsh words in the Gospel accounts. Once again, Luther,

> You say: "Well does not Christ Himself often frighten and threaten us in the Gospel? For example, when He says, (Matt, 4:17): 'Repent!' Or in Luke 13:5: 'I tell you, unless you repent, you will all likewise perish.'" Why, these are Christ's own words, and a faint and saddened conscience must constantly worry lest they pertain to it. It must declare: "Say what you will, Christ Himself makes this statement. Who can ignore it?"[87]

The words of Christ to the rich young ruler could be added to this list, "You lack one thing: go, sell all that you have and give to the poor, and you will have treasure in heaven; and come, follow me" (Mark 10:21b). The demand of the law can be heard in the voice of Jesus, and the law accuses anyone outside of Christ. What can we do? Luther instructs us in the following:

> When he [the devil] attempts to frighten us in the name of Christ, we must always say: "I will not listen now to any terrifying and threatening words; for I know that this is not according to the will and intention of Christ my Lord, who bids me and all believers in Him be of good cheer. Therefore even though Christ Himself does speak threatening and frightening works here and there, I am not to apply these words to myself. For they pertain only to the smug, impenitent, hardened, and wicked scorners of His Word and His grace. Therefore since I am a Christian and a disciple of my Savior, do not try to harass me with these verses. For even though they are Christ's words, you are not quoting them at the right time and at the proper place; nor are you applying them to the person to whom they refer. You are not using the words as Christ does;

but they are being perverted by the lying spirit, the devil, who diverts both the threatening and the comforting words from the group to which they apply, just as he perverts all God's Words and transforms truth into a lie."[88]

The art of distinguishing between the suggestions of Christ and the devil comes with and in the experience, or perhaps we could say it is an agonizing struggle carried out on the battlefield of the conscience. The experienced know that even the words of Christ can be twisted and made to do service to the devil. To quote the words of Christ at the wrong time or the improper place is to not distinguish properly between law and gospel, the word of accusation or the word of promise. The struggle is really one of experiencing the Holy Scripture as it is meant to be heard. This takes place through the testimony and the illumination of the Holy Spirit.

Luther was fond of using direct first-person discourse in his teaching to highlight proper doctrinal distinctions. Casting an issue in the form of a dialogue or an answer for the devil, the world, the papacy, or the Anabaptists depicts a realism and an urgency hard to achieve in more descriptive third-person prose. We have seen examples of direct defiance of the devil. We end this section with a few examples of a slightly different kind.

The first is a passage that shows the stark contrast between the privilege of the Christian and the boasting of the world. The Christian regards as magnificent the ability to comfort and save hearts through the preaching of the gospel and the help extended to others through prayer. The world, however, is attracted to silver and gold and anything that glitters and strikes the eye. Against this, a Christian could defiantly exclaim,

> Good and well, dear world, be rich, and count your guldens! I, a Christian, may have nothing on earth; yet you are indebted to me and my prayer for whatever you own. For my Christ is your Liege Lord; without Him you can possess nothing. And though I may appear to be a beggar in your sight, I still own a great treasure, compared with which all your wealth is not worth a penny. I can help everyone to know where to remain in the hour of death and in every trouble, and to have enough for all eternity. You are far from doing this with all your wealth, your crown, and your splendor.[89]

In this short paragraph, Luther addresses the important question, "Which is the greater treasure, silver and gold or the possession of the gospel?" It speaks to the everyday matter of a Christian's attitude toward wealth and the claims of the world. The answer Luther gives, of course, is that our Christian estate is higher and more glorious than the mere admiration of gold.

In this final example, Luther teaches about the giving of another Comforter (John 14:16), again through words he attributes to Christ:

> This is what you are to look for and expect from the Father and from Me. If, as Christians who believe in Me and hold to Me, you suffer or are assailed, whether it be by the devil or by your conscience, then the Holy Spirit will be

your Comforter and will address Himself to your heart as follows: "Be unafraid, and do not fear; for you are baptized, and you believe in Christ. Therefore you need not be frightened either by the devil with all his angels in hell, by your own thoughts, or by your anxiety about your relation to God. No, do not think otherwise than that God's anger and all hell are totally extinguished. For that is surely true for believers, even though they still feel sin and weakness."[90]

Since the Comforter, together with the Father and Christ, is ours, we have all we should desire. This is reason to let our hearts be glad. Hearing, knowing, and being able to repeat this cheerful word of Scripture is enough to make Christians proficient in instructing their consciences with the gospel.

Luther's use of direct address to the laity is an effective means to teach them. These paragraphs are powerful sound bites that we can easily remember. They are moving and memorable, and they shape our thinking and touch our affections. They are nothing less than scripts for believers that can be used to banish the negative feedback loop that continually plays in our minds, warding off assaults from the devil, blocking the accusation of the law, and reminding us of the glad message of Christ.

Luther's Letters of Counsel for Spiritual Trial

So far we have seen that Luther consistently expresses spiritual trial, or struggle, as an essential aspect of life in the Spirit. We have seen this in his explicit presentation of the three rules in 1539, when he says that spiritual trial is the touchstone that makes Scripture come alive. We have seen how *Anfechtung*, especially in the monastery and his struggle in family life, played out in Luther's personal experience. We have also seen how through his sermons Luther preaches the gospel to the laity, preparing them to deal with reversals in life and contradiction in spiritual matters.

We now have opportunity to take a brief look at some examples of how Luther deals with others in the midst of their own particular troubles and trials. In Luther's time, the art of the rhetorically crafted letter was still in vogue, and Luther proved himself to be adept in employing its subtleties. But not all of the three thousand letters he authored were sophisticated—some were direct and to the point. As we might imagine, much of the correspondence is official in nature. As the dean of the theological faculty, communication via letter was necessary. Luther wrote numerous letters to government officials, the Elector of Saxony, fellow reformers, printers, and even the pope![91] Mixed into this surprising output are also a number of letters of spiritual counsel to friends and acquaintances.

Through the years, the value of these letters has been recognized. The first collection of Luther's letters of spiritual counsel was published shortly after his death, and every generation since has seen the appearance of at least one new collection.[92] These collections tend to vary with the age and its particular interests and points of pressure. The most prominent current collection in English appears in the multivolume collection of the Library of Christian Classics.[93]

Luther's magnificent letters cover a multitude of situations, including comfort for the sick and dying, consolation for the bereaved, encouragement for those dealing with depression, and advocacy for the dispossessed and the refugee. In his letters to magistrates and various rulers, Luther addresses issues ranging from what to do with abandoned monastic properties to the degree that government should be involved in reform. It is well known that Luther played an important role in helping escaped nuns find suitable husbands (including himself!). It is also true that he offered spiritual advice to several who had to make difficult choices regarding marriage in a climate in which views on this important institution were changing.

Elector Frederick the Wise of Saxony (1486–1525) played a crucial role in the early phases of the Reformation movement. When the controversy with Rome escalated, considerable pressure had been put on him to hand over Luther. The elector was reticent to give up his star professor and soon proved himself as an adroit political leader. During the Peasant's War, however, he fell gravely ill and died. Rule then fell to his brother, John of Saxony (1525–32), later known as John the Constant or Johann the Steadfast.

After Frederick's death, Luther wrote to the new elector, addressing him with the official title that rightfully belonged now to John: "Serene, highborn Prince, gracious Lord."[94] In this letter, Luther acknowledges the difficulty of losing a beloved leader in the midst of "perilous times," but he encourages John with a reminder of God's faithfulness. He cites relevant scriptures from the Psalms, reminding John that although afflictions come to the righteous, the Lord delivers. He then rehearses the words of Christ, which often appear in his letters, "In the world you will have tribulation. But take heart; I have overcome the world" (John 16:33). With written clarity and wisdom of his perspective on leadership in God's cause, Luther says:

> This is the school in which God chastens us and teaches us to trust in him so that our faith may not always stay in our ears and hover on our lips but may have its true dwelling place in the depth of our hearts. Your Grace now is in this school. And without doubt God has taken away our Leader in order that God may himself take the deceased man's place and draw nearer to Your Grace, and in order to teach Your Grace to give up and surrender your comforting and tender reliance upon that man and draw strength and comfort only from the goodness and power of Him who is far more comforting and tender.[95]

Luther writes this letter with good reason. In the first instance, it allows him the opportunity to voice his love and appreciation for Frederick, while at the same time affirming John's role as the new elector. More importantly, his words frame the future in the light of God's kingdom and the work of the elector in the midst of the school that "chastens us and teaches us to trust in him so that our faith may not always stay in our ears and hover on our lips but may have its true dwelling place in the depth of our hearts." Luther points out that the exercise of faith is an experiential wisdom that grows in the hothouse of struggle and pressure. This is the bold word Luther offers to his "Serene, highborn Prince." He ends his letter asking for the elector to accept his letter of consolation, hoping he might find more joy in the Psalter and the Holy Scriptures.

Caspar Mueller was the chancellor of Mansfeld and a friend of Luther who had served as a sponsor at the baptism of Luther's oldest child. A few years later, Caspar fell ill, which weighed heavily upon Luther. After expressing his sorrow for his illness, Luther writes how Caspar should glorify and carry in his body him who gained the victory over the world, the devil, sin, death, flesh, sickness, and all evils:

> The exchange is to be accepted cheerfully. He is a good merchant and a gracious tradesman who sells us life for death, righteousness for sin, and lays a momentary sickness or two upon us by way of interest and as a token that he sells more reasonably and borrows at more favorable rates than the Fuggers [bankers] and the tradesmen on earth. Well, then, our Lord Jesus Christ is the valiant man who fights for us, conquers for us, triumphs for us. He is and must be the man, and we must be with him and in him. There is no other way, no matter how much the gates of hell rage.[96]

He then urges Caspar to drink cheerfully from the cup of his difficulties and to bear his misfortune with gladness and singing.

In yet another instance, Luther gave spiritual counsel to Jerome Weller, a young man who began a study of law but through contact with Luther decided instead to study theology. For a period of time he lived in Luther's home and served as tutor for his children. His shy temperament made him susceptible to bouts of depression, prompting Luther to write the following letter to him. Almost all of it is reproduced here to demonstrate the tone of Luther's very personal communication.

Grace and peace in Christ,

My Dear Jerome:

You must believe that this temptation of yours is of the devil, who vexes you so because you believe in Christ. You see how contented and happy he permits the worst enemies of the gospel to be. Just think of Eck, Zwingli, and others. It is necessary for all of us who are Christians to have the devil as an adversary and enemy; as Saint Peter says, "your adversary, the devil, walketh about." (1 Peter 5:8)

Excellent Jerome, you ought to rejoice in this temptation of the devil because it is a certain sign that God is propitious and merciful to you. You say that the temptation is heavier than you can bear, and that you fear that it will so break and beat you down as to drive you to despair and blasphemy. I know this wile of the devil. If he cannot break a person with his first attack, he tries by persevering to wear him out and weaken him until the person falls and confesses himself beaten. Whenever this temptation comes to you, avoid entering upon a disputation with the devil and do not allow yourself to dwell on those deadly thoughts, for to do so is nothing short of yielding to the devil and letting him have his way. Try as hard as you can to despise those thoughts which are induced by the devil. In this sort of temptation and struggle, contempt is the best and easiest method of winning over the devil. Laugh your adversary to scorn and ask who it is with whom you are talking. By all means flee solitude, for the devil watches and lies in wait for you most of all when you are alone. This devil is conquered by mocking and despising him, not by resisting and arguing with him. Therefore, Jerome, joke and play games with my wife and others. In this way you will drive out your diabolical thoughts and take courage.

This temptation is more necessary to you than food and drink. Let me remind you what happened to me when I was about your age. When I first entered the monastery it came to pass that I was sad and downcast, nor could I lay aside my counsel with Dr. Staupitz (a man I gladly remember) and opened to him what horrible and terrible thoughts I had. Then said he: "Don't you know, Martin, that this temptation is useful and necessary to you? God does not exercise you thus without reason. You will see that he intends to use you as his servant to accomplish great things." And so it turned out. . . . Be of good courage, therefore, and cast these dreadful thoughts out of your mind. Whenever the devil pesters you with these thoughts, at once seek out the company of men, drink more, joke and jest, or engage in some other form of merriment. Sometimes it is necessary to drink a little more, play, jest, or even commit some sin in defiance and contempt of the devil in order not to give him an opportunity to make us scrupulous about trifles. We shall be overcome if we worry too much about falling into sin.

Accordingly if the devil should say, "Do not drink," you should reply to him, "On this very account, because you forbid it, I shall drink, and what is more, I shall drink a generous amount." Thus one must always do the opposite of that which Satan prohibits. What do you think is my reason for drinking wine undiluted, talking freely, and eating more often if it is not to torment and vex the devil who made up his mind to torment and vex me? Would that I could commit some token sin simply for the sake of mocking the devil, so that he might understand that I acknowledge no sin and am conscious of no sin. When the devil attacks and torments us, we must completely set aside the whole Decalogue. When the devil throws our sins up to us and declares that we deserve death and hell, we ought to speak thus: "I admit that I deserve death and hell. What of it? Does that mean that I shall be sentenced to eternal damnation? By no means. For I know One who suffered and made satisfaction in my behalf. His name is Jesus Christ, the Son of God. Where he is, there I shall be also."

Yours,
Martin Luther[97]

Luther's thoughts to his friend are direct, bold, theological, and personal. There is an open and honest faith, even a sweetness and joy on display in this intimate exchange. Luther's spiritual counsel is given not from the position of special authority in the church derived from an official position. The authority that beats throughout this letter comes from one who has himself experienced vexation, struggle, and trial. He writes as a fellow sojourner on the path of faith, directing his friend to the one source of help, Jesus Christ.

Luther frames the temptation in terms of the devil, saying he "vexes you so because you believe in Christ." Yet, in the case of Caspar Mueller, Luther said that he was sorry *God* had heaped more sickness on him to try him. So, in Luther's mind, what is the source of temptation and trial? Is it God or is it the devil? The fact is that it is impossible in this world marked by sin to know for sure the exact source of the trial or the temptation. God in his hiddenness looks a lot like the devil. More important for Luther than answering this question is his sure conviction of the decisive victory of Christ that reveals the unconquerable love, the compassionate mercy, and the infinite grace of God— Father, Son, and Holy Spirit. This reality established in the Person and work of Jesus Christ is the catalytic reality and fundamental change that allows—indeed, induces—a change of heart in the believer. On the new ground of the victory of Christ every circumstance in life, whether good or bad, is seen in a new light. Although Luther's world is described as a conflict between Jesus and the devil, it is merely an expression of this underlying truth. This same truth can be described in a more direct biblical way. Scripture teaches that the work of Christ is to overturn the work of the devil. First John 3:8 says, "The devil has been sinning from the beginning. The reason the Son of God appeared was to destroy the works of the devil." Since Luther is firmly focused on Jesus Christ and his victory, it is no surprise that there are times in his theology when the devil appears in his negative role.

Jerome's temptation to despair and blasphemy is an action that threatens to separate him from belief in God. This potential act of despair fulfills the definition of "diabolical" in that it seeks to separate from God. For this reason, Luther is content to say that this temptation is from the devil, and he proceeds to speak of the appropriate tactics to meet the challenge. Negatively, Luther advises Jerome to avoid disputation and evil thoughts—simply leave off! Positively, he is to practice disdaining the devil. "This devil is conquered by mocking and despising him, not by resisting and arguing with him." Contempt of the devil, or the despising of the devil, is a concept we have noted in Luther's sermons and other writings. We see it applied here yet again.

In this letter, Luther advises Jerome to do the opposite of what the devil tells him to do. If the devil says he should not drink, then Luther says Jerome should drink and in "a generous amount." This advice might seem a bit odd on the surface. Is Luther leading this young man, who suffers from depression, to the potentially worse difficulties associated with drinking? Clearly not, for there are lots of places in Luther's writings where he decries drunkenness. The source of

Luther's advice has a different starting point. Not surprisingly, it is the distinction between law and gospel. Christian identity is grounded and rooted in Jesus Christ. Where he is present, sin is overcome and banished. When assaults and accusations of the law drive the believer to depression or despair, the solution is not to conform but to flee to Christ. Instead of agreeing with the devil—who in this instance says, "You are not pious enough"—Jerome is to thumb his nose at the devil and thus live out his true identity in Christ. That is why Luther can say, "We shall be overcome if we worry too much about falling into sin." The point of Luther's words of encouragement is not to help Jerome live up to a vision of popular religious sentiment that was expected of him. That would be to worry about outward action, when in reality it is faith that is at stake. The idea is not to adjust his "religious" life so as to be "proper" and acceptable in suitable society. Luther's letter is a written form of consolation—believing friend to believing friend. It is a preaching of Christ to engender faith so that his friend might live in the Spirit, as opposed to succumbing to the law and to despair.

Jerome found it difficult to hear the gospel in the midst of his vexatious trial, and Luther was well aware of that feeling. There are times when it is impossible for us to preach the gospel into our own ears. In fact, Luther was convinced that it is God's way to make his will known through other human beings. The mutual consolation of the body of Christ is an important source of hearing the gospel in times of need. In this instance, Luther could do for Jerome what he could not do for himself. The living voice of God travels best from one person to another.

The Town of Wittenberg, in spite of its relatively small size, attracted numbers of people, many of whom were students seeking an education at the newly founded university. Interestingly enough, Wittenberg was famous enough for Shakespeare to make passing mention of it in *Hamlet* (Act I, Scene 2). It was natural that there would be an influx of national and international students into the town, but there were others as well, and many of them were in trouble or in need. Luther did what he could to relieve their distress; sometimes that meant interceding with the magistrates, and at other times it meant organizing relief through his own network of friends and acquaintances.

Among the many who appealed to him for help were widows and orphans, exiles from surrounding territories, unemployed workers, underpaid clergy, and monks and nuns who had abandoned monastic life and found it difficult to adjust themselves to secular life. He interceded on behalf of those who had run afoul of the law, for persons whose property had been confiscated, and for those who had lost their means of making a living. He advocated for foreign students, who upon arriving in town found that Wittenberg did not hold up to their expectations. He wrote letters of introduction and tried to find stipends for those who could not stay without aid. He interceded with parents on behalf of their children, and pleaded with women and men on behalf of their respective spouses. He assisted refugees, mitigated the pressure of oppression and persecution, and called upon the authorities to assist in times of famine.

In all of the letters of spiritual counsel that Luther wrote, we find a clear commitment to a ministry of the gospel. Whether it is a matter of inner turmoil and depression, as in the case of Jerome Weller, or whether it is the pressing external needs of a refugee or a foundling, it is all of a piece. Luther's loving concern led him to true evangelical advice—sensitive but never sentimental, positive yet flexible, consistently rooted in the word. His aim was to help hearers grapple with the word of God and to have faith as members of the universal priesthood, exercising the love and patience that come from faith.

The Spirit and Spiritual Trial

While life in the Spirit is not always placid, it is always oriented to the promise of God in Jesus Christ. We have seen how Luther himself experienced inner struggle in one of the most difficult periods of his life, as well as at the time of Magdalene's death. We have also seen how he preached to the laity in such a way that the text of Scripture interprets life and lays bare the reality of God's goodness, in spite of the immediate circumstances that may distract and obscure sight of the gracious God. And we have had a glimpse of how Luther comforted others through his personal and pastoral letters of spiritual counsel. Now we have the chance to hear how Luther describes the role of the Holy Spirit.

One of the striking things about Luther's view is the close connection between the Holy Spirit and human experience. Without the enlightenment of the Holy Spirit, no one could correctly understand the word of God. "But no one can receive it from the Holy Spirit without experiencing, proving, and feeling it. In such experience the Holy Spirit instructs us as in His own school, outside of which nothing is learned but empty words and prattle."[98] Throughout his writings, Luther depicts the "school" of the Holy Spirit as the place to learn experience.[99] The truths of the faith are not abstract but real in the individual history of our lives as Christians. This is not an easy matter, but through trial and struggles of many kinds the work of the Holy Spirit is accomplished.

In his sermons on the Gospel of John, Luther follows the lead of Jesus, who was preparing his disciples for the time when they would no longer see him and would undergo hardship and persecution. Luther is quite certain that trials will come: "Anyone who is deeply rooted and well grounded will often imagine that he has neither God nor Christ. He will feel nothing but death, the devil, and sin passing over him like a violent storm and dark cloud."[100] Here, Luther may be thinking that apostolic trials are greater than those experienced by the average layperson. Yet still, in these moments, believers—whether apostolic or not—are not to fear that they are forsaken: "Such trials and strife are to let us experience something that preaching alone is not able to do, namely, how powerful Christ is and how sincerely the Father loves us."[101]

Once we hear this sermon of Jesus, the Holy Spirit then applies it to our hearts:

Thus this is a sermon not only of words but of experience as well. To be sure, Christ begins with the Word, when He lets us hear the gospel and receive Baptism and the Sacrament. But the devil comes on the heels of this; he assails and hinders us on all sides, in an attempt to check and obstruct the Word. At this point experience must enter in and enable a Christian to say: "Hitherto I have heard that Christ is my Savior, who conquered sin and death, and I believed this. Now my experience bears this out. For I was often in the agony of death and in the bonds of the devil, but He rescued me and manifested Himself. Now I see and know that He loves me and that what I believe is true."[102]

Following Paul (Rom. 5:4–5), Luther makes the point that suffering produces endurance and endurance produces hope—the kind that springs from faith and does not disappoint. In Luther's view, the Holy Spirit is our instructor in the school of experience. He takes the words of Jesus and applies them to the life of the believer so that the goodness of Jesus might be tested and found true in life.

Luther summarizes the role of the Holy Spirit as Comfort, Truth, and Witness. These three biblical terms, with an occasional reference to the third article of the creed, serve Luther well as he paints a vivid picture of the work produced by the Spirit. He is able to do so in a more leisurely manner in the sermons than the more compact theological presentation of the Spirit's work that appears in the Large Catechism.

Comfort is given and granted to Christians and the whole Christian church in and with the abiding presence of the Holy Spirit. Christendom has the promise that the Spirit will teach Christians and bring all Christ's words to their remembrance. The internal work of the Holy Spirit is thus connected and flows out of the external work and word of Christ, keeping the ministry a matter of public record rather than a matter of secret knowledge or self-styled spirituality. The Spirit does not speak or act apart from the word. This is a critical point that Luther makes plain.

> Thus we confess: "I believe in the Holy Spirit and the holy Christian Church." With these words we affirm that the Holy Spirit dwells with Christendom and sanctifies it, namely, through Word and sacrament, through which He works faith in it and the knowledge of Christ. Those are the tools and the means through which He continuously sanctifies and purifies Christendom. This also makes Christians holy before God, not by virtue of what we ourselves are or do but because the Holy Spirit is given to us.[103]

Luther does not want Christians to look for the Holy Spirit above the clouds in heaven, but down here on earth where Christ came to live, die, and rise again for the sake of the church. It is precisely through the word and the sacraments that the Holy Spirit enlightens the heart, creates the knowledge of Christ in faith, and in this way makes sinners pure and holy. Further, the Holy Spirit is present wherever word and sacrament are present, and whoever receives them certainly receives the Holy Spirit as well.

Christian holiness and the comfort brought by the Holy Spirit are achieved as the saving work of Christ is applied to the life of the Christian. In the Large Catechism, Luther says, "Just as the Son obtains dominion by purchasing us through his birth, death, and resurrection, etc., so the Holy Spirit effects our being made holy through the following: the community of saints or the Christian church, the forgiveness of sins, the resurrection of the body, and the life everlasting."[104] Genuine holiness is a gift that comes from God.

Luther celebrates the fact that the Holy Spirit sanctifies the believer and the whole Christian church: "Therefore I am a member of a holy order, not that of St. Francis but that of Christ, who makes me holy through His Word and sacraments." Knowing that this claim would provoke a response, Luther places into the mouth of a monkish saint the following reply, "May God preserve me from such presumption! I am a poor sinner." But Luther goes on to point out that since we are sinful, the Holy Spirit must perform his work in us. He does that in such a way that the believer says, "I am not holy through myself but through Christ's blood, with which I have been sprinkled, yes, washed in Baptism, and also through His Gospel, which is spoken over me daily."[105]

With his characteristic bluntness, Luther speaks against the false humility of the monkish saints:

> Thus there is nothing laudable about that stupid, false, and harmful humility which makes you want to say that your sins prevent you from being holy. That would be a denial of Christ's blood and Baptism; that would deny that you have the Holy Spirit and are a member of the Christian Church, in which we are to assemble for the Gospel, for Baptism, and for the Sacrament.[106]

Luther's observation is that to speak in this way succumbs to a way of thinking about holiness that is undertaken outside of Christ and based on human works. It may have a pious ring about it, heightened by self-deprecation, but it removes Christ's teaching about the Spirit and the Christian church.

In the Gospel of John, the Holy Spirit is referred to as the Comforter (John 14:26; 15:26; 16:7). Luther therefore takes great delight in depicting the Holy Spirit as a Comforter against the evil spirit who rules the world and who tries to terrorize Christians.

> Therefore God has been gracious to us and has given us a Comforter to counteract this spirit of terror—a Comforter, who, as God Himself, is much stronger with His comfort than the devil is with his terror. And now when the devil also comes along with God's Law, advances against your works and your life, and shatters these so thoroughly that even your good works appear to be evil and condemned—an art in which he is a master and an excellent theologian—the Holy Spirit on the other hand, will come and whisper consolingly to your heart. "Be of good cheer and unafraid. Go, preach, do what you have been commanded to do; and do not fear the terrors of sin, death, or the devil, even if these terrors present themselves in the name of God. God does not want

to be angry with you, nor does He want to reject you; for Christ, God's Son, died for you. He paid for your sins; and if you believe in Him, these will not be imputed to you, no matter how great they are. Because of your faith your works are pleasing to God; they are adjudged good and well done even though weakness does creep in. Why do you let your sins be falsely magnified? Christ your Righteousness is greater than your sins and those of the whole world; His life and His consolation are stronger and mightier than your death and hell."[107]

Luther, who has a knack for direct and heartfelt communication, sets forward the joy, freedom, and wonder of the Holy Spirit's presence.

The Holy Spirit is also called the Spirit of truth who opposes false arguments, factions, and anything that would lead us away from Christ. The world cannot accept the Spirit of truth (John 14:17), because it has another truth. Convinced that the world was full of other spirits, Luther was fond of citing the proverb, "Wherever God erects a church, the devil builds his chapel or tavern next to it."[108] He was convinced that wherever the word of God springs up in its purity, the devil ushers in sects, factions, and many false spirits. These factions and sects mimic the church and parade themselves as that which is authentic and to be sought after.

But Christ sends the Holy Spirit, who makes Christians sure about sin, judgment, and righteousness. There is no longer any need for doubt regarding the truth of any article of faith, and the Spirit will make his Christians competent to judge all doctrines. "Thus he will not only make you warriors and heroes, but He will also confer the doctorate on you and call you doctors and masters who can determine with certainty what is true or false doctrine in Christendom."[109] Such is the role of the Holy Spirit that discernment of the essentials becomes clear and judgment in matters of faith and practice have basis.

We know already that Luther affirms the work of the Holy Spirit, who gives us the ability to defend and preserve against the devil's lies and whisperings on an individual level. The struggle can be difficult in those moments, however, because the devil has the power to present his arguments so attractively that it is hard to tell the truth from a lie. But here Luther is referring to making judgments on doctrine—not in the moment of personal attack, so much as in discerning between the devil's tavern and the true church. As Luther puts it, "What would we have done if we had not had this sure conviction, given to us by the Spirit of truth? Who would have had the courage to chide and condemn such great and glorious semblance of truth as found in the papacy?"[110]

It is the confidence that the Holy Spirit gives that allows Luther to critique the position of the Roman Church. They maintain two corollaries that determine the relationship between the Holy Spirit and the Christian church. First, they maintained that Christ declares that the Holy Spirit is with the Christian church and teaches it everything. This is an assertion with which Luther can heartily agree. This is correct and in alignment with the confession of the creed that says, "I believe in the holy Christian Church." The second part of Roman teaching goes on to say that whatever the Christian church decrees is decreed by the Holy Spirit. To this, Luther takes exception.

To think in this way identifies the true church of Christ with historical Christendom and binds the Holy Spirit to the church and its decrees in a manner that restricts the freedom of the Spirit. Luther's concern is that the Roman Church privileges human traditions over the pure teaching of Christ as set forward in baptism, the gospel, and the sacrament. Instead of leading people toward Christ and his word, Luther is convinced they do the very opposite under the pretext of the name of Christ and the Holy Spirit.

> Christ did not say that I must believe and accept every resolution of the pope, the cardinals, and the bishops. He said that I should hearken to the Christian Church, which has the Holy Spirit, who is sent by the Father in Christ's name and teaches nothing but what Christ said. This is to be the church, and I must identify it by these marks.[111]

The apostolic succession of bishops, which the official church claims for itself, does not necessarily imply the succession of truth of the genuine apostolic gospel.

Luther recognizes that no council or gathering of bishops can cite the promise of the Holy Spirit as proof that its decrees are binding and authoritative. Only as the decrees of the church are in accordance with the teaching of Christ and Scripture can they be authoritative and reflect the mandate of the Holy Spirit. In Luther's view, the true church and historic Christendom are thus not identical. The true church is hidden with Christ's Spirit as its ruler. It is not invisible as though it is a Platonic ideal that exists only in theory; it is actual in that the church is where the gospel is preached and the sacraments administered to real people. But it is hidden in that outward forms and official statements do not tell the full story. Only the word conveys God's truth, and this takes place where and when the Holy Spirit works.

Luther is also critical of the spiritualists and enthusiasts. Whereas the Roman Church tied the decrees of the Holy Spirit to the decrees of the church, the enthusiasts claim they have the Spirit and therefore they should be believed. In both cases, a wedge is driven between the word and Spirit. In the case of Rome, the Holy Spirit is tied to the hierarchy and structure of which they have control. In the case of the enthusiasts, there is a disregard for any external criterion falling back rather to an internal mode of action not tied to Scripture. In neither case is the direction of the Holy Spirit corroborated with the teaching of Christ found in Scripture.

Finally, Luther speaks of the work of the Holy Spirit in terms of witness. After the Spirit has comforted and emboldened the mind and understanding of the Christian, one more thing is added. Even as the Spirit is a witness to the work, words, and saving power of Jesus Christ, so also the person of faith is enlisted into the same activity. The process of becoming a witness comes in two phases. The first phase is the internal witness of the Spirit that brings the reality of Christ to Christians in the form of faith, awakening our hearts and stirring our emotions. The second phase is external, in which Christians act as public witnesses to Christ through actions done for their neighbor, the corporate confession of the faith, and preaching of the gospel.

The testimony that results from the twofold witness of the Holy Spirit has parameters defined by the words of Jesus, "He will bear witness about me" (John 15:26). In other words, the witness that the Holy Spirit impels the Christian to undertake is fully Christ-centered. The life and deeds of Jesus Christ are the basis of salvation, not the life and deeds of any other. When we find ourselves being measured by the holy standard of the Ten Commandments in a moment of accusation, we will always come up short. As Luther puts it, "I must and will not remain in Moses' school."[112] In our consciences the law does not rule, only Christ.

The work of the Holy Spirit is to point the Christian away from a consideration of the self to a focus on Jesus. Or, to say it in the distinctive language of Luther, the Holy Spirit leads us from Moses to Christ. The person who has comprehended the testimony of the Holy Spirit is then able to judge doctrine well and to set into proper relationship the law and the gospel. The Holy Spirit aids the Christian in making the distinction that is at the heart of Christian theology.

> There are two types of life and work. The one is my life and work which must be carried out in accordance with the Ten Commandments; the other is that of Christ my Lord, which is recorded in my Creed. My salvation and happiness and all consolation for my conscience depend on the latter. With this differentiation I can meet the devil's attacks on me and say: "May God forgive me if my life does not conform perfectly to the Ten Commandments; but I cling to the life of this Man who died for me, whose Baptism and Sacrament I have received." This does not imply that one should not perform as many good works as possible. But now, when we are engaged in a battle with the devil and our own conscience, there must be no argument about this.[113]

The sermon of the Holy Spirit, with its sweet message and its discerning outcome, is the best way of comforting, strengthening, and instructing consciences for the good of the Christian church.

CHAPTER 5

LIFE IN THE SPIRIT

The great challenge of dealing with Luther and his theology is the expansive and complex nature of his vision. In this present study, our focus has been on the three rules, not as a particular aspect of Luther's thinking, but as a lens through which to see what it means to live before God and neighbor. The three rules Luther sets forward mark out the pathway or method he urges his hearers to follow. Prayer, meditation on the text of Scripture, and the experience of spiritual trial constitute the shape of the life of faith as animated by the Holy Spirit. Life in the Spirit, as conceived by Luther, has its origins in this holographic triad.

After God the Father addresses us through Jesus Christ, our souls spring to life in grateful response. The initiating word comes from without, establishing a dialogue between God and his creation. Prayer stands at the center of this important conversation. Prayer, as an action made possible by the Spirit, is expressed in the new life of faith as an action of the First Table of the Ten Commandments. Prayer undertaken as an action of the Second Table results in our intercession and care for others, and in prayer for the coming of God's kingdom both without and within.

Meditation on the text of Scripture is the foundation or the geography of the Christian life. In Scripture, we find the content, landmarks, and narrative coherence of God's story with Israel and the church. Luther sojourns in the world of the Bible even as he resides in his own world. Perhaps we could say that Luther inhabits his own world best as he finds himself in the scriptural landscape. To meditate on the external words, as well as from the heart, assures us that we will find the meaning the Holy Spirit intends. Meditation, as an action made possible by the Spirit, is expressed in the new life of faith as understanding.

Spiritual trial is the touchstone, as Luther puts it, which provides us with understanding and animates our experience with respect to God's word. With the Holy Spirit fighting on behalf of the believer, the objective and the subjective sides of the faith are forged together. Spiritual trial as an action undertaken with the Spirit is expressed in our new life of faith through endurance, comfort, bold defiance, and, above all, joy.

This final chapter will summarize Luther's account of life in the Spirit by way of a thought experiment using Luther's account of Abraham as a paradigm. Even as God called Abram (as he was originally named) from his original place of residence, so the work of the Spirit in creating faith in the believer is the starting point of our spiritual life. Life in the Spirit is thus a certain kind of coming home, of being at rest. When the word of the gospel is spoken and faith is created, it is in the first instance a matter of the ear and not of the hands. In the preaching of the gospel, the listener hears God's word of judgment and his forgiving will as expressed in Jesus Christ. Only after we realize that our salvation has already been won are we released into the world at the behest of God, who wills the redemption of all things. We go out under God's direction to serve our neighbor in love. This pilgrimage, or holy wandering, is not like its medieval counterpart that is an attempt to accrue merit, but it is an act of worship undertaken in freedom. It is also not geographical in nature, but a pilgrimage that realigns all of life.

Using pilgrimage as one of the overarching metaphors for Luther's account of life in the Spirit, however, may seem to be an unlikely and impractical suggestion. After all, Luther was not a particular fan of medieval pilgrimage, and we can glean from his writings several caustic accounts in opposition to the practice. Could it be that someone who spoke so strongly against the practice of pilgrimage in his own writings should in actuality be an adherent of pilgrimage on some other level?

Without too much effort, we can find passages in Luther where his disgust for certain kinds of piety and religious practices is worn on his sleeve. In his sermons on the Gospel of John, we have one such example:

> Before we had Christ, we were at peace with the devil but at war with God. At that time we ran from pillar to post, through cloisters and churches, on pilgrimages and all the rest, in search of God's peace or a gracious God; and we could not find these anywhere. On the contrary, the more we undertook, the less peace we had. And although we did have external peace with the devil, our hearts and consciences were so dismayed that we were afraid of a rustling leaf (Lev. 26:36) and were ceaselessly chased from one doctrine and work to another.[1]

Here Luther is quite clear that pilgrimages of the literal kind were ambiguous at best and apt to lead to nothing of benefit in our search for God and his peace. Clearly, Luther is not promoting literal physical pilgrimage. Luther, who is well known for his aphorisms and memorable statements, said it this way, "The Spirit does not come through fasting, praying, pilgrimages, running to and fro around the country; no, only through faith."[2]

Luther's trenchant comments regarding pilgrimage were in tension with much lay practice. The laity held pilgrimages in high regard because of the purported benefits accrued through penance, miracles that might possibly touch the pilgrim, indulgences, and the wonder of being in the presence of a venerated saint. The enthusiasm with which many different strata of society undertook pilgrimages to Rome or Compostella speaks of the cultural acceptance of this form of religious expression, even though it was not essential for the practice of Christianity proper.

The cloistered communities denied themselves the possibility of a literal pilgrimage to Jerusalem because of their commitment to their abbey and its ordered daily existence tied to its location. They did this in order to devote themselves more completely to the pilgrimage to the heavenly Jerusalem, eschewing the matter of holy sightseeing as the lower of the two enterprises. The physical city of Jerusalem was, after all, only a place in a world destined to pass away. Since true worshipers were to worship in spirit and in truth, the need to find and sanction a holy place was not critical in Christian teaching, as it was in other religions.

While the differences between lay and cloistered approaches to pilgrimages no doubt played a part in his assessment, Luther's critique goes well beyond that. In reflecting back on an earlier time, he recalls the real issue as touching on the forgiveness of sins. In this excerpt from *Table Talk*, Luther refers to Compostella (Santiago), Spain, where the cathedral of St. James was the destination and where the body of James the apostle is purportedly buried. It was a very popular site for pilgrimages during the Middle Ages and has even come back into vogue in our own time.

> God in his grace promises us the forgiveness of sins, and he adds threats and punishments: "If you don't believe you will perish" [John 8:24]. Before we believed this and accepted it as a free gift, we preferred to torment ourselves to death and went in full armor to St. James.[3]

Luther's reference to full armor may have to do with the full burden of sin a pilgrim would carry as an act of penance on the long and arduous journey, or it may have to do with an added satisfaction. Such an act of devotion, according to the Scholastic reckoning of the time, would most likely merit God's grace in a measure to undo the burden of guilt. Luther's critique amounted to this: If pilgrimage or good works save, then the pilgrim has another savior and has excluded Christ. Luther's assessment of pilgrimage is singularly negative when seen as an expression of the piety of accumulated merit.

But it should be remembered that there are at least three different definitions of pilgrimage. The first is what we have been discussing: a physical journey to a holy site out of devotion or in anticipation of a spiritual blessing or divine intervention. This is an old and common religious practice used in Christianity since early times. Jerusalem is a particularly cherished place for pilgrimage, along with other nearby sites, because Jesus walked there. There were a number of sites across Europe dedicated to pilgrims including Rome, Santiago de Compostella, Aachen, Maastricht, Lourdes, and Canterbury.[4]

The second definition is a spiritual form of pilgrimage. Life is a spiritual journey fraught with difficulties and challenges as the wanderer is caught between this world and the next. This notion of the human wayfarer (*homo viator*) has a long and venerable tradition among Christian writers. Even the Bible is not silent in this matter. For example, 1 Peter 2:11 addresses believers as "sojourners and exiles," and Hebrews 11:13 speaks of a people looking for a better country and a city whose builder and maker is God. Augustine carried this concept into his *De civitate Dei*, where he expresses the idea that the city of God (representing faith) contends with the city of man (representing unbelief) on this earth. Some early church fathers saw in Homer's story of Odysseus an illustration of the voyage of earthly life, beset by deadly encounters while being consumed with longing for a heavenly home.[5] This predates John Bunyan's famous *Pilgrim's Progress* that traces the dangerous path of the main character, Christian, as he moves toward the Celestial City. In our own time, theologians Stanley Hauerwas and William H. Willimon include a similar theme in their book, *Resident Aliens: Life in the Christian Colony*.

There is also a third way in which pilgrimage can be understood: as an inward matter of personal change and growth. A pilgrimage can be a search for our life's mission or an expression of spiritual renewal or discovery. Saint Bonaventure wrote a book titled *Itinerarium Mentis in Deum* ("The Journey of the Soul into God"), in which he describes the stages of the mind's journey toward God. The focus in this instance is on the inward journey and is somewhat speculative in nature, which is what distinguishes it from the other definitions.

In medieval Christianity, physical, mental, or spiritual pilgrimages were encouraged as acts of commemoration and veneration. In the end, there is a sense in which all three definitions have a commonality on a deeper level. Perhaps it is because they are all rooted in a pattern of *homo viator*—the individual who is headed toward some destination or some goal. This sense is deeply rooted in the human psyche and has to do with more than physical (or mental) travel. Meaning comes from outside the human being, and the pilgrim is a wanderer between two worlds.

One problem, however, became acute during this time period. The pilgrim status within the medieval system reveals the Christian suspended between God's future judgment and the past and present expressions of God's mercy and grace. In the past, the Father was merciful by sending his Son to die for the sinful human race. In the present, the grace of God is extended in the sacraments. God's judgment in the future, however, produces grave uncertainty. Luther himself experienced some of the futility of this structure as he made his own pilgrimage to Rome and visited some of the celebrated sites that granted indulgences, and as he wrestled with an even greater problem in the monastery while pondering the uncertainty of the doctrine of predestination.[6]

It might seem logical to assume that Luther's reformational discovery put him at odds with all medieval spirituality that viewed the believer as a pilgrim. After all, Luther was struck by spiritual struggle precisely at the point where he felt suspended between his present hope and fear of future judgment. Luther, as we have seen, discovered that grace was not given alongside the righteousness of God, but through it. The saving intervention of a merciful God, as revealed in Jesus Christ, is freely bestowed on sinners through faith. This reveals the unity of God's judgment and mercy in Christ, and thus the anxious pilgrim status is overcome. And while there is some truth to this depiction, historian Steven Ozment has argued that this oversimplifies both medieval and Reformation theology.[7] Ozment points out that assaults on the *viator* status of the Christian life were not uncommon in the late Middle Ages. This is especially true of those outside Scholastic medieval traditions that tended toward more mystical ways of understanding God. Saint Bernard of Clairvaux presents an order of salvation that consists of four stages of love. In the first stage, the individual knows himself or herself, and love is directed inward and only for the good of the self. As it becomes evident that seeking within the self alone is inadequate, the individual begins to seek God through faith. Although in this second stage the individual begins to know God, it is only through what God gives. In the third stage—through much prayer, meditation, and obedience, and with full participation in the life of the church—the individual comes to the love of God for his own sake. Bernard doubts that it is likely that anyone would attain to the fourth stage in this life—that of the mystical and eschatological union with God in which thoughts of the self pass away as the self knows and loves only God.

It is interesting to note the important position of faith in this process. If we add to that Bernard's ability to see Christ not as a condemning judge but as sweet Savior, then we can appreciate why Luther had special regard for Bernard. Also relevant is Johannes Tauler, who sought to overcome the *viator* status but in a different fashion from Bernard.[8] Tauler emphasizes the unity of the being of God. In the mystical union (*unio mystica*) between God and the Christian, the opposition between past mercy and future judgment is overcome. The parallel with Luther is remarkable. Substitute the mystical union with Luther's concept of a living faith, and then replace Tauler's concept of the unity of God's being with the incarnate Christ, and they both provide ways of surmounting the instability of medieval theology.

As Ozment sees it, the decisive matter lies in Luther's view of faith. Surprisingly enough, it is not because faith alone denies the necessity of good works for salvation. This is beside the point. The real issue is that the *sola fide* (faith alone) suspends the *viator* status of Christian life, while at the same time recognizing that the Christian is simultaneously righteous and sinful. Ozment writes, "This is a position maintained by no medieval theologian, whether Scholastic or mystic, Dominican or Franciscan, Thomist or nominalist."[9]

Luther retains the *viator* status—the idea of the Christian as wanderer or wayfarer. Luther, however, isolates it from the abuses it suffered with the commercial aspects of pilgrimage. In other words, Luther's notion of the wayfarer status is not an action undertaken to complete something missing in a person's nature. To be a wanderer, a pilgrim, or a wayfarer does not mean that we are attempting to do something notable for the love of God or to seek God as an act of piety or self-fulfillment. Nor is it the opportunity to exercise charity to complete a nonsaving faith, as in much Scholastic thought.

Luther's account of life in the Spirit as a pilgrimage is not a pilgrimage as a means of satisfaction for sins or according to the old merit idea of relating to God. Instead, we need to understand Luther's account of the Spirit along the lines of pilgrimage as a journey of faith. The believer at rest means that whatever pilgrimage is undertaken is based on the gift of God in Christ who brought life and the gospel to light. Pilgrimage in this sense is life born out of word and sacrament. This is a pilgrimage that is not self-chosen for the purpose of accruing merit but something else altogether. Pilgrimage is a response to being called by the Spirit into a new existence, or new creation; it is being sent back into the world to take up our place for the greater good of the society. As we will see, Luther perceives this very much along the lines of Abraham, the exemplar of faith.

Abraham's Story of Life in the Spirit

When we turn to Luther's telling of the Abraham narrative in his lectures on Genesis, we find his account consistent with the pattern we saw in his early writings. The unilateral action of God in his mercy, and his speaking that reality into the lives of people, is the source for the new creation. It is the God who speaks (*Deus dixit*) who addresses Abraham the idolater in mercy and pity. He is an idolater deserving of death and eternal damnation. "But in this wretched state God does not cast him away; He calls him and through the call makes everything out of him who is nothing."[10] Luther does not doubt that Abraham may well have had civil virtues, but these virtues are not the reason for God's call. There is nothing in Abraham that compelled God to take this action. "For what is Abraham except a man who hears God when He calls him, that is, a merely passive person and merely the material on which divine mercy acts."[11] As Luther is pleased to point out, in the case of Abraham, the Divine Majesty through his word transforms this idolater into a new human and into a patriarch. Thus we see that the story of Abraham the pilgrim, Abraham the sojourner, does not begin with actions undertaken on the part of the pilgrim to please God, but with a radical transformation of a life not looking for change.

Medieval theology in the line of Gabriel Biel (1420–95), an influential Scholastic theologian, would not have told the story as Luther did. In fact, it would have been quite the opposite. Paul's statement that Abraham was justified by faith—that he was justified by faith alone—cannot be taken at face value. James 2:28 and 1 Corinthians 3:12–14 and 13:13 indicate that the faith that justifies is one formed by love (*fides caritate formata*). While there may not be any inherent power in charity that would produce eternal blessing, according to medieval theology a sinner must have a habit of grace to be received by God. Love does not have a necessary causality, only a conditional causality, but as such it is still infused love that is the real principle of justification. Paul's claim in Romans 4 that Abraham was saved by faith must be taken as a peculiar mode of speech (*modus loquendi*) shaped for pastoral reasons. Given this explanation, it is possible to see the story of Abraham as a perfect example of the theological principle of Biel, who said, "God does not deny grace to those who do what is in them." Abraham did what was in him. He was a virtuous man who attempted to love the God who called him from Ur of the Chaldees, and who by means of his unformed faith did his best. In recognition of the good works performed, he thus merited the infused love that would make his unformed faith saving.[12] So said medieval theology.

Luther's opposition to this interpretation of the doctrine of justification could not have been more complete. Instead of saying that Abraham was accepted by God due to the works exercised by his unformed faith, Luther gives an unexpected answer. God could have chosen someone from among the company of the holy patriarch Shem, someone who had kept true in their worship of him. But God's call came precisely because "Abraham is an idolater and a very great sinner, who worships a God he does not know! The Son of God wants this ancestor in His line of descent to be exalted, just as other ancestors of Christ are noted for their great sins."[13] Luther goes on to explain:

> Why should this be the case? In the first place, in order to show that He is the Savior of sinners. In the second place, to inform us of His limitless kindness, lest we be overwhelmed by our sins and plunged into despair. In the third place, to block the road to haughtiness and pride. For when Abraham has been called in this way, he cannot say: "I have deserved this; this is my work." Even though he was guiltless before men so far as the Second Table is concerned, yet he was an idolater. He would have deserved eternal death had it not been for the call by which he was delivered from idolatry and finally granted the forgiveness of sins through faith. Therefore the statement stands (Rom. 9:16): "It depends not upon man's will or exertion but upon God's mercy."[14]

Telling the story of Abraham brings Luther back to the matter of justification by faith. Abraham is the perfect example of the truth that theology is about the God who justifies the ungodly.

In this sense, all the saints are like Abraham in that they may have the appearance of people who are guiltless as far as the Second Table of the Ten Commandments is concerned, but who nonetheless are deserving of God's wrath. "But when they have been called and enlightened through the Word, they believe, they give thanks to God, they lead a godly life, and they please God—yet in such a way that even then they need the forgiveness of sins."[15] This is the believer at home or at rest. This is the saint who has been forgiven and set at peace with God and has come into the beginnings of what it means to be a new human being.

Abraham in Luther's Lectures on Galatians

In his lectures on Galatians, Luther makes extensive comments on Abraham. In this segment of his writing, Luther builds his image of Abraham on

Paul's portrayal of him. Luther, along with Paul, presents Abraham to us as one who is reckoned righteous through faith. Abraham is honored as one who, in spite of the resistance of reason that always finds a cause to reject God's word, overcomes the opposition and finds himself following in faith through the Spirit. Luther presents Abraham in vivid fashion, and at one point Luther even gives the patriarch a special name: "Abraham the believer."[16]

Paul establishes his case with respect to the gospel using Abraham as an example. He writes in Galatians 3:6, "Abraham believed God, and it was counted to him as righteousness." In an act of theological concordance, Luther adds Romans 4:2 to this Scripture: "If Abraham was justified by works, he had something to boast about, but not before God." And from Romans 4:19–24, Luther writes:

> Without weakening in his faith, he faced the fact that his body was as good as dead, since he was about a hundred years old, and that Sarah's womb was also dead. Yet he did not waver through unbelief regarding the promise of God, but was strengthened in his faith and gave glory to God, being fully persuaded that God had power to do what he had promised. This is why "it was credited to him as righteousness." The words "it was credited to him" were written not for him alone, but also for us, to whom God will credit righteousness, for us who believe in him who raised Jesus our Lord from the dead.

Luther succinctly summarizes the full weight of these Scriptures when he says, "With these words Paul makes faith in God the supreme worship, the supreme allegiance, the supreme obedience, and the supreme sacrifice."[17] Faith, Luther says, is omnipotent; power is of great worth, and it is infinite because it gives God his due. This is something faith does and not human reason. Faith attributes glory to God, regards him as truthful, wise, righteous; in short, it allows God to be God. Faith gives up the lost cause of the human spirit that, out of envy, desires what is above it—namely, to be God. By allowing God to retain his divinity, the believing heart takes up its proper role as a glad and happy creature of God.

When God sets forward the doctrines of faith, however, there is an offense and an affront to human reason that is not yet wedded to faith. Luther sets forward Abraham as a prime example of one who is caught in this strait. When God spoke to Abraham, he did not give him an easy pathway. What, in fact, did God say?

> Things that are impossible, untrue, foolish, weak, absurd, abominable, heretical, and diabolical—if you consult reason. For what is more ridiculous, foolish, and impossible than when God says to Abraham that he is to get a son from the body of Sarah, which is barren and already dead?[18]

The challenge of faith, indeed the supreme form of worship, is to hear the voice of God and to believe. But the word of God plucks up and destroys before it gives new life. It is for good reason that Paul calls the gospel of Christ "the word of the cross." Luther complains that this is not something done by the Sophists and the followers of Erasmus, who measure God's word by human reason.

Abraham, on the other hand, is an example of one who follows in the pathway of belief. "In hope he believed against hope, that he should become the father of many nations as he had been told" (Rom. 4:18). Although struggle was present in Abraham, faith wins out. Abraham is fully a part of Paul's argument in Galatians. As such, Luther deals with the patriarch as an exemplar for every Christian who follows in the pathway of faith. "Abraham the believer" is presented as one who has passed from death to life.

> With the words "Abraham believed" Paul defines and sets before our view an Abraham who is a believer, who is righteous, who has the promise, and who is spiritual, one who is not in error and in the old flesh, one who is born not of Adam but of the Holy Spirit. About this Abraham, renewed by faith and reborn by the Holy Spirit, Scripture speaks and announces that he is to be the father of many nations, and that the Gentiles are to be given to him as an inheritance, when it says: "in you all the nations of the earth shall be blessed."[19]

Even as unbelief is a great sin and a sign of envy against God, in faith we find an incomparable righteousness that attributes glory and honor to God. The blessing of Abraham is not only for himself but for other descendants of faith as well. "From this it follows that the blessing and the faith of Abraham are the same as ours, that Abraham's Christ is our Christ, and that Christ died for Abraham's sins as well as for ours."[20]

This Abraham of faith, and thus of the promise, is to be distinguished from the Abraham of the flesh or of the world. The matter of physical descent is circumvented and rendered null and void. Claiming prerogatives on the basis of being the offspring of Abraham is not a matter of faith but of the law. So it is that Luther distinguishes between two Abrahams: there is an Abraham who does works, and an Abraham who has faith. "The outstanding good deeds of Abraham did not help him to be pronounced righteous in the sight of God; in the same way imitation of the example of Christ does not make us righteous in the sight of God."[21] The Abraham of faith is the exemplar of all who follow this same path in faith. Since Scripture attributes righteousness to Abraham only as a believer, it is faith that is important. Luther presents this both negatively and positively.

Negatively, faith does not correspond to reason and the law. Reason has the ability to see, understand, and use those things that are beneath it. But in the case of God, whose majesty is removed from simple inquiry, reason is entirely inadequate to the task of knowing him. And, although God attaches himself to the word, arrogant reason is not willing to hear that word. According to Luther, arrogant reason denies God's glory, wisdom, righteousness, truthfulness, and mercy. "In short, God has none of His majesty or divinity where faith is absent."[22]

Luther speaks of "the self-righteous, who do not have faith," filling the void with many things. They fast and employ various rituals in an attempt to placate God and his wrath. But these self-chosen works reveal a fundamental misunderstanding and distance from God. Rather than ascribing to God his glory and recognizing him as merciful, they mistakenly consider him as an angry judge who must be placated. "In this way they despise God, accuse Him of lying in all His promises, and deny Christ and all His blessings. In short, they depose God from His throne and set themselves up in His place. Neglecting and despising the Word of God, they select acts of worship and works that they themselves like."[23]

Another way Luther speaks of the absence of faith is in his lively discussion regarding what it means "to do" the law. Here, Luther makes the observation that there are two different ways to approach the matter. A philosophical approach to the question will proceed on the basis of Aristotelian logic, which says that one becomes a virtuous person by doing virtuous deeds. This is not so in theology, for it is not merely the work done but the attitude of the heart of the one doing the work that is important.

> Thus, the "doer of the Law" is not one who becomes a doer on the basis of his deeds; he is one who, having already become a person through faith, then becomes a doer. For in theology those who have been made righteous do righteous things, not as in philosophy, where those who do righteous things are made righteous.[24]

Positively, faith attributes glory to God. "To attribute glory to God is to believe in Him and to regard Him as truthful, wise, righteous, merciful and almighty, in short, to acknowledge Him as the Author and Donor of every good. Reason does not do this but faith does."[25] Faith allows the reality of God to exist and considers him truthful; this in turn begins to root out unbelief, doubt, uncleanness, hatred of God, and the like, which make up the fountainhead of all evils.

Faith corresponds to the promise. The highest honor we can give to God is to hear his word and believe it. So when the promise of God comes to Abraham, as difficult as it is, and he takes it for his own, this becomes an example of living life in the promise. Faith takes the position that arrogant reason used to hold, and faith remains there by having as its object the word of God that directs the believer to reality outside the self where doing the law is made possible.

Faith renews the believer precisely because in faith the believer and Christ are joined. Luther presents to us Abraham, who is reborn and renewed by the Holy Spirit. This is a transformation no less dramatic than that of death to new life. In the following text, we find Luther emphasizing the fact that Abraham grasps Christ through faith:

> We must be blessed solely with Abraham and by his faith in the promise. Therefore it is necessary above all to take refuge in the promise, so that we may hear the sound of blessing, that is, the Gospel. This must be believed. The sound of

the promise to Abraham brings Christ; and when He has been grasped by faith, the Holy Spirit is granted on Christ's account. Then God and our neighbor are loved, good works are performed, and the cross is borne.[26]

As a result of grasping Christ through faith, Abraham enters into the fullness of the Christian life and receives the Spirit; he begins to perform good works, serve his neighbor, and bear the cross. Faith brings Christ and Abraham together. Here, Luther presents Abraham as sharing in the person of Christ through faith.

This idea is confirmed and made more intensive in the quotation that follows below. Here, Luther speaks of Christ and the believer as one person. The *unio personalis* strikes a note that recalls the central impulse of late medieval mysticism—the desire for a direct, personal, and holistic experience of the nearness of God.[27] The idea of the union that takes place between Christ and the believer should not be seen as an exaggeration in Luther.[28] Rather, the idea of union is an important and abiding element in his doctrine of justification.

> But faith must be taught correctly, namely, that by it you are so cemented to Christ that He and you are as one person, which cannot be separated but remains attached to Him forever and declares: "I am as Christ." And Christ, in turn, says: "I am as that sinner who is attached to Me, and I to him. For by faith we are joined together into one flesh and one bone." Thus Eph. 5:30 says: "We are members of the body of Christ, of His flesh and of His bones," in such a way that this faith couples Christ and me more intimately than a husband is coupled to his wife. Therefore this faith is no idle quality; but it is a thing of such magnitude that it obscures and completely removes those foolish dreams of the sophists' doctrine—the fiction of a "formed faith" and of love, of merits, our worthiness, our quality, etc.[29]

There is no doubt that Luther's view of faith includes the idea of the real presence of Christ. Only where Christ is present are sins forgiven; where he is absent they are retained. To be divided from Christ is to live within the framework of the law and to be outside the promise. As Luther puts it,

> It is unprecedented and insolent to say: "I live, I do not live; I am dead, I am not dead; I am a sinner, I am not a sinner; I have the Law, I do not have the Law." But this phraseology is true in Christ and through Christ. When it comes to justification, therefore, if you divide Christ's Person from your own, you are in the Law; you remain in it and live in yourself, which means that you are dead in the sight of God and damned by the Law.[30]

Through faith, Christ and the believer become one. Under the sheltering care of Christ, the believer is safe from the damning ways of the law. This union is not to be divided, for what is at stake is nothing less than salvation.

At this point in the discussion, the mystical elements in Luther's theology cannot be dismissed. Luther's insistence on the union with Christ hearkens back to his *On the Freedom of the Christian*, in which the bride and bridegroom language is prominent. And once again, we are confronted with the fact that Luther is comfortable with some of the concepts and terminology of mysticism.

The Christian mysticism of the premodern West sought an immediate experience of the nearness of God that would seize all of the senses. With the spirit, the imagination, the intellect, and the physical senses enraptured in such an experience, the subject would enter into communion with God. Past obstacles would be swept aside in this all-encompassing moment, and the comforting, joyful, and blessed presence of God would become foremost. In the medieval period, any theology that focused on this experience was designated as mystical theology (*theologia mystica*). The emphasis here is on experiential wisdom (*spiritualis experientia*), and not discursive and speculative elements as it is in Scholastic theology.

Luther stood within the stream of mystical theology, drawing on its various sources. In fact, he goes on record saying that the *theologia mystica* represents the highest and truest form of theology.[31] On the other hand, Luther can bring excoriating critique to mystical theologians such as Dionysius the Areopagite (a first-century Greek convert of Paul's in Athens, who became the first bishop of Athens). Of the Areopagite, Luther urged wariness, saying, "He is more a Platonist than a Christian."[32] This tells us that Luther's relationship to the mystical tradition is nuanced. He learns from the humility theology of Staupitz, but he goes beyond him. He draws from the mystical vision of Tauler, but he distances himself in the end. Berndt Hamm, in summing up Luther's movement through various stages, suggests that Luther actually transformed the mystical tradition in such a way that we can say he founded a new type of Western mysticism.[33]

In the 1531 *Lectures on Galatians*, there are three texts that are particularly interesting because they all speak of or allude to the darkness of faith (*tenebra et caligo est fides*). In the first of these (Gal. 2:13), Luther uses the motif of Moses' ascent of Mount Sinai (Exod. 19; 20:18–21) to give advice to his students on how to properly distinguish between law and gospel. In the second (Gal. 2:16), Luther refers to faith as a darkness in which Christ himself dwells. In the third (Gal. 3:6), Luther speaks of how all devout people enter with Abraham into the darkness of faith.[34]

First, the darkness of faith is used to illustrate the necessity of the distinction between law and gospel. When a believer wrestles with the judgment of God, neither reason nor the law should be consulted. Instead, believers need to rely on grace and the word of comfort that comes through the gospel. Luther instructs his students to take a stand and then urges them in the following way:

> Ascend into the darkness, where neither the Law nor reason shines, but only the dimness of faith (1 Cor. 13:12), which assures us that we are saved by Christ alone, without any Law. Thus the Gospel leads us above and beyond the light of the Law and reason into the darkness of faith, where the Law and reason have no business. The Law, too, deserves a hearing, but in its proper place and time. When Moses was on the mountain speaking with God face to face, he neither

had nor established nor administered the Law. But now that he has come down from the mountain, he is a lawgiver and rules the people by the Law. So the conscience must be free from the Law, but the body must obey the Law.[35]

The context for this ascent into the darkness is Luther's explication of the doctrine of justification and the distinction between law and gospel. If faith and the gospel are to be kept inviolate, then reason and the law must be kept far away. This is true, because in the temptations of sin and death, neither reason nor the law rely on the righteousness of faith. In a discussion regarding justification, there is no room for speaking of the law. The sole matter that counts is the gift given in Christ. The Christian is pronounced righteous by faith alone, not by the works of the law or by love.

Luther reminds his hearers that when Moses was on the mountain speaking with God face to face, the law had not been given and was not being administered. In fact, it would never be used on the mountaintop, only down below. In the valley, where all the work is done, the law applies to the individual and to society as a whole. In a bit of shorthand, Luther can refer to the law with all its demands and burdens as the quintessential beast of burden, the donkey:

> But when you ascend into heaven, leave the ass with his burdens on earth; for the conscience has no relation to the Law or to works or the earthly righteousness. Thus the ass remains in the valley; but the conscience ascends the mountain with Isaac, knowing absolutely nothing about the Law or its works but looking only to the forgiveness of sins and the pure righteousness offered and given in Christ.[36]

Luther uses the language of ascent in order to teach the "deep" things of the faith. (I am sure Luther would forgive us the paradoxical reference here; perhaps he would even approve!) It is not the process of affirmation and negation on its way to an experience of God apart from the Word incarnate that is highlighted, as it would be in Dionysian mystical theology, but rather it is the gospel of the Son come in the flesh that leads us into the cloud where neither the law nor reason have a voice. The assurance of salvation comes in the darkness of faith that relies on faith rather than sight (2 Cor. 5:7).

Luther's second text is set in his exposition of Galatians 2:16, where he ranges widely over topics on the relation of faith and love. Central in this regard is the Scholastic understanding of *fides formata charitate*, or faith formed by love. Scholastic teaching asserts that faith alone is not saving. One might have faith, but if it stays unformed, then one remains in a state of mortal sin. For the Scholastics, love must add its living colors to complete faith for salvation to take hold. Formal righteousness comes with acts of love. For his part, Luther argues that "faith takes hold of Christ. . . . He is the form that adorns and informs faith as color does the wall." In this view, faith is not idle nor is it "an empty husk in the heart."

But if it is true faith, it is a sure trust and firm acceptance in the heart. It takes hold of Christ in such a way that Christ is the object of faith, or rather not the object but, so to speak, the One who is present in the faith itself. Thus faith is a sort of knowledge or darkness that nothing can see. Yet the Christ of whom faith takes hold is sitting in this darkness as God sat in the midst of darkness on Sinai and in the temple. Therefore our formal righteousness is not a love that informs faith, but it is faith itself, a cloud in our hearts, that is, trust in a thing we do not see, in Christ, who is present especially when He cannot be seen.[37]

Here, Luther confesses that Christ is present in faith, but he does not say how or in what way Christ is present. Moses was not allowed to look directly upon God, but only as he passed by (Exod. 33:20–23); likewise, Christ is present in faith but in the mystery of the darkness and cloud. The Finnish School of Luther interpretation views the theme of the reality of Christ in faith as central to the doctrine of justification by faith and has pointed out its affinities with the Eastern Orthodox doctrine of theosis.[38]

In this passage, we find Luther referencing God as he "sat in the midst of darkness on Sinai." He speaks of faith as "a cloud in our hearts" and "darkness that nothing can see." It would seem Luther has brought us back once again to that critical place of Sinai that elicits cognition of divine transcendence, human weakness, and the darkness or hiddenness of the cloud. Luther does not use this language in a Dionysian manner. Luther leads with faith and its importance. Sure trust and acceptance in the heart takes hold of Christ so that he is not an object as such (for how can God in the proper sense be an object?), but is "the One who is present in the faith itself." According to Luther, Christ is the form and the content of faith, and this is why faith alone is saving.

Luther says that the Christ whom faith takes hold of is present in hiddenness. Here, Luther alludes to the presence of God on Sinai and in the temple and the mystery of that presence. Luther conveys the hiddenness of Christ by saying he sits in darkness comparable to Sinai. Dionysius would speak of the "darkness of unknowing"—that is, the experience beyond word or logic in which we experience the darkness as God absent and incomprehensible (*absconditus et incomprehensibilis*). Here, however, Luther points to a divine hiddenness due to the "clothing" of God in the incarnation; it is a circumstance in which God is not seen but heard.[39] For Luther, God is not absent and incomprehensible, but he is present or near in hiddenness. The matter of Christian spirituality is thus not controlled by a humanly constructed ascent toward God, but by a divinely chosen descent in love in the person of his Son to claim his creation.

Luther's third passage appears in his explanation of Galatians 3:6, "Abraham believed God, and it was counted to him as righteousness." In this passage, Luther emphasizes the opposition between faith that accepts the word of God and human reason that is unwilling and unable to receive it. Faith, as it grasps Christ, is a victory over reason, especially in matters that defy worldly logic such as the incarnation of the Son of God, the virgin birth, and resurrection.

Thus all devout people enter with Abraham into the darkness of faith, kill reason, and say: "Reason, you are foolish. You do not understand the things that belong to God (Matt. 16:23). Therefore do not speak against me, but keep quiet. Do not judge; but listen to the Word of God, and believe it." Thus devout people, by their faith, kill a beast that is greater than the world, and so they offer a highly pleasing sacrifice and worship to God.[40]

Faith as the highest form of sacrifice and worship displaces reason and thus slays it.[41] In fact, Luther can say that faith "consummates the Deity; and, if I may put it this way, it is the creator of the Deity, not in the substance of God but in us."[42] A negative way of saying the same thing can be found in one of Luther's more colorful comments, "As soon as reason and the Law are joined, faith immediately loses its virginity."[43] Faith that partners with something more than Jesus Christ alone denies Christian righteousness.

Luther celebrates the sacrifice of faith begun in Abraham, but he asserts that it had only a beginning in this life. While faith begins to give God his due, it is imperfect and so vacillates, and at times is weak. "We have received the first fruits of the Spirit, but not the tithes. Nor is reason completely killed in this life. Hence, lust, wrath, impatience, and other fruits of the flesh and of unbelief still remain in us."[44] Thus it is necessary for God to cover the remnant of sin for the sake of Christ. That is how Luther understands Paul as he says, "Abraham believed God, and it was counted to him as righteousness" (Gal. 3:6).

The righteousness of Christ imputed through faith reveals a contradictory or paradoxical fact: a Christian is righteous and a sinner at the same time (*simul iustus et peccator*). The darkness of faith protects the Christian from considering the works of the law in the matter of salvation. Not only that, but the darkness of faith cuts short any attempt to place trust in good works as well. The idea of Christ present in the darkness of faith therefore works in two directions: on the one hand, it comforts those who despair of living up to the demands of the law; and on the other hand, it disarms any claim of those who falsely imagine they have something to boast about.

As we have seen, Luther's presentation in his Galatians lectures features Abraham the believer, the exemplar of faith. Abraham is granted a venerable spot in the minds of the apostolic writers and in Luther's thinking as well. He could very well be called the second father of the race. Luther portrays the alien or Christian righteousness of Abraham in multiple ways: as one to whom faith is reckoned as righteousness, as the two Abrahams (one of faith and one of works), and as the Abraham of mystical experience. Abraham's ascent into the darkness is not the action of religious aspiration, from uninitiated to initiated, but it is an escape from all self-virtue to the grace of Christ. Faith is the passive experience of being led along the pathway of Christ and his cross. As such, Abraham claims nothing for himself; in fact, he cannot even consider the spiritual virtues his own. All of this shows him as one who has nothing but who is justified by God.

Abraham in Luther's Lectures on Genesis

As we have seen, Luther moves quickly in his exposition of Genesis 12 to establish the doctrine of grace over against the worth of merits and works. Before Abraham was called, he may well have been an honorable man in civil virtues, but he was an idolater and not even one of the priests of his religion. Even though he is in this wretched state, God does not cast him away but calls him and through that call makes everything out of him who is nothing. God brings about something from nothing. "Abraham is merely the material that the Divine Majesty seizes through the Word and forms into a new human being and into a patriarch."[45]

It might seem curious that God would choose someone who is an idolater and has no particular standing among his people to be placed in the genealogy of the coming Savior. After all, this is someone who does not even know the God he worships. To this, Luther answers, "The Son of God wants this ancestor in His line of descent to be exalted, just as other ancestors of Christ are noted for their great sins."[46]

> Why should this be the case? In the first place, in order to show that He is the Savior of sinners. In the second place, to inform us of His limitless kindness, lest we be overwhelmed by our sins and plunged into despair. In the third place, to block the road to haughtiness and pride. For when Abraham has been called in this way, he cannot say: "I have deserved this; this is my work."[47]

Once Abraham is established on this footing of grace and faith, Luther then builds the Abraham of works into the subsequent narrative. In the first few pages of his discussion of Abraham, he produces out of his rhetorician's bag a string of three memorable tags that he places on Abraham. These titles are impressive as they push Luther's theological argument forward, and they are memorable as they fill in a picture of the diverse range of vocational expressions that Abraham embraces.

In contrast to a works-oriented monasticism, Luther calls Abraham "our own monk."[48] Two things indict the monastic orders in Luther's view: first, they proceed without any word in a kind of manufactured religion; and second, they maintain that an outward change will bring about a change in the heart. Abraham, on the contrary, has a word from God that mandates and directs his course of action. First, he forsakes everything in true faith on the basis of the word of God. Second, he was not justified because he forsook everything. He had already been justified when he believed the promise of God. "Therefore he heard the Word and believed the Word; and later on, after he had been justified thereby, he also became a righteous doer of works by wandering about and following Christ, who had called him."[49] The monks reverse the order that Abraham follows. That is why Luther rejoices in calling Abraham "our monk," for his example is far better.

The second title Luther uses for Abraham is "exile." After tracing the toil and the hardships that accompanied the many moves the patriarch makes, Luther says that he is a wonderful example of someone who undertook the journey only by his trust in the mercy of God. He adds that the extraordinary works of the saints are "stinking filth in comparison with the works and faith of our sojourner or exile."[50] Abraham journeys without knowing where he will be allowed to make a home. "It is, therefore, an admirable example of faith that the holy man does not become weary but continually comforts himself with the Word of the Lord, relies on it, and does not think that what God has once promised is futile."[51]

The third title Luther gives Abraham is "bishop" or "priest." Luther gives this title to Abraham when he builds an altar on the site where the Lord had appeared to him (Gen. 12:7). "Abraham builds an altar; that is, he himself is the bishop or priest, and he himself teaches the others and gives them instruction about the true worship of God."[52] "Therefore we shall call these companions of Abraham not simply his household but the true and holy church, in which Abraham was the high priest."[53] In this church, Abraham instructed, prayed, and preached. Abraham's companions followed their holy head of the household rather than forfeit the promise, even though they possessed it only in hope.

These three titles clearly do not exhaust the riches of Luther's exposition on Abraham. But they do indicate a trajectory for what the account of Scripture sets forward, and they provide some small indication of the manner in which Luther handles the text. From the starting point of justification, Abraham is presented as the exemplar of faith. He begins his journey with an act of leaving his homeland and becoming a sojourner and a wanderer with only God's word to sustain his actions and his resolve. He lives before God on the basis of the promise and before men with his actions. In all of this, we see faith under trial. Abraham becomes an example of how these two realities can exist in a life of faith. And there is no episode in Abraham's life that exemplifies the struggle of faith like his call to sacrifice Isaac.

In this dark and difficult story of the sacrifice of Isaac, Luther sets forward the holy patriarch Abraham as he undergoes an incredible trial. Luther is at his narrative finest as he paints in full colors what Abraham had to endure. Precisely as one who received everything graciously at the hands of God, Abraham knows he owes everything to God in return. In this account, we find Abraham responding in the obedience of faith to the word that had come to him from God. And if ever there was an example of disbelieving while believing, this is it.

Luther begins the story with Abraham in good spirits, "happy and confident," "altogether carefree,"[54] and taking joy in his grown son Isaac. The conflict with Ishmael is long since over, and Abraham's hope of an heir rests on his miracle son, Isaac. But then everything changes when God calls Abraham to a test. "Take your son, your only son Isaac, whom you love, and go to the land of Moriah, and offer him there as a burnt offering on one of the mountains of which I shall tell you" (Gen. 22:2).

Luther personalizes the storytelling of the great love both parents have for their son. Their old age has been blessed and made secure by the promise of God and this special birth. He even adds details about how Abraham and Sarah entertained pleasing thoughts about the marriage of their son. But all these plans are "upset and confounded by a single word, namely, by the Lord's command to Abraham to take his son and sacrifice him."[55]

> Therefore Abraham's heart was wounded far more deeply now than previously, when he cast out Ishmael. But it is impossible for us to comprehend the greatness of this trial. The reason is that Isaac had the promise of the future blessing. Therefore the command to kill him was all the more painful.[56]

Even though it is impossible for us to comprehend the greatness of this trial, Luther does his best to set the matter before his students and readers, sharply stating the problem.[57] According to Luther, what Abraham faced was nothing short of a contradiction of Holy Scripture. "Here God is clearly contradicting Himself; for how do these statements agree: 'Through Isaac shall your descendants be named' (Gen. 21:12) and 'Take your son, and sacrifice him'?"[58]

In this situation, it is inevitable that murmuring should arise and fill the heart. Luther thinks alongside Abraham as he squirms under the pressure of the circumstance:

> This is not a command of God; it is a trick of Satan. For God's promise is sure, clear, and beyond doubt: "From Isaac you will have descendants." Why, then, does God command that he should be killed? Undoubtedly God is repenting of His promise. Otherwise He would not contradict Himself. Or have I committed some extraordinary sin, with which I have deeply offended God, so that He is withdrawing the promise?[59]

Luther helps us feel Abraham's pain. In fact, it is as though Luther is the friend at the shoulder of Abraham, interpreting his thoughts to us. Luther fills in the gaps left by Scripture. He adds the emotional side of this human story. He makes Abraham live again so we can experience what he experienced.

The trial of Abraham is no small matter; it is spiritual struggle of the deepest kind. Luther tries to put into words just how expansive the matter really is:

> This trial cannot be overcome and is far too great to be understood by us. For there is a contradiction with which God contradicts Himself. It is impossible for the flesh to understand this; for it inevitably concludes either that God is lying—and this is blasphemy—or that God hates me—and this leads to despair. Accordingly, this passage cannot be explained in a manner commensurate with the importance of the subject matter.[60]

Abraham is hemmed in. The contradiction of the Holy Scriptures may present him with an intellectual impasse, yet that intellectual impasse does not remain merely intellectual but ultimately leads to an existential crisis. The accusation of the conscience rises up—first to the offense itself. "God, how can you tell me to kill my only son when he is the one through whom my descendants are to be named? This makes no sense. This seems to be a trick of the devil." Next, Abraham feels the rising objection within himself in a visceral sense and as a murmuring in the heart. "There is no way out! The lights have gone out, and there is no way to see forward." Abraham finds himself between despair and blasphemy, for reason can arrive only at one of those two answers. Abraham is in the dark about God's intention, and he sits in the dark cloud of faith:

> But in this situation there is need of the fervent prayer that God may give us His Spirit, in order that the promise may not be wrested from us. I am unable to resolve this contradiction. Our only consolation is that in affliction we take refuge in the promise; for it alone is our staff and rod, and if Satan strikes it out of our hands, we have no place left to stand. But we must hold fast to the promise and maintain that, just as the text states about Abraham, we are tempted by God, not because He really wants this, but because He wants to find out whether we love Him above all things and are able to bear Him when He is angry as we gladly bear Him when He is beneficent and makes promises.[61]

Luther personally testifies that he is "unable to resolve this contradiction." Although Luther had not endured the same spiritual struggle as Abraham, he did have a similar experience. Here, he makes a statement about the very nature of these kinds of events. When God's promise is in jeopardy, the believer is cast back on prayer through the Spirit, clinging to the promise in the midst of spiritual struggle. In this case, Abraham is left without hope, confronted only with a contradiction. "And God, who formerly seemed to be his best friend, now appears to have become an enemy and a tyrant."[62]

Luther submits that Abraham is actually being more severely tried than Mary when she lost her young son Jesus in Jerusalem! This is a trial of patriarchal proportions where God seems to be speaking in earnest, and in such a way that the promise itself is challenged. This is what Luther means when he speaks of "a contradiction with which God contradicts Himself." Surely Abraham did not know he was being tested, for in those moments God only seems to be angry. He is doing a strange work (Isa. 28:21) and only simulates anger in order to work mortification in the believer for the believer's good.

In narrating the events of Abraham's fateful trial, Luther never tires of coming back to the real problem—namely, the contradiction of the promise.

> Human reason would simply conclude either that the promise is lying or that the command is not God's but the devil's. For there is a plain contradiction. If Isaac must be killed, the promise is void; but if the promise is sure, it is impossible that this is a command of God. Reason cannot do anything else, as experience shows in less important matters.[63]

Luther never minimizes the difficulty and the strain of the circumstance. In fact, he goes to great pains to help his readers empathize with the natural human emotions such a circumstance might evoke.

At the same time, Luther marvels at the faith of Abraham, for he keeps counsel within himself. He follows the word of God in simple obedience. He does not delay in carrying out the instructions, and he does not argue.

> Therefore his faith shines forth with special clarity in this passage, inasmuch as he obeys God with such a ready heart when He gives him the command. And although Isaac has to be sacrificed, he nevertheless has no doubt whatever that the promise will be fulfilled, even if he does not know the manner of its fulfillment. Yet he is also alarmed and terrified. For what else could the father do? Nevertheless, he clings to the promise that at some time Isaac will have descendants.[64]

As Luther points out, Abraham relies on the attributes of the Divine Majesty and the fact that he can restore his dead son to life. If God can bring forth from a barren woman and an ancient man the son of promise, then surely this slain son can be restored again.

> Accordingly, Abraham understood the doctrine of the resurrection of the dead, and through it alone he resolved this contradiction, which otherwise cannot be resolved; and his faith deserves the praise it receives from the prophets and apostles. These were his thoughts: "Today I have a son; tomorrow I shall have nothing but ashes. I do not know how long they will lie scattered; but they will be brought to life again, whether this happens while I am still alive or a thousand years after my death. For the Word declares that I shall have descendants through this Isaac, even though he has been reduced to ashes."[65]

Abraham's resolution to the contradiction comes in the form of faith that reaches above and beyond what he can see. The promise of the resurrection of the dead is not obvious to reason. It certainly is not an experience confirmed from everyday life. Faith, however, clings to the promise and is not drawn away from the fact that it is true and dependable.

Abraham experienced the contradiction in the most direct and forceful way. This was not a matter of speculation, but a matter of life and death. Yet Abraham believed God, even though he could not see God's promises. At the last moment, when Abraham had taken up the knife to slay his son, the angel of the Lord called out telling him not to lay a hand on the boy. In an instant, the long ordeal that caused Abraham to die seven times over was done. One can only imagine the deafening silence in his ears, the swelling relief in his heart, and the newfound energy of his hand that quickly replaced the knife to its sheath. The struggle was over, and the ram caught in the thicket became the substitute and sacrifice.

While Luther may be an expositor of the text, at the same time he is retelling the story for the edification of his audience. As he puts it, "These trials of the saintly patriarch have been set before us in order that we may be encouraged in our own trials."[66] Luther does not try to separate the life of Abraham from the life of every believer, even though this was a trial like no other. He is not taken up with the demands of what we would call scientific objectivity. He would no more think to treat Abraham in that way than to treat Jesus as a mere object of intellectual pursuit. But he sought to give a faithful and accurate account of the message of the gospel contained in the word. The Holy Scriptures are the world in which Luther operates—the holy geography of his fertile mind. These are his people. Luther takes Paul seriously when he says, "But the words 'it was counted to him' were not written for his sake alone" (Rom. 4:23). Luther moves back and forth seamlessly from exposition of the Abraham narrative to what this means "for us."

Luther's exposition goes from the text to himself and back again. The rich tapestry of Abraham's life becomes the canvas of his exposition. In Abraham, Luther recognizes the conflicts, contradictions, and joys of his own life. To gaze through the eyes of this saintly patriarch reveals the pathway of the cross, a pathway that makes space for faith.

If we were to distill the vigorous, theological, emotive, and at times enrapturing exposition of Abraham given to us by Luther, the following items stand out. In the *Lectures on Galatians*, Luther single-mindedly and voluminously sets forward Abraham, the one reckoned righteous through faith. Justification by faith is thoroughly explored as Luther describes his subject as "Abraham the believer," "the two Abrahams—the one of faith and the one of works," and "the Abraham who enters the dark cloud of faith where Christ is present, especially when he cannot be seen." In the Genesis lectures, Luther presents us with Abraham who is reckoned righteous through faith and who kept faith in the midst of trials. Here, Luther is afforded more opportunity to depict Abraham in his vocation: among other things, he sets him out as a peacekeeper when a dispute arises between his men and the men of Lot, as a priest as he intercedes for others, as someone who deals with kings, and a prince who has responsibility over an extended camp of people and flocks. Over the course of his life, Abraham did many things; but the shape of his theological existence consisted in prayer, meditation, and spiritual struggle.

Abraham as Practitioner of the Three Rules

Abraham was called out of Ur of the Chaldees to a place that he knew nothing about, with nothing to rely upon except God's word. His great trial of faith required him to listen to the voice of God and be led to a foreign land rather than follow his own path. By the obedience of faith, "Abraham gave a supreme example of an evangelical life, because he left everything and followed the Lord."[67] Preferring the word of God to anything else, and regarding it as more important than anything else, he became a stranger and a wanderer subject to the dangers of the journey.

Luther deals with Abraham as one who exercises faith, who clings to the promise, and who through trial is practiced in prayer and meditation. The "saintly patriarch," as Luther liked to call him, is used as an exemplar of the faith to teach the people under Luther's own care. It should come as no surprise, therefore, that Luther presents Abraham as a practitioner of the three rules.

Mary Jane Haemig highlights Luther's use of Abraham as a means of understanding and practicing prayer:[68] "In the Genesis lectures Luther saw prayer as a key element in the lives of the patriarchs and matriarchs and used their examples to teach prayer in his time."[69] As early as 1520, fifteen years before his Genesis lectures, Luther extolled Abraham's petition to God on behalf of the people in the cities of Sodom and Gomorrah, which were set for destruction.

Although prayer is not the central focus of the Genesis lectures, we still find memorable comments that demand attention. For example, Luther asserts that God is able to give far more than we think. "Therefore God's title and true name is this, that he is a hearer of prayers. But we the petitioners are called those who do not know how to pray or what to pray for."[70] The human heart is uncertain and deterred from approaching the infinite and eternal God. Venturing to ask God is risky.

> Such are truly the sentiments of all human beings. Yet we must learn that we should pray even in the most desperate evils and hope for the unexpected and the impossible. And it is for this reason that those examples of the holy patriarchs are set before us. They show that the patriarchs too were afflicted by sundry cares and trials and yet received more good than they either understood or had been bold enough to ask for.[71]

We are not to be hampered either by the grandeur of the One who bestows or by the unworthiness of the one who prays. "For we have a God who is able to give more than we understand or ask for."[72]

The Genesis account records for us Abraham's bold prayer for Sodom and Gomorrah, which were under the judgment of God. With "fervor and driving emotion,"[73] Abraham presents his case before the Lord. Animating his advocacy for the people, including women and children, Abraham asks, "Will you indeed sweep away the righteous with the wicked?" (Gen. 18:23). In an exchange unmatched in all of Scripture, Abraham implores God to save the cities if fifty who are righteous are found in them. God agrees that for the sake of fifty righteous people, the cities will be spared. In humility, Abraham persists and approaches the Lord six times, hoping to reduce the number until finally it stands at ten. For the sake of ten who are righteous, God agrees that the cities will be spared. The rhetorical power of the story builds as Abraham's entreaty is repeated six times for each expression of the mercy of God. Abraham becomes an example for us of someone who is persistent in prayer. Although he did not know the outcome in advance, he was bold to pray on behalf of others even when the prospects looked bleak.

In commenting on this passage, Luther heaps up a number of descriptions. He says it is a "foolish prayer," because Abraham almost speaks as though God does not know how to make a distinction between the righteous and the unrighteous. On the other hand, it is a "forceful and impulsive prayer, as if Abraham wanted to compel God to forgive."[74] Abraham knows that the cruelty so characteristic of tyrants, who destroy in order to indulge their wrath, does not apply to God. This is what causes Abraham to become anxious as he considers the possible destruction of so many. On the basis of the goodness of God, Abraham is bold to pray and he does so with great emotion of heart. "Shall not the Judge of all the earth do that which is just?" (Gen. 18:25).

Not wanting to waste any teaching opportunity, Luther uses this prayer of Abraham as an example. We have seen that Abraham appeals to the justice of God, but Luther also tells us that he prays and does not stop because of his ardent love for "very wicked people."[75] We see Abraham interceding on behalf of others in a priestly manner, not because it is a religious act, but because it reflects his status as one called by God, who was given a certain promise and is now sent back into the world. Luther points out, "Prayer must be bold. Therefore Abraham continues to pray."[76] "Consider this example whenever you pray, and learn that persistence is needed in praying. It does not offend God; it pleases Him."[77] Abraham is one who practices prayer and is an exemplar for bold, persistent prayer.

Luther also depicts Abraham as one who meditates on the word of God. In this case, Abraham is not seen poring over a biblical manuscript with a lexicon in hand. The word of God that has come to Abraham is a spoken word, given in his encounters with the Almighty: in his calling to leave his country and the promise that he would be made into a great nation (Gen. 12); the covenant renewal with a promise of a son (Gen. 15); and again in the covenant confirmation, the giving of the sign of circumcision, and the changing of Sarai's and Abram's names (Gen. 17). Abraham's call and receipt of the promise shape his life dramatically. Once he hears and believes the promise, everything about his life changes. We find that at every point, God's promise speaks into his life, and it continues to be a lodestone as Abraham continues his saintly wanderings.

In his retelling of Genesis 17, Luther points out that it was on account of the promise that Abram's name was changed to Abraham and Sarai's name to Sarah. Also on account of the promise, Abraham will be called by the new name of "father" due to the explicit promise of a son through his wife. The promise of a son to a couple of old age past childbearing years is more than shocking. As Luther puts it, "What this story sets forth is analogous to the resurrection of the dead."[78] The reiteration of this promise also conditions the role Ishmael will play as it continues to shape Abraham's thinking and acting. "Therefore it is a most extraordinary account. In it we must direct our attention chiefly to the

Word of God. Here God speaks with Abraham at such length and so intimately that the reader is compelled to forget the Divine Majesty and to think of a guest or an intimate friend."[79]

But more importantly from Luther's point of view, the promise extends well beyond what Abraham will see in his lifetime. "Moreover, it must be noted especially that these promises include Christ Himself, yes, eternal life, even though they appear to be speaking not of Christ but of Isaac."[80] While God's promise to Abraham may have been temporal in its immediate manifestation, it points to something more. Luther says this is "like a nut which covers the kernel, namely, Christ and eternal life. When Christ comes, the shell or hull in which the kernel is enclosed is broken, that is, the temporal blessing comes to an end, and the spiritual blessing takes its place."[81] Luther follows the thinking of the apostle Paul, who says, "And if you are Christ's, then you are Abraham's offspring, heirs according to promise" (Gal. 3:29). So we see that God's promise determines the course of Abraham's life with its cares and concerns, as well as the certainty it produces. Abraham's wrestling with and believing in the promise is his lifelong meditation on God's word with its trials and comforts.

Luther also portrays Abraham as living through the struggles of life in faith. Abraham is no stranger to spiritual trials. We have only to be reminded of his conflict with Lot and the dividing of their property, his fear that the promise would be diverted away from his offspring to his servant, the story of Hagar and Ishmael, and the trial he experienced in the call to sacrifice Isaac. Some ordeals were greater than others, but the worst put Abraham in a place where the promise was his only hope.

Abraham believed, even though he could not see the promises of God fulfilled. At times, Luther describes this intense spiritual experience as a withdrawing into the darkness of faith. Walking by faith and not by sight, Abraham was thus sustained by the sighs and groanings of the Holy Spirit, who "procures inexpressible and incomprehensible things."[82] "Accordingly, these matters transcend all eloquence and have to do with experiences that are spiritual. Just as no one can put the sorrow of afflicted hearts in words, so this exultation and joy of the spirit is altogether inexpressible."[83]

While some of the patriarch's trials are placed upon him by the hidden actions of God, Abraham is not only an onlooker but also the cause of some of his misfortune. He is someone whom Luther would describe as being indwelt by the Holy Spirit, yet also as someone who possesses great faults that lead to sin. Some of the affliction that follows his life is thus meant to lead him to repentance, while some leads to the mortification of the sinful self that hinders living out the active obedience of faith.[84]

The positive counterpart to repentance and mortification is that the believer can live out God's commands in the context of his calling.

> But the real chief points of godliness and of true religion are these: faith toward God, through which we receive remissions of sins; invocation; thanksgiving;

and confession; next the works of our calling with reference to our neighbor, that you rule, prescribe, teach, comfort, exhort, make a living by working, etc.[85]

Faith produces a life of love that benefits others. This happens "when it is recognized that God is gracious, placable, and kind, then I go out and turn my face from God to human beings, that is, I tend to my calling. If I am a king, I govern the state. If I am the head of a household, I direct the domestics; if I am a schoolmaster, I teach pupils, mold their habits and views toward godliness."[86]

Luther presents Abraham as an exemplar of the faith and, as such, a practitioner of the three rules. Abraham may be occupied with sad thoughts and prayers in the middle of the night while learning the truth that "affliction is the teacher of such praying."[87] Or, through meditation on the promise of God, he may be caught up in the spiritual experience of exultation and joy. He may be in the midst of a trial of patriarchal proportions. Life is never static; it moves continually from challenge to challenge. But whatever the challenge, the holy wanderings of Abraham—the pathway or *ductus* of faith—are negotiated with prayer, meditation, and spiritual struggle.

The True Pilgrimage of Faith

When Luther uses the term "pilgrimage" in his writings, we often find it in a list of practices that are detrimental and that distract from faith. One of the rare occasions of a positive use is found in the dedicatory letter attached to his booklet on Psalm 117. Luther wrote this letter to Hans von Sternberg, a knight who had gone on pilgrimage to the Holy Land and had told Luther about it. In response, after explaining a little about performing his own pilgrimage to Rome, Luther says the following:

> Well, that is what we used to do; we did not know any better, and the Holy See did not punish such gross lies. Now however, thanks be to God, we have the gospels, psalms, and other parts of the holy scriptures, to which we can make pilgrimages with profit and salvation. We want to see and visit the proper blessed land, the true Jerusalem—yes, the true paradise and heaven—not via the physical locations of the saints, their graves, but by gazing through their hearts, thoughts, and spirits. With this I commend you and yours to God.[88]

Here Luther speaks of making pilgrimages to various portions of the Holy Scripture with profit and salvation. In a parallel passage in *Table Talk*, he says that we go on true pilgrimages in faith when we diligently read the Psalms, the Prophets, the Gospels, and so on.[89] Indeed, this is precisely what Luther is doing when he spends time meditating on Holy Scripture. In his lectures on Galatians, Luther spent hours gazing through the heart of Paul as he looked on Abraham, the father of faith. In his lectures on Genesis, we saw how Luther felt the pulse of Abraham in his trials and measured his spirit as he acted as a priest, interceding for Sodom and Gomorrah.

Luther desires believers to undertake the true pilgrimage of faith, and not the medieval pilgrimage where believers seek God's presence in a particular place, hoping for divine intervention or the satisfaction of sins. For Luther, "performing" a pilgrimage to Compostella or Rome thus pales in comparison with the real pilgrimage of diligently reading and exploring the sacred page.

In a sermon on John, Luther continues this theme of an inward versus an outward pilgrimage. "This is the right way to go daily to the holy sepulcher, and for such a pilgrimage it is not necessary to travel many days or to have many possessions." From the historical account of the Lord's burial and resurrection, the Christian should turn with the inward eyes of faith and "make a true and Christian pilgrimage to the holy sepulcher and kiss it, not in external and physical pilgrimage, such as took place in the papacy at great expense, effort, and labor, but one in spirit and truth . . . such an exercise of faith and thanksgiving is the true pilgrimage and the true kiss."[90]

In spite of Luther's fierce rhetoric against the forms of pilgrimage undertaken for the satisfaction of sins and his trenchant critique of monasticism overall, he retains a positive view of spiritual or mental pilgrimage. His personal commitment and his public recommendation of an inward exercise of faith and thanksgiving do not cease. Going daily to the holy sepulcher in one's mind is not only advised but recommended. For there is a true pilgrimage that is reflective of a theology of the cross in which we see ourselves humbled and lifted up by looking to Jesus Christ who, when we touch his flesh and embrace his divine will, sanctifies the true holy relics of our faith—namely, suffering and the cross.[91]

While Luther recommends an inward pilgrimage, he also advocates worship in word and sacrament as the proper replacement for the abuses of pilgrimage. Since pilgrimage is often the cover for self-chosen works that deflect from the gospel, the solution is for the believer to embrace the will of God as revealed in the word of God.

> Remember how, previously, you ran to see the graves of the saints, their clothes and their bones: Do you recall how eagerly pilgrimages were made to Rome, to Jerusalem, to St. James, only to see a stone, a bone, wood, and earth, and nothing was thought of Christ? And here in your city or village, in front of your door, Christ himself is present with his body and blood, with his remembrance, alive to receive praise and glory, and you do not desire to go there and to assist in giving thanks and praise? You are surely not a Christian, not even a human being, but a devil or the devil's servant.[92]

True pilgrimage, according to Luther, is a Christ-centered activity that is a matter of faith. Here he places the uncertainty of pilgrimages made to Rome, Jerusalem, and St. James over against the certainty of the presence of Christ presented in the sacrament of the altar. "Self-chosen devotions are to be condemned, and men should be reminded that they should direct their eyes where God has revealed Himself."[93] Preferring pilgrimages instead of baptism, the Lord's Supper, and the preaching of remission of sins—all those means where God promises to be found—is wrongheaded. "In the Word, in the Lord's Supper, and in Baptism you have the remission of sins. With these you will have to be satisfied if you wish to be saved."[94] The alternative to a false pilgrimage is found in Christian worship.

Luther also contrasts the negative example of pilgrimage with the positive example of the command and calling to follow Christ. In a sermon on John, he begins by painting the picture of a fellow eager to perform a pilgrimage because he has heard that certain saints were praised for doing the same. He abandons his wife and children, who are his real responsibility, in order to chase after whatever can be found at Compostella. Luther points out that the way of God does not tolerate three things: first, a human doctrine or command; second, self-chosen works; and third, the examples of the saints.

Instead, Luther reminds his hearers that God teaches the way he has chosen and shows the humble his way (cf. Ps. 25:8–9). From these comments, he moves directly into a discussion of Christian vocation, which is the cure for the misguided notion of pilgrimage of his time.

> Then you may reply: "but if I am not called, what shall I do then?" Answer: How is it possible that you are not called? You will always be in some estate; you are a husband or a wife, or a son or a daughter, or a servant or a maid. Take the lowest for yourself. Are you a husband, and you think you do not have enough to do in that estate with governing your wife, children, domestics, and property so that all may be obedient to God and that you do no one any wrong? Even if you had four heads and ten hands, you would still be too little either to make a pilgrimage or to take some saint's work as your own.[95]

Luther is adamant in his advice yet still quite humorous. He spends the next three pages driving this point home in his typical lively fashion. In this particular example we discover that medieval pilgrimage, with its desire to emulate the saints, is a misplaced vocation.

Luther's position on true pilgrimage, gathered together in one place, comprises at least three elements. First, pilgrimage can profitably be made in Holy Scripture; that is to say, the holy geography of the sacred text is the terrain that shows us the true land of promise. The exercise of faith and thanksgiving in an inward activity of prayer and meditation through spiritual pilgrimage is profitable for the Christian. Second, true pilgrimage lives in the assured presence of God through word and sacrament found in public worship. Being rooted and at home in God's word places the Christian in the community of faith that turns its back on self-seeking piety and engages in service on behalf of the world. Third, true pilgrimage is a holy wandering in which we do the next right thing, living before God in faith, fulfilling our vocation, and acting in love toward our neighbor. Thus the inner life of faith connects in an intrinsic way with the outer life of the world—in the world and for the sake of the world.

Abraham's pilgrimage becomes the pattern and ideal for all Christian pilgrimage. For those who wrote the New Testament, Abraham is the type of true piety. Apostolic Christianity finds its own attitude to God anticipated or reflected in him. Paul proves this in his references to Abraham in his letters to the Romans and the Galatians. James demonstrates this in his discussion of faith and works, and the writer of Hebrews says in sublime and memorable fashion, "By faith Abraham obeyed when he was called to go out to a place that he was to receive as an inheritance. And he went out, not knowing where he was going" (Heb. 11:8). Luther renovates and rejuvenates the view of Abraham in his time, making it possible to view the life of Abraham as an example of faith alone. Abraham is the believer who tenaciously clings to God's promise and then goes out into the world and exercises himself in works that fulfill his vocation.

This pattern begins with the word of promise God spoke to Abraham and his response of faith. To believe in the promise, though it meant to count unreal all that was most real to other men, was the only right thing to do; and as Abraham lived out his long life still believing, still counting God's promise the final reality, it made and kept him right with God. He stood before God justified, the friend of God (Isa. 41:8). Abraham knew and treated God as the last and absolute reality in life, and God's unconditional acceptance then makes possible a life of thanksgiving and praise, fighting against sin, and living out daily life in God's calling. To live and believe in this way is to take our place among the children of Abraham. This is the true pilgrimage that does not derive its essential meaning through geography but is real nonetheless, filled with the joys and challenges of living in faith.

Early in Luther's career, we find the following comment emphasizing that we are not the ones making progress toward the kingdom; it is the kingdom that draws near to us:

> Therefore, we do not pray, "Dear Father, let us come into your kingdom," as though we might journey toward it. But we do say, "May thy kingdom come to us." If we are to receive it at all, God's grace and his kingdom, together with all virtues, must come to us. We will never be able to come into this kingdom. Similarly, Christ came to us from heaven to earth; we did not ascend from earth into heaven to him.[96]

This picture of the gospel is purely one of gift. Christ came into the world to save sinners (1 Tim. 1:15). It is Christ's descent, his journey to the cross, and the victory of his resurrection that wins salvation, not the ascent from earth to heaven on the part of the religious devotee. We are not as pilgrims under our own power, moving with resolution toward the kingdom; the kingdom is moving toward us in Christ. As wayfarers and wanderers, we keep our eyes peeled and our ears open. We are members of the kingdom through baptism and thus forgiven and at home, but we are also sojourners in this life, struggling against sin and against being overcome by the law and the devil. It is in this posture and status of not being at home that we restlessly look to return home, to the city that has foundations, whose designer and builder is God (Heb. 11:10).

Further, we find in Luther that we make progress in the kingdom as the kingdom makes progress in us. "God must have his way in us, that he alone must be, dwell, and reign in us. We must strive for that goal first and foremost. We are saved only when God reigns in us and we are his kingdom."[97] The negative example of wayward Israel during the time of the exodus was a topic Luther preached on. In the following excerpt from a sermon on 1 Corinthians 10:6–10, Luther urges his hearers against pride and presumption, referring them rather to the sustaining power of the forgiveness of sins and the grace of Christ:

> Now, if such a frightening, horrible verdict and punishment came on these very great people, then, "dear friends, let us not be proud and arrogant," says St. Paul, since we are far from being equal to them and cannot now at these last times of the world have the same great gifts and very glorious miracles they had. Rather, let us see ourselves in them and learn from their example, so that, when we boast about Christ, the forgiveness of sins, and God's grace, we also take care to remain in it and not again lose what we have received, and thus fall into God's punishment and damnation. We are not yet completely through or on the other side, where we ought to be. Rather, we are still on the road, where we must always continue in the struggle we have begun against all the dangers and hindrances we meet.
>
> Our deliverance has certainly been begun, but it has not yet been completed. You have come out of Egypt and gone through the Red Sea (that is, you have been led out of the devil's power through Christ's Baptism into God's kingdom). However, you have not yet come through the wilderness into the promise land, and you can still stray along the road, so that you are struck and lose your deliverance.[98]

Here, Luther observes that Christians are privileged to glory in Christ and the forgiveness of sins, but this is all the more reason to pay attention. We are to be careful and faithful not to fall into the same fate as those who fell away. The world in which we live still has its dangers, and we would be foolish not to recognize this. Like Abraham, we are to cling to the promise, experience the darkness of faith, and resolutely move forward in the power of the Spirit who intercedes for us.

In the following passage, Luther emphasizes the ongoing nature of salvation and refers to the pathway of faith as a continual passing through the desert of Egypt to the Promised Land:

> For the sake of those who are not yet sufficiently instructed in Christ I repeat what I have said rather more often above, namely, that these expressions "to

redeem," "that we might receive adoption," "you are sons," "He has sent the Spirit," "He is son and heir, not a slave," and similar expressions are not to be understood as having been fulfilled in us, but that Christ has fulfilled this in order that it may also be fulfilled in us; for they have all been begun in such a way that from day to day they are achieved more and more. For this reason it is also called the Passover of the Lord, that is, a passing through (Ex. 12:11–12), and we are called Galileans, that is, wanderers, because we are continually going forth from Egypt through the desert, that is, through the way of the cross and suffering to the Land of Promise. We have been redeemed, and we are being redeemed continually. We have received adoption and are still receiving it. We have been made sons of God, and we are and shall be sons. The Spirit has been sent, is being sent, and will be sent. We learn, and we shall learn.

And so you must not imagine that the Christian's life is a standing still and a state of rest. No, it is a passing over and a progress from vices to virtue, from charity to charity, from virtue to virtue. And those who have not been en route you should not consider Christians either.[99]

For Luther, the true pilgrimage, or what we might call "spirituality" in our own time, begins as God redeems us and sends his Spirit. Having begun in faith and been proclaimed as righteous, it is a sojourn, an all-embracing response to the promise of God in Christ that remains in faith—not merely a truth to be believed, but a gift to be lived in joy. Our glad response recognizes that our destiny of fulfilling the law is still being worked out; it is, as it were, a "passing over." But step by step, this will be completed as we as holy wayfarers live life in the Spirit in quiet confidence, joy, love, and hope.

We live much of our lives in the day-to-day activities of our earthly vocation, which may not have the appearance of anything especially religious. But in this Christian life, we will certainly have spiritual struggles that drive us back to Scripture. It is then we realize that it is our true vocation as members of the household of faith to continue in our Christian pilgrimage—walking the pathway marked by prayer, meditation, and spiritual trial.

BIBLIOGRAPHY

Books

Althaus, Paul. *The Theology of Martin Luther*. Minneapolis: Fortress, 1963.

Arand, Charles. *That I May Be His Own: An Overview of Luther's Catechisms*. St. Louis: Concordia Academic, 2000.

Augustine. *Enchiridion on Faith, Hope, and Charity*. In *The Works of Saint Augustine: A Translation for the 21st Century*. Edited by Edmund Hill and John E. Rotelle, in three series. Hyde Park, NY: New City, 1990ff.

————. *The Rule of Saint Augustine: With Introduction & Commentary*. Translated by Raymond Canning O.S.A. London: Darton, Longman & Todd, 1984.

Aulen, Gustav. *Christus Victor: An Historical Study of the Three Main Types of the Idea of the Atonement*. New York: Macmillan, 1954.

Bainton, Roland. *Here I Stand: A Life of Martin Luther*. Nashville: Abingdon, 1950.

Barth, Hans Martin. *Der Teufel und Jesus Christus in der Theologie Martin Luthers*. Göttingen: Vandenhoeck & Ruprecht, 1967.

Bayer, Oswald. *Martin Luther's Theology: A Contemporary Interpretation*. Translated by Thomas H. Trapp. Grand Rapids: Eerdmans, 2008.

————. *Theology the Lutheran Way*. Edited and translated by Jeffery G. Silcock and Mark C. Mattes. Grand Rapids: Eerdmans, 2007.

Bell, Theo. *Divus Bernhardus. Bernhard von Clairvaux in Martin Luthers Schriften*. Mainz: P. von Zabern, 1993.

Boyle, Marjorie O'Rourke. *Rhetoric and Reform: Erasmus' Civil Dispute with Luther*. Harvard Historical Monographs 71. Cambridge, MA: Harvard University Press, 1983.

Braaten, Carl, and Robert Jenson, eds. *Union with Christ: The New Finnish Interpretation of Luther*. Grand Rapids: Eerdmans, 1998.

Brecht, Martin. *Martin Luther: His Road to Reformation, 1483–1521*. Translated by James L. Schaaf. Minneapolis: Fortress, 1985.

————. *Martin Luther: The Preservation of the Church, 1532–1546*. Minneapolis: Fortress, 1993.

————. *Martin Luther: Shaping and Defining the Reformation, 1521–1532*. Minneapolis: Fortress, 1990.

Brigitta, Saint. *Mystical Visions of St. Bridget.* Translated by Leroy Butler. Mahwah, NJ: Paulist, 1998.

Caruthers, Mary. *The Book of Memory: A Study of Memory in Medieval Culture.* Cambridge Studies in Medieval Literature 10. Cambridge: Cambridge University Press, 1990.

Cyprian. *The Fathers of the Church.* Vol. 36. New York: Fathers of the Church, 1958.

Ellul, Jacques. *To Will and to Do.* Philadelphia: Pilgrim, 1969.

Erasmus of Rotterdam. *Enchiridion of a Christian Knight* (1501). In *Collected Works of Erasmus.* Edited by John W. O'Malley. Toronto: University of Toronto Press, 1974ff.

Forde, Gerhard O. *On Being a Theologian of the Cross: Reflections on Luther's Heidelberg Disputation, 1518.* Grand Rapids: Eerdmans, 1997.

_____. *Where God Meets Man: Luther's Down-to-Earth Approach to the Gospel.* Minneapolis: Augsburg, 1972.

Gerrish, Brian. *Grace and Reason: A Study in the Theology of Luther.* Oxford: Oxford University Press, 1962.

Hagen, Kenneth. *Luther's Approach to Scripture as Seen in His "Commentaries" on Galatians 1519–1538.* Tübingen: J. C. B. Mohr [Paul Siebeck], 1993.

Hamm, Berndt. *The Early Luther: Stages in a Reformation Reorientation.* Grand Rapids: Eerdmans, 2014.

Helmer, Christine, ed. *The Global Luther: A Theologian for Modern Times.* Minneapolis: Fortress, 2009.

Irenaeus. *On the Apostolic Preaching.* Popular Patristics Series 17. Crestwood, NY: St. Vladimir's Seminary Press, 1997.

Isaac, Gordon L. *Left Behind or Left Befuddled: The Subtle Dangers of Popularizing the End Times.* Collegeville, MN: Liturgical, 2008.

Jacobs, Alan. *The Book of Common Prayer: A Biography.* Lives of Great Religious Books. Princeton: Princeton University Press, 2013.

James, William. *Varieties of Religious Experience.* Edited by Matthew Bradley. Oxford World's Classics. Oxford: Oxford University Press, 2012.

Janz, Denis R. *The Westminster Handbook to Martin Luther.* Westminster Handbooks to Christian Theology. Louisville, KY: Westminster John Knox, 2010.

Jenson, Robert W. *Canon and Creed: Interpretation: Resources for the Use of Scripture in the Church.* Louisville: Westminster John Knox, 2010.

Kant, Immanuel. *Critique of Pure Reason.* Translated by Norman Kemp Smith. New York: St. Martin's, 1965.

Kolb, Robert. *Luther and the Stories of God: Biblical Narratives as a Foundation for Christian Living.* Grand Rapids: Baker Academic, 2012.

Kolb, Robert, and Christian Neddens. *Gottes Wort vom Kreuz, Luthers Theologie als Kritische Theologie.* Oberurseler Hefte 40. Oberursel: Lutherische Theologische Hochschule, 2001.

Kolb, Robert, Irene Dingel, and L'Ubomir Batka, eds. *Oxford Handbook on Luther's Theology.* Oxford: Oxford University Press, 2014.

Koslofsky, Craig. *The Reformation of the Dead: Death and Ritual in Early Modern Germany, 1450–1700.* Early Modern History. Edited by Rab Houston, Edward Muir, and Bob Scribner. New York: St. Martin's, 2000.

Kürschner, Mathias J. *Martin Luther als Ausleger der Heiligen Schrift.* Edition Ichthys Band 3—in der Reihe TVG—Orientierung. Giessen: Brunnen Verlag, 2004.

Leclercq, Jean. *The Love of Learning and the Desire for God: A Study of Monastic Culture.* New York: Fordham University Press, 1983.

Leppin, Volker. *Die fremde Reformation: Luthers mystische Wurzeln.* Munich: Beck, 2016.

Leroux, Neil R. *Luther's Rhetoric: Strategies and Style from the Invocavit Sermons.* St. Louis: Concordia Academic, 2002.

Lienhard, Marc. *Luther: Witness to Christ—Stages and Themes of the Reformer's Christology.* Minneapolis: Augsburg, 1982.

Lindhardt, Jan. *Martin Luther: Knowledge and Mediation in the Renaissance.* Texts and Studies in Religion. Vol. 29. Lewiston, NY: Edwin Mellon, 1986.

Lohse, Bernhard. *Martin Luther's Theology: Its Historical and Systematic Development.* Minneapolis: Fortress, 1999.

Luther, Martin. *Luther's Spirituality.* The Classics of Western Spirituality. Edited and translated by Philip D. W. Krey and Peter D. S. Krey. Mahwah, NJ: Paulist, 2007.

Mannermaa, Tuomo. *Christ Present in Faith: Luther's View of Justification.* Minneapolis: Fortress, 2005.

Mathesius, Johann. *Ausgewählte Werke/Johannes Mathesius.* Selected, explained, and introduced by Georg Loesche. Prague: F. Tempsky, 1896–1904.

McKim, Donald, ed. *The Cambridge Companion to Martin Luther.* Cambridge: Cambridge University Press, 2003.

Ngien, Dennis. *Luther as a Spiritual Advisor: The Interface of Theology and Piety in Luther's Devotional Writings.* Studies in Christian History and Thought. Milton Keynes, UK: Paternoster, 2007.

Nichol, Martin. *Meditatio bei Luther.* Göttingen: Vandenhoeck & Ruprecht, 1984.

Oberman, Heiko A. *Luther: Man between God and the Devil.* New Haven: Yale University Press, 1989.

Otto, Rudolf. *The Idea of the Holy.* Translated by John W. Harvey. Oxford: Oxford University Press, 1958.

Pettegree, Andrew. *Brand Luther: 1517, Printing, and the Making of the Reformation.* New York: Penguin, 2015.

Posset, Franz. *The Front-Runner of the Catholic Reformation: The Life and Words of Johann von Staupitz.* Farnham, Surrey, UK: Ashgate, 2003.

———. *Pater Bernhardus: Martin Luther and Bernhard of Clairvaux.* Cistercian Studies Series 168. Kalamazoo, MI: Cistercian Studies Quarterly, 1999.

Prenter, Regin. *Spiritus Creator.* Translated by John Jensen. Philadelphia: Muhlenberg, 1953.

Quintilian. *The Institutio Oratoria of Quintilian.* Translated by H. E. Butler. The Loeb Classical Library. Cambridge, MA: Harvard University Press, 1922.

Rahner, Hugo. *Greek Myths and Christian Mystery.* New York: Biblo-Moser, 1963.

Reinis, Austra. *Reforming the Art of Dying: The ars moriendi in the German Reformation (1519–1528).* St. Andrews Studies in Reformation History. Farnham, Surrey, UK: Ashgate, 2007.

Rupp, Gordon. *The Righteousness of God.* London: Hodder & Stoughton, 1953.

Sider, Ronald, ed. *Karlstadt's Battle with Luther: Documents in a Liberal-Radical Debate.* Philadelphia: Fortress, 1978.

Steinmetz, David C. *Luther in Context.* Bloomington: Indiana University Press, 1986; Grand Rapids: Labyrinth Books, 1995.

———. *Taking the Long View: Christian Theology in Historical Perspective.* Oxford: Oxford University Press, 2011.

Stjerna, Kirsi I., and Brooks Schramm, eds. *Encounters with Luther: New Directions for Critical Studies.* Louisville: Westminster John Knox, 2016.

Stolt, Birgit. "Laßt uns fröhlich springen!" *Gefühlswelt und Gefühlsnavigierung in Luthers Reformationsarbeit.* Berlin: Weidler Buchverlag, 2012.

Trueman, Carl. *Luther on the Christian Life: Cross and Freedom.* Wheaton, IL: Crossway Books, 2015.

Vaino, Olli-Pekka, ed. *Engaging Luther: A (New) Theological Assessment.* Eugene, OR: Cascade, 2010.

Wengert. Timothy. *Martin Luther's Catechisms: Forming the Faith.* Minneapolis: Fortress, 2009.

———, ed. *The Pastoral Luther: Essays on Martin Luther's Practical Theology.* Lutheran Quarterly Books. Grand Rapids: Eerdmans, 2009.

———. *Reading the Bible with Luther: An Introductory Guide.* Grand Rapids: Baker Academic, 2013.

Wesley, John. *The Works of John Wesley.* Vol. 18: *Journals and Diaries* (1735–1738). Edited by W. Reginald Ward and Richard P. Heizenrater. Nashville: Abingdon, 1988.

Wilson, Andrew. *Here I Walk: A Thousand Miles on Foot to Rome with Martin Luther.* Grand Rapids: Brazos, 2016.

Wriedt, Marcus. *Gnade und Erwählung.* Mainz: P. von Zabern, 1991.

Articles or Chapters in Books

Alfsvag, Knut. "Luther as Reader of Dionysius the Areopagite." *Studia Theologica* 65 (2011): 101–14.

———. "*Notae Ecclesiae* in Luther's *Von den Konsiliis und Kirchen.*" *International Study of the History of the Christian Church* 8, no. 1 (February 2008): 32–41.

Andersson, Bo. "Luther's Tower Experience: The Case for a Rhetorical Approach." *Lutheran Quarterly* (1987): 205–13.

Arand, Charles. "The Battle-Cry of Faith: The Catechisms' Cry of Faith." *Concordia Journal* 21, no. 1 (January 1995): 42–65.

Asendorf, Ulrich. "Holy Scripture and Holy Spirit." In *Ad Fontes Lutheri: Toward the Recovery of the Real Luther: Essays in Honor of Kenneth Hagen's Sixty-Fifth Birthday*, 1–16. Edited by Timothy Maschke, Franz Posset, and Joan Skokir. Milwaukee: Marquette University Press, 2001.

Bayer, Oswald. "*Oratio, Meditatio, Tentatio*. Eine Besinnung auf Luthers Theologiverständnis." In *Martin Seils zum 60. Geburtstag*, 7–59. Göttingen: Vandenhoeck & Ruprecht, 1988.

Cousins, Ewert. "The Humanity and the Passion of Christ." In *Christian Spirituality: High Middle Ages and Reformation*. Vol. 17, *World Spirituality: An Encyclopedic History of the Religious Quest*, 375–91. New York: Crossroad, 1987.

Dieter, Theo. "Martin Luther's Understanding of Reason." *Lutheran Quarterly* 25 (2011): 249–78.

Dubbelman, Sam. "The Darkness of Faith: A Study in Luther's 1535 Commentary on Galatians." *Trinity Journal* 37NS (2016): 213–32.

Goez, Werner. "Luthers 'Ein Sermon von der Bereitung zum Sterben' und die spätmittelalterliche *ars moriendi*." *Luther Jahrbuch* (1981): 97–114.

Haemig, Mary Jane. "Prayer as Talking Back to God in Luther's Genesis Commentary." *Lutheran Quarterly* 23 (2009): 270–95.

Hagen, Kenneth. "Changes in the Understanding of Luther: The Development of the Young Luther." *Theological Studies* 29 (1968): 472–96.

Haussleiter, Johannes. "Luthers Trostbriefe." In *Allgemeine Evangelisch-Lutherische Kirchenzeitung*, 434–87. Leipzig: Evangelische Verlagsanstalt, 1917.

Isaac, Gordon L. "The Changing Image of Luther as Biblical Expositor." In *Ad Fontes Lutheri: Toward the Recovery of the Real Luther: Essays in Honor of Kenneth Hagen's Sixty-Fifth Birthday*, 67–85. Edited by Timothy Maschke, Franz Posset, and Joan Skocir. Marquette: Marquette University Press, 2001.

———. "Monastic *Memoria* in the Preface to the Complete Edition of Luther's Latin Writings 1545." *Luther Digest: An Annual Abridgment of Luther Studies* 20, supplement (St. Louis: Luther Academy, 2012): 127–40.

Janz, Denis R. "To Hell (and Back) with Luther: The Dialectic of *Anfechtung* and Faith." In *Encounters with Luther: New Directions for Critical Studies*, 17–29. Edited by Kirsi I. Stjerna and Brooks Schramm. Louisville: Westminster John Knox, 2016.

Junghans, Helmar. "The Center of the Theology of Martin Luther." In *Martin Luther in Two Centuries: The Sixteenth and the Twentieth*, 29–44. St. Paul, MN: Lutheran Brotherhood Foundation Reformation Research Library at Luther Northwestern Theological Seminary, 1992.

———. "Das Wort Gottes bei Luther während seiner ersten Psalmenvorlesung." *Theologische Literaturzeitung* 100 (1975): 161–74.

———. "Luther als Bibelhumanist." *Lutherjahrbuch* 53 (1982): 1–9.

———. "Luther's Development from Biblical Humanist to Reformer." In *Martin Luther in Two Centuries: The Sixteenth and the Twentieth*, 1–14. St. Paul, MN: Lutheran Brotherhood Foundation Reformation Research Library at Luther Northwestern Theological Seminary, 1992.

Kleinig, John. "The Attentive Heart: Meditation in the Old Testament." *Reformed Theological Review* 51 (May-August 1992): 50–63.

———. "The Indwelling Word: Meditation in the New Testament." *Reformed Theological Review* 51 (September-December 1992): 81–90.

———. "The Kindred Heart: Luther on Meditation." *Lutheran Theological Journal* 20 (1986): 142–54.

———. "Meditation." *Logia* 10, no. 2 (2001): 45–50.

———. "*Oratio, Meditatio, Tentatio*: What Makes a Theologian?" *Concordia Theological Quarterly* 66, no. 3 (2002): 255–67.

Kolb, Robert. "Luther's Theology of the Cross Fifteen Years after Heidelberg: The Psalms of Ascent." *Journal of Ecclesiastical History* 61, no. 1 (2010): 69–85.

———. "Models of the Christian Life in Luther's Genesis Sermons and Lectures." *Lutherjahrbuch* 76 (2009): 193–220.

Köpf, Ulrich. "Wurzeln reformatorischen Denkens in der Theologie Bernhards von Clairvaux." In *Reformation und Mönchtum: Aspeckte eines Verhältnisses über Luther hinaus*. Edited by Athina Lexutt, Volker Mantey, and Volkmar Ortman. Late Middle Ages, Humanism, Reformation 43, 29–56. Tübingen: Mohr Siebeck, 2008.

Leppin, Volker. "Luther on the Devil." In *Encounters with Luther: New Directions for Critical Studies*, 30–41. Edited by Kirsi I. Stjerna and Brooks Schramm. Louisville: Westminster John Knox, 2016.

———. "Luther's Roots in Monastic-Mystical Piety." In *The Oxford Handbook of Luther's Theology*, 49–61. Edited by Robert Kolb, Irene Dingel, and L'Ubomir Batka. Oxford: Oxford University Press, 2014.

———. "Luther's Transformation of Late Medieval Mysticism." *Lutheran Forum* 44 (2010): 25–28.

Małysz, Piotr J. "Luther and Dionysius: Beyond Mere Negations." In *Re-Thinking Dionysius the Areopagite*, 149–62. Edited by Sarah Coakley and Charles Stang. Malden, MA: Wiley-Blackwell, 2009.

Maschke, Timothy. "Contemporaneity: A Hermeneutical Perspective in Martin Luther's Work." In *Ad Fontes Lutheri: Toward the Recovery of the Real Luther: Essays in Honor of Kenneth Hagen's Sixty-Fifth Birthday*, 165–82. Marquette Studies in Theology 28. Edited by Timothy Maschke, Franz Posset, and Joan Skokir. Milwaukee: Marquette University Press, 2001.

Mueller, Bernard. "Piety in Germany Around 1500." In *The Reformation in Medieval Perspective*, 50–75. Edited with an introduction by Steven Ozment. Chicago: Quadrangle Books, 1971.

Nestingen, James Arne. "The Lord's Prayer in the Catechism." *Word & World* 22, no. 1 (Winter 2002): 36–48.

Ozment, Steven. "*Homo Viator*: Luther and Late Medieval Theology." In *The Reformation in Medieval Perspective*, 142–54. Chicago: Quadrangle Books, 1971.

Posset, Franz. "Bible Reading 'With Closed Eyes' In the Monastic Tradition: An Overlooked Aspect of Martin Luther's Hermeneutics." *American Benedictine Review* 38:3 (1987): 293–306.

———. "Luther's Journey to Rome 1511–1512: In Commemoration of Its 500th Anniversary and in Search of the Historical Luther—A Sequel to *The Real Luther*." *Luther Digest: An Annual Abridgment of Luther Studies* 20, supplement (St. Louis: Luther Academy, 2012): 9–24.

———. "The Sweetness of God." *American Benedictine Review* 44:2 (1993): 143–78.

Rorem, Paul. "Martin Luther's Christocentric Critique of Pseudo-Dionysian Spirituality." *Lutheran Quarterly* 11 (1997): 291–307.

Stolt, Birgit. " . . . And Feel It in the Heart. . . . Luther's Translation of the Bible from the Perspective of the Modern Science of Linguistics and Translating." *Lutheran Quarterly* 28 (2014): 373–400.

———. "Luther's 'Faith of the Heart': Experience, Emotion, and Reason." In *The Global Luther: A Theologian for Modern Times*, 131–50. Minneapolis: Fortress, 2009.

Vercruysee, Jos. E. "Eine Rechte Weise in Der Theologia zu Studieren: Oratio, Meditatio, Tentatio, Luthers Vorrede von 1539." In *Denkender Glaube in Geschichte und Gegenwart: Festschrift aus Anlass der Gründung der Universität Erfurt von 600 Jahren und aus Anlass des 40 jährigen Bestehens des Philosophisch-Theologischen Studiums Erfurt*, 297–307. Edited by Wilhelm Ernst and Konrad Feiereis. Leipzig: Benno Verlag, 1992.

Wengert, Timothy. "Forming the Faith Today through Luther's Catechisms." *Lutheran Quarterly* 11 (1997): 379–96.

———. "Luther's *Freedom of a Christian* for Today's Church." *Lutheran Quarterly* 28 (2014): 1–21.

———. "Luther on Prayer in the Large Catechism." *Lutheran Quarterly* 18 (2004): 249–74.

ABBREVIATIONS

AL	*The Annotated Luther.* 6 vols. Eds. Hans. J Hillerbrand, Kirsi I. Stjerna, Timothy Wengert. Minneapolis: Fortress, 2015ff.
CA	Augsburg Confession
CR	*Corpus Reformatorum. Philippi Melanthonis Opera quae supersunt omnia.* 28 vols. Edited by C. G. Bretschneider and H. E. Bindseil. Halle: C. A. Schwetschke & Sons, 1834–60
DBWE	*Dietrich Bonhoeffer Works.* 17 vols. Edited by Wayne Whitson Floyd Jr. Minneapolis: Fortress, 1998–2014
Kolb-Wengert	Robert Kolb and Timothy J. Wengert, eds. *The Book of Concord: The Confessions of the Evangelical Lutheran Church.* Minneapolis: Fortress, 2000
LC	Large Catechism
LCC	Library of Christian Classics. Edited by John T. McNeill and Henry P. van Dusen. Philadelphia: Westminster, 1953ff.
LW	*Luther's Works: American Edition.* Vols. 1–30, edited by Jaroslav Pelikan. Saint Louis: Concordia, 1955–76. Vols. 31–55, edited by Helmut Lehmann. Philadelphia/Minneapolis: Fortress, 1957–86. Vols. 56–82, edited by Christopher B. Brown. Saint Louis: Concordia, 2009ff.
SA	Smalkald Articles
SC	Small Catechism
WA	*D. Martin Luthers Werke: Kritische Gesamtausgabe (Weimarer Ausgabe).* 73 vols. Weimar: H. Böhlau, 1883–1993
WA Br	*D. Martin Luthers Werke: Briefwechsel.* 18 vols. Weimar: H. Böhlau, 1930–85
WA DB	*D. Martin Luthers Werke: Deutsche Bible.* 12 vols. Weimar: H. Böhlau, 1906–61
WA TR	*D. Martin Luthers Werke: Tischreden.* 6 vols. Weimar: H. Böhlau, 1912–21

NOTES

Chapter 1

1. *Preface to the Wittenberg Edition of Luther's German Writings* (1539), *WA* 50:659.1–4; *LW* 34:285.

2. To this effect, see Jos E. Vercruysee, "Eine Rechte Weise in Der Theologia zu Studieren: *Oratio, Meditatio, Tentatio,* Luthers Vorrede von 1539," in *Denkender Glaube in Geschichte und Gegenwart: Festschrift aus Anlass der Gründung der Universität Erfurt von 600 Jahren und aus Anlass des 40 jährigen Bestehens des Philosophisch-Theologischen Studiums Erfurt,* ed. Wilhelm Ernst and Konrad Feiereis (Leipzig: Benno Verlag, 1992), 299, 301.

3. *Preface to the Wittenberg Edition of Luther's German Writings* (1539), *WA* 50:658.29–34; *LW* 34:285.

4. See the Heidelberg Disputation (1518), *WA* 1:353–374; *LW* 31:39–70.

5. Gerhard O. Forde, *On Being a Theologian of the Cross: Reflections on Luther's Heidelberg Disputation, 1518* (Grand Rapids: Eerdmans, 1997), 10.

6. Vercruysse, "Eine Rechte Weise in Der Theologia Zu Studieren," 298.

7. *Preface to the Wittenberg Edition of Luther's German Writings (1539),* WA 50:658.5–12; *LW* 34:284.

8. Ibid.

9. Ibid.

10. Ibid., *WA* 50:657.25–27; *LW* 34:284.

11. Ibid., *WA* 50:658.21–28; *LW* 34:285.

12. Ibid., *WA* 50:658.29–30; *LW* 34:285.

13. Ibid., *WA* 50:660.17–19; *LW* 34:287.

14. God is not gendered. By using masculine pronouns in reference to God, I am following the precedent of the Bible and Luther, and because it aids in reflecting the personal God who seeks and saves the lost. For more on inclusive language, see David C. Steinmetz, "Inclusive Language and the Trinity," in *Taking the Long View: Christian Theology in Historical Perspective* (Oxford: Oxford University Press, 2011), 27–36.

15. Ibid., *WA* 50:659.10–12; *LW* 34:285–86.

16. *Preface to the Epistle of St. Paul to the Romans* (1522/46), *WA* 7:2.8–11; *LW* 35:365. "We can never read it or ponder over it too much; for the more we deal with it, the more precious it becomes and the better it tastes." In the monastic context, contemplating Scripture meant to draw out its savor and application to life, not simply for science of what the text says. Luther also describes the change in his understanding of the biblical words "repentance" and "righteousness" as "sweet" to the taste in his Letter to Staupitz, May 30, 1518, *LW* 48:6, and in the *Preface to*

the Complete Edition of Luther's Latin Writings (1545), *LW* 34:337. He depicts both of these discoveries as a result of intense meditation on Scripture. For the monastic/mystical background behind the concept of "sweetness," see Berndt Hamm, *The Early Luther: Stages in a Reformation Reorientation* (Grand Rapids: Eerdmans, 2014), 46, 50, 53, 226.

17. Sermon for the Funeral of the Elector, Duke John of Saxony, August 18, 1532, *WA* 36:253.24–28; *LW* 51:242.

18. Heidelberg Disputation (1518), *WA* 1:354.13–22; *LW* 31:40.

19. Ibid., *WA* 1:362.24–25; *LW* 31:53.

20. *Explanations of the Ninety-Five Theses* (1518), *WA* 1:614.17–27; *LW* 31:227.

21. Heidelberg Disputation (1518), *WA* 1:362.15–19; *LW* 31:53.

22. *Explanations of the Ninety-Five Theses* (1518), *WA* 1:613.21–33; *LW* 31:225–26.

23. Robert Kolb, "Luther on the Theology of the Cross," *Lutheran Quarterly* (Winter 2002): 443. See also, *Martin Luther: Confessor of the Faith*, Christian Theology in Context (Oxford: Oxford University Press, 2009), 55–59; "Luther on the Theology of the Cross," in *The Pastoral Luther: Essays on Martin Luther's Practical Theology*, ed. Timothy Wengert, Lutheran Quarterly Books (Grand Rapids: Eerdmans, 2009), 33–56. The last essay appears in substantially the same form under the title "*Deus revelatus—Homo revelatus*, Luthers theologia crucis für das 21. Jahrhundert," in Robert Kolb and Christian Neddens, *Gottes Wort vom Kreuz, Luthers Theologie als Kritische Theologie, Oberurseler Hefte 40* (Oberursel: Lutherische Theologische Hochschule, 2001), 13–34.

24. *The Bondage of the Will* (1526), *WA* 18:685.3–6; *LW* 33:139.

25. *Commentary on Psalm 51* (1532/38), *WA* 40/II:329.20–26; *LW* 12:312.

26. *Die Promotionsdisputation von Palladius und Tilemann* (1537), *WA* 39/I:217.9–16.

27. *Vorlesung über die Stufenpsalmen* (1532/33[40]), *WA* 40:56.31–57.21. As quoted in Robert Kolb, "Luther's Theology of the Cross Fifteen Years after Heidelberg: The Psalms of Ascent," *Journal of Ecclesiastical History* 61, no. 1 (2010): 76.

28. Heidelberg Disputation (1518), *WA* 1:354.24; *LW* 31:41.

29. Ibid., *WA* 1:362.29–31; *LW* 31:53.

30. Ibid., *WA* 1:363.30; *LW* 31:55.

31. Ibid., *WA* 1:363.16–17; *LW* 31:41.

32. Ibid., *WA* 1:363.31–32; *LW* 31:55.

33. Ibid., *WA* 1:363.35–37; *LW* 31:55.

34. Ibid., *WA* 1:354.29–30; *LW* 31:41.

35. Ibid., *WA* 1:364.15–16; *LW* 31:56.

36. *Von Ehesachen* (1530), *WA* 30/III:213.34–35.

37. *Commentary on Psalm 118* (1530), *WA* 31/I:91.21–92.15; *LW* 14:58.

38. Sermon in Lichtenberg, September 15, 1536, *WA* 41:675.8. *Er stelt sich ut Teufel.*

39. Kolb, "Luther's Theology of the Cross Fifteen Years after Heidelberg," 80.

40. *Vorlesung über die Stufenpsalmen* (1532/33 [1540]), *WA* 40/III:59.34.

41. *Church Postil* (1525), Gospel for the Second Sunday in Lent [Matt. 15:21–28], *WA* 17/II:200–204; *LW* 76:378–82.

42. Ibid., *WA* 17/II:202:2–4; *LW* 76:379.

43. Ibid., *WA* 17/II:203; *LW* 76:380.

44. Kolb, "Luther's Theology of the Cross Fifteen Years after Heidelberg," 85.

45. Forde, *On Being a Theologian of the Cross*, 10–18.

46. Forde, *On Being a Theologian of the Cross*, 16.

47. This idea was suggested in a conversation I had with Robert Kolb.

48. Oswald Bayer, "*Oratio, Meditatio, Tentatio. Eine Besinnung auf Luthers Theologiverständnis*," in Martin Seils zum 60. Geburtstag (Göttingen: Vandenhoeck & Ruprecht, 1988), 7–59. See also, *Theology the Lutheran Way*, ed. and trans. Jeffery G. Silcock and Mark C. Mattes (Grand Rapids: Eerdmans, 2007); *Martin Luther's Theology: A Contemporary Interpretation*, trans. Thomas H. Trapp (Grand Rapids: Eerdmans, 2008).

49. Bayer, "*Oratio, Meditatio, Tentatio.*"

50. *An Exposition of the Lord's Prayer for Simple Laymen* (1519), WA 2:80–130; *LW* 42:15–81.

51. See the introduction to this work in *WA* 2:74–80 and *LW* 42:17–18.

52. Ibid., *WA* 2:105.5–9; *LW* 42:48.

53. Ibid., *WA* 2:111.30–33; *LW* 42:56.

54. Ibid., *WA* 2:95.16–18; *LW* 42:37.

55. Ibid., *WA* 2:123.11–16; *LW* 42:71.

56. Ibid., *WA* 2:124.6–7; *LW* 42:72.

57. Ibid., *WA* 2:124.30–32; *LW* 42:73.

58. *A Sermon on the Three Kinds of Good Life for the Instruction of Consciences* (1521), WA 7:795–802; *LW* 44:233–42.

59. See also *The Magnificat* (1521), WA 7:551; *LW* 21:304.

60. A conflation of John 16:7 and 26.

61. *A Sermon on the Three Kinds of Good Life for the Instruction of Consciences* (1521), WA 7:801.14–802.2; *LW* 44:241–242.

62. Ibid., *WA* 7:802.15–18; *LW* 44:242.

63. *The Estate of Marriage* (1522), WA 10/II:275–304; *LW* 45:11–49.

64. Ibid., *WA* 10/II:294.16; *LW* 45:38.

65. Ibid., *WA* 10/II:295.16–18; *LW* 45:39.

66. Ibid., *WA* 10/II;293.27–296.11; *LW* 45:39–40.

67. Ibid., *WA* 10/II:301.23–30; *LW* 45:46.

68. Johann Mathesius, *Ausgewählte Werke/Johannes Mathesius*, selected, explained, and introduced by Georg Loesche (Prague: F. Tempsky, 1896–1904); *Dritten Band: Luthers Leben in Predigten* (1898), 293. I am indebted to Sam Dubbelman for referring me to this quotation.

69. *Dritten Band: Luthers Leben in Predigten*, 292–93.

Chapter 2

1. *Preface to the Wittenberg Edition of Luther's German Writings* (1539), *LW* 34:285–6 (translation altered); *WA* 50:659.5–21. Compare this to the English translation of this passage by Thomas Trapp, in Oswald Bayer, *Martin Luther's Theology*, 32–33.

2. *The Seven Penitential Psalms* (1517), WA 18:479–530; *LW* 14:137–205.

3. Ninety-Five Theses (1517), *WA* 1:233.10–11; *LW* 31:25.

4. *An Exposition of the Lord's Prayer for Simple Laymen* (1519), WA 2:80–130; *LW* 42:15–81.

5. Martin Bertram's introduction to the exposition in the American Edition of Luther's Works *LW* 42:7 relates this account from the *Weimarer Ausgabe* (*WA* 2:75).

6. *Personal Prayer Book* (1522), *WA* 10/II:375–428; *LW* 43:3–45.

7. For further information, see the introduction on *Personal Prayer Book* by Martin Bertram, who also includes comments on its initial reception (*LW* 43:5–10).

8. For an account of the history of the Book of Common Prayer, see Alan Jacobs, *The Book of Common Prayer: A Biography*, Lives of Great Religious Books (Princeton: Princeton University Press, 2013).

9. *Personal Prayer Book* (1522), *WA* 10/II:375.5–9; *LW* 43:11.

10. *Personal Prayer Book* (1522), *WA* 10/II:376.5–10; *LW* 43:12–13. For more on Saint Bridget, see *Mystical Visions of St. Bridget*, trans. Leroy Butler (Mahwah, NJ: Paulist, 1998).

11. The Small Catechism (1529), Kolb-Wengert, 345–375; The Large Catechism (1529), Kolb-Wengert, 377–480.

12. For more on the catechisms, see Charles Arand, *That I May Be His Own: An Overview of Luther's Catechisms* (St. Louis: Concordia Academic, 2000).

13. *A Simple Way to Pray* (1535), *WA* 38:358–375; *LW* 193–211.

14. Ibid., *WA* 38:358.5–359.9; *LW* 43:193.

15. Ibid., *WA* 38:359.33; *LW* 43:194. *Lafs und faul, kalt und uberdrüssig zum gebet.*

16. James Arne Nestingen, "The Lord's Prayer in the Catechism," *Word & World* 22, no. 1 (Winter 2002): 36–48.

17. Charles Arand, "The Battle-Cry of Faith: The Catechisms' Cry of Faith," *Concordia Journal* 21, no. 1 (January 1995): 42–65.

18. Bayer, *Theology the Lutheran Way*, 67ff.

19. Timothy Wengert, *Martin Luther's Catechisms: Forming the Faith* (Minneapolis: Fortress, 2009).

20. Timothy Wengert, "Forming the Faith Today through Luther's Catechisms," *Lutheran Quarterly* 11 (1997): 382.

21. *Personal Prayer Book* (1522), *WA* 10/II:376–77, *LW* 43:13–14.

22. LC III.5; Kolb-Wengert, 441.

23. LC III.9; Kolb-Wengert, 441.

24. SC II.4; Kolb-Wengert, 352.

25. LC III.11; Kolb-Wengert, 442.

26. Gordon Rupp suggests that if we want to translate *Anfechtung* into English, "we may employ John Bunyan's tremendous phrase 'the bruised conscience.'" Gordon Rupp, *The Righteousness of God* (London: Hodder & Stoughton, 1953), 105.

27. LC III.19; Kolb-Wengert, 443.

28. LC III.22; Kolb-Wengert, 443.

29. LC III.56; Kolb-Wengert, 447.

30. *Lectures on Isaiah* (1528/31), *WA* 31/II:11–16; *LW* 17:392.

31. LC III.22; Kolb-Wengert, 443.

32. LC III.27; Kolb-Wengert, 444.

33. Ibid.

34. LC III.28; Kolb-Wengert, 444.

35. It should be noted that the order of the Ten Commandments varies among the Roman, Lutheran, and Reformed versions.

36. *Lectures on Genesis* (1535–45), *WA* 42:242.6–30; *LW* 1:329.

37. Ibid., *WA* 42:242, 27–29; *LW* 1:329; cf. Matt. 7:15–20.

38. Charles Arand, "The Battle-Cry of Faith," 45.

39. *Sermons on the Gospel of St. John, Chapters 14–16* (1537–38), *WA* 46:24.34–39; *LW* 24:325.

40. Martin Brecht, *Martin Luther: His Road to Reformation 1483–1521*, trans. James L. Schaaf, 3 vols. (Philadelphia: Fortress, 1985), 1:65.

41. *An Exposition of the Lord's Prayer for Simple Laymen* (1519), WA 10/ II:84.11–18; *LW* 42:23–4.

42. *Sermons on the Gospel of St. John, Chapters 14–16* (1537–38), WA 45:681.4–6; *LW* 24:241.

43. At one point, Luther says that the monks seem to be more fearful of the laws of the pope than the laws of Christ, which causes them to be more diligent in repenting about not finishing their canonical hours fully than they are about vital matters such as adultery, murder, and envy. *Lectures on the First Epistle of Saint John* (1527), WA 20:731.11–13; *LW* 30:288.

44. *Viximus in Synodis et jam moriemur in illis.*, CR 3:828; *Table Talk* no. 5058 (1540), *WA TR* 4:639; *Table Talk* no. 5365 (1540), 5:95.

45. *Annales Vitae et Indices*, June 10, 1540, CR 28:69–70. Allda, saget Lutherus, mußte mir unser Herr Gott herhalten. Denn ich Warf ihm den Sack für die Thüre, und rieb ihm die Ohren mit allen *promissionibus exaudiendarum precum*, die ich in der heil. Schrift zu erzählen mußte, daß er mich mußte erhören, wo ich anders seinen Verheisungen trauen sollte.

46. Timothy Wengert, "Luther on Prayer in the Large Catechism," *Lutheran Quarterly* 18 (2004): 250.

47. *Annales Vitae*, CR 28:69–70.

48. A plot of land recently purchased by Luther from his brother-in-law, Hans von Bora.

49. The colloquial terms "fressen" and "saufen" recommend this translation.

50. Letter to Käthe Luther, July 2, 1540, *WA Br*, 9:168.1–6; *LW* 50:208–9.

51. *Table Talk* no. 6751, *WA TR* 6:163.2–4. Und der kirchen Gebet thut große Miracula. Es hat zu unser Zeit ihr drei von den Todten auferweckt: Mich, der ich oft bin todtkrank gewesen; meine hausfrau Kätha, die auch todtkrank war; und M. Philippum Melanchthonem, welcher Anno 1540 zu Weimar todtkrank lag. See also, *Table Talk* no. 5047. (1540), *WA TR* 5:129; *Table Talk* no. 5565 (1543), *WA TR* 5:244; *LW* 54:453–4; and Wengert, "Luther on Prayer in the Large Catechism," 251.

52. *Table Talk* no. 3605 (1537), *WA TR* 3:448.6–11.

53. Ibid., *WA TR* 3:448.15–17.

54. *An Exposition of the Lord's Prayer for Simple Laymen* (1519), WA 2:82.23–26; *LW* 42:21.

55. The Franciscan Crown was a seven-decade rosary, consisting of an Our Father and ten Hail Marys for each decade.

56. *An Exposition of the Lord's Prayer for Simple Laymen* (1519), WA 2:83.5–7; *LW* 42:22.

57. Ibid., *WA* 2:83.10–11; *LW* 42:19.

58. Ibid., *WA* 2:81.13–19; *LW* 42:19–20.

59. Cyprian, "The Lord's Prayer," in *The Fathers of the Church*, vol. 36 (New York: Fathers of the Church, 1958), ch. 4, 129–30.

60. Ibid., ch. 5, 130.

61. *An Exposition of the Lord's Prayer for Simple Laymen* (1519), WA 2:85.17–24; *LW* 42:25.

62. *The Rule of Saint Augustine: With Introduction & Commentary*, trans. Raymond Canning O.S.A. (London: Darton, Longman, & Todd, 1984), 13. See also, Augustine, *Letter 211*.

63. *An Exposition of the Lord's Prayer for Simple Laymen* (1519), *WA* 2:83.14–23; *LW* 42:22.

64. *Personal Prayer Book* (1522), *WA* 10/II:396.14–25; *LW* 43:30. "Moreover, since you are not a physical father here on earth but a spiritual Father in heaven, not like an earthly, mortal father who is not always dependable and cannot be of help by himself, show us what an immeasurably better Father you are and teach us to regard earthly fatherhood, fatherland, friends, possessions, body and blood as far less in value than you."

65. *An Exposition of the Lord's Prayer for Simple Laymen* (1519), *WA* 2:84.6–9; *LW* 42:23.

66. SC III.4; Kolb-Wengert, 356.

67. LC III.38; Kolb-Wengert, 445.

68. SC III.5; Kolb-Wengert, 356.

69. LC III.41; Kolb-Wengert, 445.

70. LC III.43; Kolb-Wengert, 445.

71. LC III.45; Kolb-Wengert, 446.

72. SC III.7; Kolb-Wengert, 356.

73. LC III.51; Kolb-Wengert, 446.

74. LC III.54–55; Kolb-Wengert, 447.

75. LC III.55–56; Kolb-Wengert, 447.

76. SC III.8; Kolb-Wengert, 357.

77. *An Exposition of the Lord's Prayer* (1519), *WA* 2:100.30–101.3; *LW* 42:43–4.

78. *Lectures on Hebrews* (1517–18), *WA* 57:109.7–23; *LW* 29:118–19.

79. LC III.67; Kolb-Wengert, 449.

80. SC III.13; Kolb-Wengert, 357.

81. LC III.72; Kolb-Wengert, 449–50.

82. LC III.77; Kolb-Wengert, 451.

83. LC III.77; Kolb-Wengert, 451.

84. LC III.80–81; Kolb-Wengert, 451.

85. LC III.88; Kolb-Wengert, 452.

86. LC III.89; Kolb-Wengert, 452.

87. LC III.91; Kolb-Wengert, 452.

88. LC III.94; Kolb-Wengert, 453.

89. LC III.96; Kolb-Wengert, 453.

90. LC III.98; Kolb-Wengert, 453.

91. LC III.100; Kolb-Wengert, 453.

92. Ibid.

93. LC III.102; Kolb-Wengert, 454.

94. LC III.103; Kolb-Wengert, 454.

95. LC III.104; Kolb-Wengert, 454.

96. Ibid.

97. LC III.106; Kolb-Wengert, 454.

98. LC III.110–11; Kolb-Wengert, 455.

99. LC III.113; Kolb-Wengert, 455.

100. *An Exposition of the Lord's Prayer for Simple Laymen* (1519), *WA* 2:127, 19–27; *LW* 42:77.

101. *Preface to the Psalter* (1528/45), *WA DB* 10/I:99.24–100.2; *LW* 35:254.

102. Augustine, *Enchiridion on Faith, Hope, and Charity*, in *The Works of Saint Augustine: A Translation for the 21st Century*, ed. Edmund Hill and John E. Rotelle, in three series (Hyde Park, NY: New City, 1990ff.), I/8:265–343; see also, Erasmus of

Rotterdam, *Enchiridion of a Christian Knight* (1501), in *Collected Works of Erasmus*, ed. John W. O'Malley (Toronto: University of Toronto Press, 1974ff.), 66:1–127.

103. *WA DB* 10/I:103.33–104.4; *LW* 35:256.

104. Ibid., *WA DB* 10/I:103.15–19; *LW* 35:254.

105. Dietrich Bonhoeffer takes up this idea in *Prayer Book of the Bible: An Introduction to the Psalms*, *DBWE* 5:141–77.

106. *Preface to the Psalter* (1528/45), *WA DB* 10/I:104.5–9; *LW* 35:256–57.

107. *Commentary on Psalm 118* (1530), *WA* 31/I:69.3–13; *LW* 14:47.

108. Ibid., *WA* 31/I:69.18–70.1; *LW* 14:47–48.

109. Ibid., *WA* 31/I.70.4–5; *LW* 14:48.

110. Ibid., *WA* 31/I:71.1; *LW* 14:48.

111. Ibid., *WA* 31/I:72.15–73.6; *LW* 14:49.

112. Ibid., *WA* 31/I:93.13–94.5; *LW* 14:59.

113. Ibid., *WA* 31/I:97.6–98.1; *LW* 14:61.

114. *The Seven Penitential Psalms* (1517), *WA* 18:526.11–18; *LW* 14:201.

115. The Nicene-Constantinopolitan Creed, "*Et unam, sanctam, catholicam et apostolicam ecclesiam.*"

116. CA VII.1–2; Kolb-Wengert, 43.

117. *On the Councils and the Church* (1539), *WA* 50:509–653; *LW* 41:3–178. See also Knut Alfsvag, *Notae Ecclesiae*, in Luther's *Von den Konsiliis und Kirchen*, *International Study of the History of the Christian Church* 8, no. 1 (February 2008): 32–41.

118. *On the Councils and the Church* (1539), *WA* 50:520.12–13; *LW* 41:20.

119. Ibid., *WA* 50:541–42; *LW* 41:47.

120. Ibid., *WA* 50:628.29–30; *LW* 41:148.

121. Ibid., *WA* 50:629.32–36; *LW* 41:150. Oswald Bayer directs attention to the phrase, *Ubi est Verbum, ibi est ecclesia*—"Where the Word is, there is the church"—as the shortest definition of Luther's understanding of the church. See Oswald Bayer, *Martin Luther's Theology: A Contemporary Interpretation*, trans. Thomas Trapp (Grand Rapids: Eerdmans, 2008), 257ff.

122. *Confession Concerning Christ's Supper* (1528), *WA* 26:507.7–16; *LW* 37:368.

123. *On the Councils and the Church* (1539), *WA* 50:625.24–29; *LW* 41:144.

124. Ibid., *WA* 50:626.15–16; *LW* 41:145.

125. Ibid., *WA* 50:628.16–17; *LW* 41:148.

126. *Against Hanswurst* (1541), *WA* 51:469–572; *LW* 41:179–256.

127. *On the Councils and the Church* (1539), *WA* 50:641.20–34; *LW* 41:164.

128. SC I.3–4; Kolb-Wengert, 352.

129. *A Simple Way to Pray* (1535), *WA* 38:364.28–365.4; *LW* 43:200.

130. Ibid., *WA* 38:372.26–27; *LW* 43:209.

131. Ibid., *WA* 38:374.30–375.8; *LW* 43:211.

132. Bernhard Lohse, *Martin Luther's Theology: Its Historical and Systematic Development* (Minneapolis: Fortress, 1999), 235.

133. Ibid.

134. *Lectures on Romans* (1515–16), *WA* 56:368.12–18; *LW* 25:358.

135. LC I.50; Kolb-Wengert, 392.

136. *Church Postil* (1544), "Epistle for the Eight Sunday after Trinity [Rom. 8:12–17]," *WA* 22:137.33–138.3; *LW* 78:274–75.

137. Ibid., *WA* 22:138.19–25; *LW* 78:275.

138. *Lectures on Galatians* (1531/35), *WA* 40:580.15–21; *LW* 26:380–81.

139. Ibid., *WA* 40:582.11–19; *LW* 26:382.

140. Ibid., *WA* 40:582.26–33; *LW* 26:382.

Chapter 3

1. *Preface to German Writings* (1539), *WA* 50:659.22–29; *LW* 34:286 (trans. altered).

2. On this point, see Martin Nichol, *Meditatio bei Luther* (Göttingen: Vandenhoeck & Ruprecht, 1984), 73–75. Oswald Bayer, *Theology the Lutheran Way*, Lutheran Quarterly Books (Grand Rapids: Eerdmans, 2007), 52.

3. *An Exposition of the Lord's Prayer for Simple Laymen* (1519), *WA* 2:85.20–24; *LW* 42:25.

4. *Lectures on Psalms 1 and 2* (1519/21), *WA* 5:22.28–29; *LW* 14:284.

5. Jean Leclercq, *The Love of Learning and the Desire for God: A Study of Monastic Culture* (New York: Fordham University Press, 1983), 89.

6. This translation of John Kleinig, which departs from the *LW*, helps to point out that Luther's meditation on Scripture was meant to touch the emotions as well as the intellect. For further comments, see John Kleinig, "The Kindred Heart: Luther on Meditation," *Lutheran Theological Journal* 20 (1986): 142–54.

7. Bayer, *Theology the Lutheran Way*, 53.

8. *Sermons on John* (1537–38), *WA* 45:678.38–679.12; *LW* 24:238–39.

9. *Preface to German Writings* (1539), *WA* 50:659.30–35; *LW* 34:286.

10. Initially, Karlstadt was a friend and ally of Luther and then a bitter foe. Some emphasize the theological differences that stood between the two as the cause of the sharp divide; others emphasize the difference in tactics, strategy, and timing in implementing the Reformation changes. See Ronald Sider, ed., *Karlstadt's Battle with Luther: Documents in a Liberal-Radical Debate* (Philadelphia: Fortress, 1978).

11. Luther delivered The Eight Sermons, otherwise known as The Invocavit Sermons, in March 1522. This remarkable series of sermons touched on questions relating to the Mass, images, private confession, and the nature of the gospel. They had the effect of restoring tranquility in the wake of destructive disturbances. For a full length study, see Neil R. Leroux, *Luther's Rhetoric: Strategies and Style from the Invocavit Sermons* (St. Louis: Concordia Academic, 2002).

12. *Against the Heavenly Prophets in the Matter of Images and Sacraments* (1525), *WA* 18:37–214; *LW* 40:73–223; see also Luther's preface to Augustine, *On the Spirit and the Letter* (1533?), *WA Br* 12:387–88; *LW* 60:35–44.

13. *Against the Heavenly Prophets* (1525), *WA* 18:139.5–6; *LW* 40:149.

14. Ibid., *WA* 18:137.13–19; *LW* 40:147.

15. *This Is My Body* (1527), *WA* 23:261.11–13; *LW* 37:135.

16. "To Abraham he gave the word including with it his son Isaac. To Saul he gave the word including with it the slaying of the Amalekites. To Noah he gave the word including with it the rainbow. And so on. You find no word of God in the entire Scriptures in which something material and outward is not contained and presented." Ibid., *WA* 23.261.13ff.; *LW* 37:135ff.

17. Ibid., *WA* 23:193.31–33; *LW* 37:95.

18. *Against the Heavenly Prophets* (1525), *WA* 18:139.13–25; *LW* 40:149.

19. *Preface to the Complete Edition of Luther's Latin Writings* (1545), *WA* 54:179.24–27; *LW* 34:328.

20. Ibid., *WA* 54:180.2–3; *LW* 34:328.

21. Ibid., *WA* 54:185.12–186.2; *LW* 34:336–7 (trans. altered).

22. The felicitous phrase comes from Roland Bainton, *Here I Stand: A Life of Martin Luther* (Nashville: Abingdon, 1950), 30.

23. See especially Franz Posset, "The Sweetness of God," *American Benedictine Review* 44:2 (1993): 143–78.

24. *Table Talk* no. 526 (1533), *WA TR* 12:45.9–12; *LW* 54:97; *Table Talk* no. 1490 (1532), *WA TR* 2:112.9–11; *Table Talk* no. 173 (1532), *WA TR* 1:80.6. See Franz Posset, *The Front-Runner of the Catholic Reformation: The Life and Words of Johann von Staupitz* (Farnham, Surrey, UK: Ashgate, 2003), and Marcus Wriedt, *Gnade und Erwählung* (Mainz: P. von Zabern, 1991).

25. *Preface to Latin Writings* (1545), *WA* 54:186.3–20; *LW* 34:336–7 (trans. altered).

26. For the "tower experience," see *Table Talk* no. 3232c (1532), *WA TR* 3:228; *LW* 54:193–94; *Table Talk* no. 4007 (1538), *WA TR* 4:72–73; *LW* 54:308–9.

27. For a review of the different positions taken by Luther scholars on the timing of the "tower experience," see Kenneth Hagen, "Changes in the Understanding of Luther: The Development of the Young Luther," in *Theological Studies* 29 (1968): 472–96. In his later work, Hagen states that he wishes the problematic using of the preface of 1545 as historical value for the early Luther would go away. In *Luther's Approach to Scripture*, as seen in his "Commentaries" on Galatians 1519–1538 (Tübingen: J. C. B. Mohr [Paul Siebeck], 1993), 120.

28. Markus Wriedt makes this move in his article "Luther's Theology," in *The Cambridge Companion to Martin Luther*, ed. Donald K. McKim (Cambridge: Cambridge University Press, 2003), 86–119. For a different approach to the same issue, see Helmar Junghans, "The Center of the Theology of Martin Luther," in *Martin Luther in Two Centuries: The Sixteenth and the Twentieth* (St. Paul, MN: Lutheran Brotherhood Foundation Reformation Research Library at Luther Northwestern Theological Seminary, 1992), 29–44.

29. Bo Andersson, "Luther's Tower Experience: The Case for a Rhetorical Approach," *Lutheran Quarterly* (1987): 205–13

30. Carl Trueman, *Luther on the Christian Life: Cross and Freedom* (Wheaton, IL: Crossway, 2015), 133–34.

31. *First Lectures on the Psalms* (1513/15), *WA* 3:397.9–11; *LW* 10:332 as quoted by Oswald Bayer, 71.

32. *Preface to Latin Writings* (1545), *WA* 54:186.27–29; *LW* 34:338.

33. Mary Caruthers, *The Book of Memory: A Study of Memory in Medieval Culture*, Cambridge Studies in Medieval Literature 10 (Cambridge: Cambridge University Press, 1990).

34. Quintilian, *The Institutio Oratoria of Quintilian*, trans. H. E. Butler, The Loeb Classical Library (Cambridge: Harvard University Press, 1922), XI.ii.1: *omnes disciplina memoria constat*.

35. Ibid., XI.ii.20.

36. Caruthers, *The Craft of Thought*, 4.

37. For the connections between the theologies of Luther and Bernard, see the two full-length works by Theo Bell and Franz Posset. Theo Bell, *Divus Bernhardus. Bernhard von Clairvauz in Martin Luthers Schriften* (Mainz: P. von Zabern, 1999), and Franz Posset, *Pater Bernhardus: Martin Luther and Bernard of Clairvaux*, Cistercian Studies Series 168 (Boone, IA: Cistercian Studies Quarterly, 1999). Both authors have also contributed articles on specific aspects of these two theologians. See also Ulrich Köpf, "Wurzeln reformatorischen Denkens in der Theologie Bernhards von Clairvaux," in *Reformation und Mönchtum: Aspeckte eines Verhältnisses über Luther hinaus*, ed. Athina Lexutt, Volker Mantey, and Volkmar Ortman, Late Middle Ages, Humanism, Reformation 43 (Tübingen: Mohr Siebeck, 2008), 29–56.

38. Gordon L. Isaac, "Monastic *Memoria* in the Preface to the Complete Edition of Luther's Latin Writings 1545," in *Luther Digest: An Annual Abridgment of Luther Studies*, vol. 20, supplement 2012 (St. Louis: Luther Academy): 127–40.

39. "Piety in Germany Around 1500," in *The Reformation in Medieval Perspective*, edited with an introduction by Steven Ozment (Chicago: Quadrangle Books, 1971), 50–75.

40. For more on this topic, see Ewert Cousins, "The Humanity and the Passion of Christ," in *Christian Spirituality: High Middle Ages and Reformation*, vol. 17 of *World Spirituality: An Encyclopedic History of the Religious Quest* (New York: Crossroad, 1987), 375–91.

41. *A Meditation on Christ's Passion* (1519), *WA* 2:137.12–14; *LW* 42:8.

42. Ibid., *WA* 2:136.5; *LW* 42:7.

43. Ibid., *WA* 2:136.8; *LW* 42:7 (trans. altered).

44. Ibid., *WA* 2:136.24–25; *LW* 42:8.

45. Ibid., *WA* 2:136.16; *LW* 42:7.

46. Analysis of this treatise can also be found in Marc Lienhard, *Luther: Witness to Christ—Stages and Themes of the Reformer's Christology* (Minneapolis: Augsburg, 1982), 103; and Dennis Ngien, *Luther as a Spiritual Advisor: The Interface of Theology and Piety in Luther's Devotional Writings,* Studies in Christian History and Thought (Milton Keynes, UK: Paternoster, 2007), 4–19.

47. *A Meditation on Christ's Passion* (1519), *WA* 2:137.10–21; *LW* 42:8–9.

48. Important for this topic is Birgit Stolt, "Laßt uns fröhlich springen!" *Gefühlswelt und Gefühlsnavigierung in Luthers Reformationsarbeit* (Berlin: Weidler Buchverlag, 2012), 33f. A chapter of her book appears in English as ". . . And Feel It in the Heart. . . . Luther's Translation of the Bible from the Perspective of the Modern Science of Linguistics and Translating, " in *Lutheran Quarterly* 28 (2014): 373–400.

49. Matt. 16:13–23; Mark 8:27–33; Luke 9:18–22.

50. For example, see Luther's comments on verse 1 of his *enarratio* on Psalm 90 (1534/35), *WA* 40/3:469–507; *LW* 13:83–91.

51. Mary Caruthers, *The Book of Memory,* 193.

52. See Hagen, *Luther's Approach to Scripture,* 50–63; and Timothy Maschke, "Contemporaneity: A Hermeneutical Perspective in Martin Luther's Work," in *Ad Fontes Lutheri: Toward the Recovery of the Real Luther: Essays in Honor of Kenneth Hagen's Sixty-Fifth Birthday*, ed. Timothy Maschke, Franz Posset, and Joan Skokir, Marquette Studies in Theology 28 (Milwaukee: Marquette University Press, 2001): 165–82.

53. *A Meditation on Christ's Passion* (1519), *WA* 2:137.22–23; *LW* 42:9.

54. Ibid., *WA* 2:138.17; *LW* 42:10.

55. Ibid., *WA* 2:139.14–18; *LW* 42:11.

56. Ibid., *WA* 2:139.36–38; *LW* 42:12.

57. Ibid., *WA* 2:141.8–10; *LW* 42:13.

58. Ibid., *WA* 2:141.30–31; *LW* 42:14.

59. *A Treatise on the New Testament, that is, the Holy Mass* (1520), *WA* 6:355.21–27; *LW* 35:82.

60. Ibid., *WA* 6:362.28–29; *LW* 35:90.

61. *The Babylonian Captivity of the Church* (1520), *WA* 6:516.30–32; *LW* 36:42.

62. Luther often uses a harmony of the Gospels when setting out the Words of Institution.

63. *A Treatise on the New Testament, that is, the Holy Mass* (1520), *WA* 6:357.14–15; *LW* 35:84.

64. Ibid., *WA* 6:358.18–23; *LW* 35:85.

65. Ibid., *WA* 6:364.21–22; *LW* 35:93.

66. Ibid., *WA* 6:367.13–19; *LW* 35:97.

67. Ibid., *WA* 6:369.6–8; *LW* 35:99.

68. Ibid., *WA* 6:374.4–7; *LW* 35:106.

69. See the introduction to the treatise by Timothy J. Wengert in *AL* 1:467–473. Also, Timothy J. Wengert, "Luther's *Freedom of a Christian* for Today's Church," *Lutheran Quarterly* 28 (2014): 1–21.

70. Andrew Pettegree, *Brand Luther: 1517, Printing, and the Making of the Reformation* (New York: Penguin, 2015).

71. For a summary of some of the ways Luther's approach to Scripture has been described, see Gordon L. Isaac, "The Changing Image of Luther as Biblical Expositor," in *Ad Fontes Lutheri: Toward the Recovery of the Real Luther: Essays in Honor of Kenneth Hagen's Sixty-Fifth Birthday*, ed. Timothy Maschke, Franz Posset, and Joan Skocir (Marquette: Marquette University Press, 2001), 67–85.

72. *On the Freedom of a Christian* (1520), *WA* 7:50.33–51.3; *AL* 1:490–91; *LW* 31:345.

73. Irenaeus, *On the Apostolic Preaching*, Popular Patristics Series 17 (Crestwood, NY: St. Vladimir's Seminary Press, 1997).

74. *A Brief Instruction on What to Look for and Expect in the Gospels* (1521), *WA* 10/1:17.7–12; *LW* 35:123.

75. Ibid., *WA* 7:53.34–36; *AL* 1:497; *LW* 31:351.

76. Ibid., *WA* 7:54.21–23; *AL* 1:499; *LW* 31:351.

77. Ibid., *WA* 7:54.31–38; *AL* 1:499–500; *LW* 31:351.

78. *AL* 1:500.

79. Volker Leppin, "Luther's Transformation of Late Medieval Mysticism," *Lutheran Forum* 44 (2010): 25–28. More recently, Volker Leppin, *Die fremde Reformation: Luthers mystische Wurzeln* (Munich: Beck, 2016).

80. The mystical roots of Luther are undeniable. The only question is to what extent he retains mystical elements and to what degree these concepts are altered.

81. Ibid., *WA* 7:59.7–20; *AL* 1:509; *LW* 31:357–8.

82. Ibid., *WA* 7:66.7–12; *AL* 1:524; *LW* 31:367.

83. Ibid., *WA* 7:66.34–36; *AL* 1:525; *LW* 31:368.

84. *A Brief Instruction on What to Look for and Expect in the Gospels* (1521), *WA* 10/1:9.3–5; *LW* 35:117.

85. Ibid., *WA* 10/1:9.16–18; *LW* 35:117–18.

86. Ibid., *WA* 10/1:10.8–9; *LW* 35:118.

87. Ibid., *WA* 10/1:10.11; *LW* 35:118.

88. Ibid., *WA* 10/1:10.20–11.1; *LW* 35:119.

89. Ibid., *WA* 10/1:12.17–13.2; *LW* 35:120.

90. Ibid., *WA* 10/1:11.1–12.1; *LW* 35:119.

91. Ibid., *WA* 10/1:13.4–6; *LW* 35:120.

92. *Enrrationes epistolarum et euangeliorum* (1521), *WA* 7:502.34–35. For helpful discussions of law and gospel, see Lohse, *Martin Luther's Theology*, 267–76; Bayer, *Martin Luther's Theology*, 58–67; Paul Althaus, *The Theology of Martin Luther* (Minneapolis: Fortress, 1963), 251–73; and Wengert, *Reading the Bible with Martin Luther*, 22–46.

93. "A Sermon on the Day of John the Baptist," June 24, 1532, *WA* 36:25.21–26.

94. *Lectures on Galatians* (1531/35), *WA* 40/1:207.3–4; *LW* 26:115.

95. Jacques Ellul, *To Will and to Do* (Philadelphia: Pilgrim, 1969), 201.

96. The Heidelberg Disputation (1518), *WA* 1:364.18–19; *LW* 31:41. Thesis 26.

97. *Sermons on John* (1537–38), *WA* 45:618.28–33; *LW* 24:172.

98. *On the Freedom of a Christian* (1520), *WA* 58.38–59.6; *LW* 31:357.

99. *Table Talk* no. 590 (1533), *WA TR* 1:275–80; *LW* 54:106.

100. Ibid.

101. *Preface to the New Testament* (1522/46), *WA DB* 6:3.7–11; *LW* 35:357.

102. For a good resource on this topic, see Robert W. Jenson, *Canon and Creed: Interpretation: Resources for the Use of Scripture in the Church* (Louisville: Westminster John Knox, 2010).

103. *Prefaces to the New Testament* (1522/46), *WA DB* 7:11.6–15; *LW* 35:370.

104. *The Works of John Wesley*, ed. W. Reginald Ward and Richard P. Heizenrater, vol. 18: *Journals and Diaries (1735–1738)* (Nashville: Abingdon, 1988), 249–50.

105. *Preface to the New Testament* (1522/46), *WA DB* 6:4–11; *LW* 35:358.

106. *Preface to the Epistles of St. James and St. Jude* (1522/46), *WA DB* 7:385.25–32; *LW* 35:396 (altered).

107. *Lectures on Galatians* (1531/35), *WA* 40/1:119; *LW* 26:57–58.

108. Oswald Bayer, *Martin Luther's Theology*, 78. This is also the force of the work by Kenneth Hagen, *Luther's Approach to Scripture*, according to Ulrich Asendorf, "Holy Scripture and Holy Spirit," in *Ad Fontes Lutheri: Toward the Recovery of the Real Luther: Essays in Honor of Kenneth Hagen's Sixty-Fifth Birthday*, ed. Timothy Maschke, Franz Posset, and Joan Skokir (Milwaukee: Marquette University Press, 2001), 1–16.

109. Bayer, *Theology the Lutheran Way*, 36.

110. This organization suggested itself from Luther's exposition of John 16:13, *Sermons on John* (1537–1538), *WA* 46:52–65; *LW* 24:357–71.

111. Ibid., *WA* 46:55.23–37; *LW* 24:359–60.

112. LC 2:38–39; Kolb-Wengert, 436.

113. Lohse, *Martin Luther's Theology*, 237.

114. On the rhetorical nature of the dispute between Luther and Erasmus, see Marjorie O'Rourke Boyle, *Rhetoric and Reform: Erasmus' Civil Dispute with Luther*, Harvard Historical Monographs 71 (Cambridge, MA: Harvard University Press, 1983).

115. *The Bondage of the Will* (1526), *WA* 18:605.27–34; *LW* 33:24.

116. Ibid., *WA* 18:609.1–14; *LW* 33:28.

117. *Sermons on John* (1537–38), *WA* 46:57.21; *LW* 24:362.

118. Ibid., *WA* 45:726.19–23; *LW* 24:291.

119. Ibid., *WA* 45:726.27–28; *LW* 24:291.

120. Ibid., *WA* 45:726.34–35; *LW* 24:291.

121. Ibid., *WA* 45:727.2–6; *LW* 24:291–92.

122. Ibid., *WA* 45:727.26–32; *LW* 24:292.

123. Ibid., *WA* 46:57.37–58.2; *LW* 24:362.

124. SA 3:8, 5.

125. SA 3:8, 10.

126. *This Is My Body* (1527), *WA* 23:244.30–32; *LW* 37:125.

127. *Sermons on John* (1537–38), *WA* 46:58.35–2; *LW* 24:363–4.

128. Ibid., *WA* 46:59.10–13; *LW* 24:364.

129. Ibid., *WA* 46:59.17–20; *LW* 24:364.

130. Ibid., *WA* 46:59.26–6; *LW* 24:364–65.

131. *Lectures on Galatians* (1519), *WA* 2:536.28–31; *LW* 27:290. Here we find one passage where Luther describes the Holy Trinity in terms of life: "We live according to the Spirit, in whom the Father and the Son rest and live, as it were."

132. *Lectures on Galatians* (1531/35), *WA* 40:345.14–15; *LW* 26:214–15.

133. Ibid., *WA* 40:275.10–11; *LW* 26:161.

134. Carl Braaten and Robert Jenson, eds., *Union with Christ: The New Finnish Interpretation of Luther* (Grand Rapids: Eerdmans, 1998), 24.

Chapter 4

1. Roland Bainton, *Here I Stand: A Life of Martin Luther* (Nashville: Abingdon, 1950), 31.

2. Oswald Bayer, *Martin Luther's Theology: A Contemporary Interpretation*, trans. Thomas H. Trapp (Grand Rapids: Eerdmans, 2008), 20–21.

3. *Preface to German Writings* (1539), *WA* 50:660.1–16; *LW* 34:286–87.

4. *Explanations of the Ninety-Five Theses* (1518), *WA* 1:557.33–558.12; *LW* 31:129.

5. Denis R. Janz, *The Westminster Handbook to Martin Luther* (Louisville: Westminster John Knox, 2010), 3. Here, Janz points out that Luther did not think that the experience of *Anfechtung* was universal.

6. Immanuel Kant, *Critique of Pure Reason*, The Transcendental Dialectic Book 1, Section 1, trans. Norman Kemp Smith (New York: St. Martin's, 1965), 312.

7. William James, *Varieties of Religious Experience*, ed. Matthew Bradley, Oxford World's Classics (Oxford: Oxford University Press, 2012). Rudolf Otto, *The Idea of the Holy*, trans. John W. Harvey (Oxford: Oxford University Press, 1958).

8. Regin Prenter, *Spiritus Creator*, trans. John Jensen (Philadelphia: Muhlenberg, 1953), 55.

9. The Heidelberg Disputation (1518), *WA* 1:354.15–16; *LW* 31:40, thesis 18.

10. *WA TR* 1:146.12–16; *LW* 54:50.

11. *Whether One May Flee from a Deadly Plague* (1527), *WA* 23:377.24–26; *LW* 43:137.

12. For the details of the following account, I am indebted to Martin Brecht, *Martin Luther: Shaping and Defining the Reformation, 1521–1532* (Minneapolis: Fortress, 1993), 204–11.

13. *WA Br* 4:228.1–8.

14. *WA Br* 4:232–233.

15. *Whether One May Flee from a Deadly Plague* (1527), *WA* 23:323.339–79; *LW* 43:119–38.

16. Brecht, *Martin Luther: Shaping and Defining the Reformation 1521–1532*, 208.

17. *WA TR* 1:47.25–48.2; *LW* 54:15–16.

18. *WA Br* 4:294–95; *LW* 49:181.

19. *WA Br* 4:307–9, 313–14, 319–20.

20. For a presentation of Luther's care of souls in light of his *Anfechtungen*, see Peter D. S. Krey, "Luther's In-Depth Theology and Theological Therapy Using Self Psychology and a Little Jung," *Encounters with Luther: New Directions for Critical Studies*, ed. Kirsi I. Stjerna and Brooks Schramm (Louisville: Westminster John Knox, 2016), 189–204.

21. Gerhard O. Forde, *Where God Meets Man: Luther's Down-to-Earth Approach to the Gospel* (Minneapolis: Augsburg, 1972), 95–97.

22. *Table Talk* no. 1615 (1532), *WA TR* 2:152–53; *LW* 54:158–59.

23. *Table Talk* no. 1631 (1532), *WA TR* 2:156; *LW* 54:159.

24. *Table Talk* no. 5494 (1542), *WA TR* 5:189; *LW* 54:430.

25. *Table Talk* no. 5498 (1542), *WA TR* 5:193; *LW* 54:432.

26. Ibid.

27. Martin Brecht, *The Preservation of the Church, 1532–1546* (Minneapolis: Fortress, 1993), 238.

28. *Table Talk* no. 623 (1533), *WA TR* 1:294; *LW* 54:109.

29. *Table Talk* no. 2982b (1533), *WA TR* 3:131; *LW* 54:188.

30. *WA TR* 2:15.35–37, quoted by Volker Leppin, "Luther on the Devil," in *Encounters with Luther: New Directions for Critical Studies*, ed. Kirsi I. Stjerna and Brooks Schramm (Louisville: Westminster John Knox, 2016), 31.

31. Heiko A. Oberman, *Luther: Man between God and the Devil* (New Haven: Yale University Press, 1989), 154–56.

32. *Table Talk* no. 352 (1532), *WA TR* 1:148; *LW* 54:51

33. *Table Talk* no. 1379 (1532), *WA TR* 2:78; *LW* 54:145–46; see also, *Table Talk* no. 222 (1532), *WA TR* 1:95; *LW* 54:29.

34. *Table Talk* no. 333 (1532), *WA TR* 1:136; *LW* 54:46.

35. *Table Talk* no. 489 (1533), *WA TR* 1:214–15; *LW* 54:82; *Table Talk* no. 5027 (1540), *WA TR* 4:620.17–24.

36. *Table Talk* no. 2529b (1532), *WA TR* 2:504.22–23; *Table Talk* no. 3953 (1538), *WA TR* 4:31; *LW* 54:298.

37. *Table Talk* no. 1252 (1531), *WA TR* 2:10; *LW* 54:128–29.

38. *This Is My Body* (1527), *WA* 23:70.8; *LW* 37:17.

39. *Table Talk* no. 3798 (1538), *WA TR* 3:623–25; *LW* 54:275–76.

40. *Sermons on John* (1537–38), *WA* 45:727.1–2; *LW* 24:291.

41. *Table Talk* no. 130 (1531), *WA TR* 1:53–54; *LW* 54:18.

42. *Table Talk* no. 1583 (1532), *WA TR* 2:140–41; *LW* 54:157.

43. *Table Talk* no. 3798 (1538), *WA TR* 3:623–25; *LW* 54:275.

44. *Table Talk* no. 4081 (1538), *WA TR* 4:121–23; *LW* 54:318.

45. *Sermons on John* (1537–38), *WA* 45:565.16–21; *LW* 24:114–15.

46. *Table Talk* no. 501 (1533), *WA TR* 1:224–26; *LW* 54:86.

47. Hans Martin Barth, *Der Teufel und Jesus Christus in der Theologie Martin Luthers* (Göttingen: Vandenhoeck & Ruprecht, 1967), 208–10.

48. *Table Talk* no. 1252 (1531), *WA TR* 2:10; *LW* 54:129.

49. For a discussion of this, see Paul Althaus, *The Theology of Martin Luther* (Minneapolis: Fortress, 1963), 161–68.

50. *Commentary on Psalm 51* (1532), *WA* 40/2:417.25–25; *LW* 12:374.

51. *Commentary on Psalms 118* (1529/30), *WA* 31/1:147, 159; *LW* 14:84, 89.

52. "Our God He is a Castle Strong," *WA* 35:455–457; *LW* 53:285.

53. "A Sermon on Preparing to Die" (1519), *WA* 2:685–697; *LW* 42:99–115.

54. Ibid., *WA* 2:685.20; *LW* 42:99.

55. Ibid., *WA* 2:685.30–686.2; *LW* 42:99.

56. Luther here refers especially to confession, The Lord's Supper, and extreme unction. His views regarding extreme unction would change over time.

57. Ibid., *WA* 2:686.36–687.10; *LW* 42:101.

58. Ibid., *WA* 2:688.33–34; *LW* 42:103.

59. Ibid., *WA* 2:688.34–689.1; *LW* 42:103–4.

60. Ibid., *WA* 2:689.11–21; *LW* 42:104.

61. Ibid., *WA* 2:690.21–22; *LW* 42:105.

62. Austra Reinis, *Reforming the Art of Dying: The ars moriendi in the German Reformation (1519–1528),* St. Andrews Studies in Reformation History (Farnham, Surrey, UK: Ashgate, 2007); see also Craig Koslofsky, *The Reformation of the Dead: Death and Ritual in Early Modern Germany, 1450–1700,* Early Modern History, ed. Rab Houston, Edward Muir, and Bob Scribner (New York: St. Martin's, 2000).

63. Werner Goez, "Luthers 'Ein Sermon von der Bereitung zum Sterben' und die spätmittelalterliche *ars moriendi,*" *Luther Jahrbuch* (1981): 114. Translation my own.

64. *WA Br* 6:318.1–5.

65. *Commentary on 1 Corinthians 15* (1532–33/34), *WA* 36:481.10–12; *LW* 28:59.

66. Ibid., *WA* 36:481.31–482.11; *LW* 28:59–60.

67. Ibid., *WA* 36:483.13–15; *LW* 28:60.

68. Ibid., *WA* 36:483.16–19; *LW* 28:60.

69. Ibid., *WA* 36:524.32; *LW* 28:94.

70. I would tend to disagree with the editor in the American Edition of Luther's Works when he says that this "is a series of sermons on the Christian view of death." The real emphasis lies in Christ's victory that is shared with the believer. *LW* 28:x.

71. Ibid., *WA* 36:501.17–20; *LW* 28:77.

72. Ibid., *WA* 36:494.5–7; *LW* 28:70.

73. Ibid., *WA* 36.494.13–20; *LW* 28:70.

74. Ibid., *WA* 36:545.12–14; *LW* 28:108.

75. Ibid., *WA* 36:545.22–546.18; *LW* 28:108.

76. See Gustav Aulen, *Christus Victor: An Historical Study of the Three Main Types of the Idea of the Atonement* (New York: Macmillan, 1954).

77. Letter to Käthe Luther, February 27, 1537, *WA Br* 8:50–51; *LW* 50:167.

78. *Sermons on John* (1537–38), *WA* 45:475:4–21; *LW* 24:16.

79. Ibid., *WA* 45:469.31–32; *LW* 24:10.

80. Ibid., *WA* 45:467:15–16; *LW* 24:7.

81. Ibid., *WA* 45:470.9–10; *LW* 24:10–11.

82. Ibid., *WA* 45:470.31–33; *LW* 24:11.

83. Ibid., *WA* 45:471.33–37; *LW* 24:12.

84. Ibid., *WA* 45:472.9–10; *LW* 24:13.

85. Ibid., *WA* 45:474:16–23; *LW* 24:15.

86. Ibid., *WA* 45:475:7–10; *LW* 24:16.

87. Ibid., *WA* 45:473.8–13; *LW* 24:14.

88. Ibid., *WA* 45:474.29–475.3; *LW* 24:15–16.

89. Ibid., *WA* 45:537.4–11; *LW* 24:84.

90. Ibid., *WA* 45:562.31–563.1; *LW* 24:112.

91. For a rhetorical analysis of the letter to Pope Leo X that serves as an introduction to the treatise *On the Freedom of a Christian,* see *AL* 1:467ff.

92. For an analysis of the five earliest collections of the sixteenth century, see Johannes Haussleiter, "Luthers Trostbriefe," in *Allgemeine Evangelisch-Lutherische Kirchenzeitung* (Leipzig: Evangelische Verlagsanstalt, 1917), 434–87.

93. *Luther: Letters of Spiritual Counsel,* ed. and trans. Theodore G. Tappert, vol. 28, *The Library of Christian Classics* (London: SCM, 1955).

94. Letter to Elector John, May 15, 1525, LCC 18:55 (*WA Br* 3:496.1).

95. Ibid., LCC 18:56 (*WA Br* 3:497.26–33).

96. Letter to Caspar Mueller, November 24, 1534, LCC 18:39 (*WA Br* 7:118.24–32).

97. Letter to Jerome Weller, July 1530, LCC 18:84–87 (*WA Br* 5:518–20).

98. *The Magnificat* (1521), WA 7:546.21–29; *LW* 21:299.

99. For example, *WA* 21:8.12–23; *WA* 33:264.14–19; *WA* 33:278.16–23.

100. *Sermons on John* (1537–38), WA 45:598.32–35; *LW* 24:151.

101. Ibid., WA 45:598.20–22; *LW* 24:150.

102. Ibid., WA 45:599.5–15; *LW* 24:151.

103. Ibid., WA 45:614.33–40; *LW* 24:168.

104. LC 3.37; Kolb-Wengert, 435.

105. *Sermons on John* (1537–38), WA 45:615.31–616.8; *LW* 24:169.

106. Ibid., WA 45:616.8–13; *LW* 24:169–70.

107. Ibid., WA 45:726.33–727.13; *LW* 24:291–92.

108. Ibid., WA 45:727.35–36; *LW* 24:292.

109. Ibid., WA 45:728.6–8; *LW* 24:293.

110. Ibid., WA 45:729.11–13; *LW* 24:294.

111. Ibid., WA 45:620.13–17; *LW* 24:174.

112. Ibid., WA 45:730:29–30; *LW* 24:295.

113. Ibid., WA 45:731.14–24; *LW* 24:296.

Chapter 5

1. *Sermons on John 14–16* (1537–1538), WA 45:626.32–267.2; *LW* 24:181.

2. "The First Sermon at the Weimar Castle Church," October 19, 1522, WA 10/III:346.25–26; *LW* 51:110.

3. *Table Talk* no. 1400 (1532), WA TR 2:85.15–18; *LW* 54:147–48.

4. For an account of a modern-day pilgrimage, see Andrew Wilson, *Here I Walk: A Thousand Miles on Foot to Rome with Martin Luther* (Grand Rapids: Brazos, 2016).

5. Hugo Rahner, *Greek Myths and Christian Mystery* (New York: Biblo-Moser, 1963), 328–30.

6. For Luther's recollection of the trip to Rome, see *Commentary on Psalm 117* (1530), *WA* 31/I:225–26; *LW* 14:6; *The Private Mass* (1533), WA 38:211–12; *LW* 38:166; *Table Talk* nos. 3478 and 3479a (1536), WA TR 3:345–49; *LW* 54:208–9; *Table Talk* no. 3582a (1537), WA TR 3:431–32; *LW* 54:237; *Table Talk* no. 3930 (1538), WA TR 4:17; *LW* 54:296; *Against the Roman Papacy* (1545), WA 54:219; *LW* 41:278–79; *Brief Confession* (1544), WA 54:166; *LW* 38:318. There is much debate over whether Luther's trip was in 1510–11 or in 1511–12. See Franz Possett, "Luther's Journey to Rome 1511–1512: In Commemoration of Its 500th Anniversary and in Search of the Historical Luther—A Sequel to *The Real Luther*," *Luther Digest: An Annual Abridgment of Luther Studies*, vol. 20, supplement 2012 (St. Louis: Luther Academy): 9–24.

7. Steven Ozment, "*Homo Viator*: Luther and Late Medieval Theology," in *The Reformation in Medieval Perspective* (Chicago: Quadrangle Books, 1971), 142–54.

8. For more on Tauler's importance for Luther's theology, see Volker Leppin, "Luther's Roots in Monastic-Mystical Piety," in *Oxford Handbook on Luther's Theology*, ed. Robert Kolb, Irene Dingel, and L'Ubomir Batka (Oxford: Oxford University Press, 2014), 49–61.

9. Ozment, *"Homo-Viator:* Luther and Late Medieval Theology," 149. See also Berndt Hamm, *The Early Luther: Stages in a Reformation Reorientation,* Lutheran Quarterly Books (Grand Rapids: Eerdmans, 2014), 59–84.

10. *Lectures on Genesis* (1535/38), *WA* 42:437.14–15; *LW* 2:246.

11. Ibid., *WA* 42:437.7–9; *LW* 2:246.

12. David C. Steinmetz, *Luther in Context* (Bloomington: Indiana University Press, 1986; repr. Grand Rapids: Labyrinth Books, 1995), 32–46.

13. *Lectures on Genesis* (1535/38), *WA* 42:438.22–24; *LW* 2:248.

14. Ibid., *WA* 42:438.25–33; *LW* 2:248.

15. Ibid., *WA* 42:438.11–13; *LW* 2:249.

16. *Lectures on Galatians* (1531/35), *WA* 40:375.13; *LW* 26:237.

17. Ibid., *WA* 40:360.17–18; *LW* 26:226–27.

18. Ibid., *WA* 40:361.15–18; *LW* 26:227.

19. Ibid., *WA* 40:383.31–384.18; *LW* 26:243.

20. Ibid., *WA* 40:385.21–22; *LW* 26:244.

21. Ibid., *WA* 40:389.32–390.13; *LW* 26:247.

22. Ibid., *WA* 40:360.27–28; *LW* 26:227.

23. Ibid., *WA* 40:363.20–24; *LW* 26:229.

24. Ibid., *WA* 40:407.30–33; *LW* 26:260.

25. Ibid., *WA* 40:360.21–24; *LW* 26:227.

26. Ibid., *WA* 40:400.35–401.19; *LW* 26:255.

27. For more, see Berndt Hamm, *The Early Luther: Stages in a Reformation Reorientation*, Lutheran Quarterly Books (Grand Rapids: Eerdmans, 2014), 190–232.

28. For more on the *unio personalis*, see Tuomo Mannermaa, *Christ Present in Faith: Luther's View of Justification* (Minneapolis: Fortress, 2005), 39–42.

29. Ibid., *WA* 40.285.24–286.20; *LW* 26:168–69.

30. Ibid., *WA* 40:285.12–17; *LW* 26:168.

31. *Lectures on Hebrews* (1517/18), *WA* 57/III:179.6–11; 197:15–20; *LW* 29:179, 200.

32. *Babylonian Captivity of the Church* (1520), *WA* 6:562.9–10; *LW* 36:109.

33. Berndt Hamm, *The Early Luther,* 190–232.

34. Sam Dubbelman, "The Darkness of Faith: A Study in Luther's 1535 Commentary on Galatians," *Trinity Journal* 37NS (2016): 213–32. The following discussion borrows extensively from this treatment.

35. *Lectures on Galatians* (1531/35), *WA* 40:204.24–205.9; *LW* 26:113–14.

36. Ibid., *WA* 40:208.9–13; *LW* 26:116.

37. Ibid., *WA* 40:228.33–229.21; *LW* 26:129–30.

38. Mannermaa, *Christ Present in Faith*. See also Carl Braaten and Robert Jenson, *Union with Christ: The New Finnish Interpretation of Luther* (Grand Rapids: Eerdmans, 1998); Olli-Pekka Vaino, ed., *Engaging Luther: A (New) Theological Assessment* (Eugene, OR: Cascade, 2010).

39. On this point, see Paul Rorem, "Martin Luther's Christocentric Critique of Pseudo-Dionysian Spirituality," *Lutheran Quarterly* 11 (1997): 291–307.

40. Ibid., *WA* 40:361.23–27; *LW* 26:228.

41. Brian Gerrish observes that one must distinguish in Luther: "(1) natural reason, ruling within its proper domain (the Earthly Kingdom); (2) arrogant reason, trespassing upon the domain of faith (the Heavenly Kingdom); (3) regenerate reason, serving humbly in the household of faith, but always subject to the Word of God." Brian Gerrish, *Grace and Reason: A Study in the Theology of Luther* (Oxford:

Oxford University Press, 1962), 87. See also Theo Dieter, "Martin Luther's Understanding of Reason," *Lutheran Quarterly* 25 (2011): 249–78.

42. *Lectures on Galatians* (1531/35), WA 40:360.24–5; *LW* 26:227; see also LC 1.2–3: "As I have often said, it is the trust and faith of the heart alone that make both God and an idol. If your faith and trust are right, then your God is the true one. Conversely, where your trust is false and wrong, there you do not have the true God. For these two belong together, faith and God. Anything on which your heart relies and depends, I say that is really your God." Kolb-Wengert, 386.

43. *Lectures on Galatians* (1531/35), WA 40:204.17–18; *LW* 26:113.

44. Ibid., WA 40:364.18–20; *LW* 26:230.

45. *Lectures on Genesis* (1535/38), WA 42:437; *LW* 2:247.

46. Ibid., WA 42:438.23–24; *LW* 2:248.

47. Ibid., WA 42:438.25–29; *LW* 2:248.

48. Ibid., WA 42:453.32, 454.36; *LW* 2:268, 270.

49. Ibid., WA 42:454.17–19; *LW* 2:269–270.

50. Ibid., WA 42:462.29–30; *LW* 2:281.

51. Ibid., WA 42:463.12–14; *LW* 2:281–82.

52. Ibid., WA 42:465.7–8; *LW* 2:284.

53. Ibid., WA 42:462.7–8; *LW* 2:280.

54. *Lectures on Genesis* (1538/42), WA 43:201.8; *LW* 4:91.

55. Ibid., WA 43:201.18–20; *LW* 4:92.

56. Ibid., WA 43:201.21–24; *LW* 4:92.

57. Luther gave this account first as lectures to students before it was published.

58. Ibid., WA 43:201.30–32; *LW* 4:92.

59. Ibid., WA 43:202.1–6; *LW* 4:92.

60. Ibid., WA 43:202.16–21; *LW* 4:93.

61. Ibid., WA 43:202.28–36; *LW* 4:93.

62. Ibid., WA 43:202.41–42; *LW* 4:94.

63. Ibid., WA 43:203.40–204.2; *LW* 4:95.

64. Ibid., WA 43:203.35–39; *LW* 4:95.

65. Ibid., WA 43:204.23–29; *LW* 4:96.

66. Ibid., WA 43:205.14–15; *LW* 4:97.

67. *Lectures on Hebrews* (1517/18), WA 57:236.4–5; *LW* 29:238.

68. Mary Jane Haemig, "Prayer as Talking Back to God in Luther's Genesis Commentary," *Lutheran Quarterly* 23 (2009): 270–95.

69. Haemig, "Prayer as Talking Back," 272.

70. *Lectures on Genesis* (1535/38), WA 42:661.8–9; *LW* 3:158.

71. Ibid., WA 42:661.37–42; *LW* 3:159.

72. Ibid., WA 42:662.1–2; *LW* 3:159.

73. *Lectures on Genesis* (1538/42), WA 43:43.5; *LW* 3:234.

74. Ibid., WA 43:43.21; *LW* 3:235

75. Ibid., WA 43:42.9; *LW* 3:233.

76. Ibid., WA 43:44.6; *LW* 3:235.

77. Ibid., WA 43:44.25–27; *LW* 3:236.

78. *Lectures on Genesis* (1535/38), WA 42:654.1; *LW* 3:148.

79. Ibid., WA 42:654.4–7; *LW* 3:148.

80. Ibid., WA 42:654.8–9; *LW* 3:148.

81. Ibid., WA 42:654.12–14; *LW* 3:148.

82. Ibid., WA 42:662.4; *LW* 3:159.

83. Ibid., *WA* 42:658.12–14; *LW* 3:154.

84. Robert Kolb, "Models of the Christian Life in Luther's Genesis Sermons and Lectures," *Lutherjahrbuch* 76 (2009): 193–220. Many of the ideas contained in this article have been presented in greater detail in Robert Kolb, *Luther and the Stories of God: Biblical Narratives as a Foundation for Christian Living* (Grand Rapids: Baker Academic, 2012). See esp. 99–168.

85. *Lectures on Genesis* (1535/38), *WA* 42:632.10–14; *LW* 3:118.

86. Ibid., *WA* 42:631.40–632.5; *LW* 3:117.

87. Ibid., *WA* 42:561.7; *LW* 3:18.

88. *Commentary on Psalm 117* (1530), *WA* 31/1:223–257; English translation found in, *Luther's Spirituality*, The Classics of Western Spirituality, ed. and trans. Philip D. W. Krey and Peter D. S. Krey (Mahwah, NJ: Paulist, 2007), 126.

89. *Table Talk* no. 3588 (1537), *WA TR* 3:434–35; *LW* 54:238.

90. *Sermons on John, Chapters 18–20:18* (1528–29/1557), *WA* 28:421.33–34;28:424.36–42; *LW* 69:279, 283.

91. *Explanations of the Ninety-Five Theses* (1518), *WA* 1:613.21–41; *LW* 31:224–26.

92. *Admonition Concerning the Sacrament* (1530), *WA* 30/2:605.8–16; *LW* 38:109–10.

93. *Lectures on Genesis* (1543/45), *WA* 44:95.27–28; *LW* 6:128.

94. Ibid., *WA* 44:96.16–17; *LW* 6:129.

95. "Sermon on St. John's Day, John 21:19–24," December 27, 1522, *WA* 10/1.1:305–324; *LW* 75:353–54.

96. *An Exposition of the Lord's Prayer for Simple Laymen* (1519), *WA* 2:98.23–28; *LW* 42:41.

97. Ibid., *WA* 2:98.36–38; *LW* 42:41.

98. *Church Postil* (1544), Ninth Sunday after Trinity [1 Cor. 10:6–13], *WA* 22:165.7–23; *LW* 78:315.

99. *Lectures on Galatians* (1519), *WA* 2:535.26–536.5; *LW* 27:289.